BIRMINGHAM

THE MAKING OF THE

SECOND CITY

1850-1939

BIRMINGHAM
THE MAKING OF THE
SECOND CITY
1850-1939

Eric Hopkins

TEMPUS

First published 2001

PUBLISHED IN THE UNITED KINGDOM BY:

Tempus Publishing Ltd
The Mill, Brimscombe Port
Stroud, Gloucestershire GL5 2QG
www.tempus-publishing.com

PUBLISHED IN THE UNITED STATES OF AMERICA BY:

Tempus Publishing Inc.
2 Cumberland Street
Charleston, SC 29401
(Tel: 1-888-313-2665)
www.arcadiapublishing.com

Tempus books are available in France, Germany from the following addresses:

Tempus Publishing Group
21 Avenue de la République
37300 Joué-lès-Tours
FRANCE

Tempus Publishing Group
Gustav-Adolf-Straße 3
99084 Erfurt
GERMANY

British Library Cataloguing in Publication Data.
A catalogue record for this book is available from the British Library.

ISBN 0 7524 2327 4

Typesetting and origination by Tempus Publishing.
PRINTED AND BOUND IN GREAT BRITAIN.

Contents

DEDICATION

In memory of my late wife Barbara,
and for our children, Ruth, Hedley and Valerie,
and the grandchildren, Heather and Simon.

INTRODUCTION

This book is essentially a continuation of my previous book on Birmingham, first published in 1989 under the title *Birmingham: The First Manufacturing City in the World, 1760-1840*. Like its predecessor, the present book is concerned primarily with the economic and social life of the city. In this respect it is different from many books on Birmingham history which concentrate rather more on political and general development, though this aspect is by no means ignored and indeed is essential to understanding the social amelioration of the period – witness the chapter on the Civic Gospel. Inevitably much space is devoted to the fortunes of the working classes, though the middle classes are not ignored; they supplied invaluable leadership to the Birmingham community, and indeed a history of Birmingham in the nineteenth century without Joseph Chamberlain would be Hamlet without the Prince. Efforts have also been made to place Birmingham history within the context of national economic and social developments, and in this way to escape the charge of mere parochialism which sometimes is levelled at local history.

The book is divided into three parts: the first takes the story up to 1914, and covers the period of Victorian and Edwardian prosperity. Chapter One sets the economic and social scene in 1850, while Chapter Two outlines the basic economic changes of the next half-century or so up to 1914. Chapter Three deals with the Civic Gospel and the transformation of Council policies which it effected. Chapters Four and Five describe and discuss the major aspects of working-class life before 1914 – that is, working and living conditions. Chapter Six on the Social Scene is concerned with specific aspects of social life not dealt with hitherto such as religion, education, and leisure activities. Part Two, Chapter Seven, is short, being devoted to the economic and social effects of the Great War. Part Three, Chapter Eight, ends the book with a survey of the inter-war years in Birmingham, covering a variety of aspects of social life. The Envoi contains some last thoughts by the author.

This book is hoped to provide a useful, up-to-date account of the period in which Birmingham became the Second City of the kingdom, focusing attention in particular on the daily lives and labours of the millions of its inhabitants who contributed so much to its prosperity and made the creation of the Second City possible.

ERIC HOPKINS
Stourbridge

Chapter One

The Mid-Century Economy and Society

How far was Birmingham a product of the Industrial Revolution? Popular conceptions of this immense industrial change are commonly based on the idea that industry in Britain was transformed during the first half of the nineteenth century as a result of technological advances which led to the development of the factory system of production. An essential part of this was the use of steam power to drive the new machinery. As the factory system spread, it is assumed that a new and rigorous work discipline manifested itself, making for increasing class conflict, especially in some of the new textile towns, such as Manchester. Industrial and social change was accelerated still further by the building of the steam railways which greatly improved on the earlier advances in communications brought by the turnpike system and by the canals. While the textile industry flourished, so did the iron, coal and engineering industries. Meanwhile the industrial towns, of which Birmingham was a prominent example, expanded greatly, producing serious health problems. All in all, at the root of an immense complex of economic and social change there lay a fundamental shift in the national economy from an economic system based essentially on agriculture to one based on industry. At the mid-century, the balance had already tipped sharply towards a predominance of industry over agriculture. By the end of the century, the transformation was complete. Britain had become the first industrial nation in the world.[1]

Where did Birmingham stand at the mid-century in all this ferment of change? First it must be noted that all recent research over the past quarter-century goes to show that the pace of change to an industrial economy in the first half of the nineteenth century has been greatly exaggerated.[2] Even in the booming textile industry, water power was not superseded by steam power until the 1830s. As for the factory system, mechanisation affected less than a quarter of the industrial workers in 1851, even if mining, where the use of machinery in the modern sense was actually minimal, is included as a mechanised industry.[3] The majority of workers were employed not in anything recognisable as factories, but in workshops, in foundries and forges, in shipyards, in building work, in the home as domestic servants, and in many other workplaces. Even in the most technologically advanced industry of all, the cotton industry, there were still 200,000 handloom weavers in the 1830s, still struggling to compete with the factory system. In 1851, the largest single occupation was still agriculture, and the second largest domestic service. Birmingham, in fact, supplies a fascinating example of a great industrial city - described by Arthur Young in 1791 as 'the first manufacturing town in the world'[4] - which singularly fails to conform to the stereotype of an industrial town based on steam-driven factory machinery.

Birmingham's industrial expansion appears to have become marked in the early and middle years of the eighteenth century, well before the spread of technological invention in the textile industry. Its growth in population has been estimated to have exceeded that of all other industrial towns of the time except Sheffield. Not only did it have a flourishing home trade commensurate with its increasing importance as a regional capital, but overseas trade was also developing fast. All this trade was based on the expanding metal industries of the town. These included the toy trade, specialising in many small items of iron, brass, and steel such as buckles, buttons, snuff boxes and trinkets of all kinds; the jewellery trade; the manufacture of pins; and the gun trade, one of the oldest industries, dating back to the sixteenth century if not earlier.

All these industries owed little directly to what Dr. Samuel Johnson called 'the fury of innovation' - certainly nothing was owed to the well-known inventions designed to speed up spinning, and later weaving. Birmingham entrepreneurs such as John Taylor and Matthew Boulton took pride in the use of an advanced hand technology in their workshops in the form of the press, the stamp, the lathe and the drawbench.[5] All these simple hand-operated machines could be worked by men, women and children without any assistance from steam power. They permitted both a significant division of labour, and the production of goods very competitively priced. Boulton's proud boast of the efficiency of production in his Soho works is well-known:[6]

> ... although in many places they have as good and as cheap materials as we have, and have labour cent per cent cheaper, yet nevertheless by the superactivity of our people and by the many mechanical contrivances and extensive apparatus wh we are possess'd of, our men are enabled to do from twice to ten times the work that can be done without the help of such contrivances & even women and children to do more than men can do without them.

It was not until after the end of the Napoleonic wars in 1815 that steam power began to be widely used in Birmingham, in spite of the fact that the Boulton & Watt steam engine patent had been renewed forty years earlier in 1775; the early Boulton & Watt engines were not even manufactured and used in Birmingham, but were built *in situ*, mostly for Cornish tin mines. In 1815 there were only about forty steam engines of all kinds in use in the town, and about 120 by 1830. After this, the rate of use speeded up, one authority giving a figure of 169 steam engines in 1835, another 240 by 1838.[7] In the toy industry, the size of these engines was quite small, though they were larger in the primary metal industries, where they were used for hammering, rolling and blowing purposes. By 1839, the most important use of steam power was for rolling copper, brass and other metals (570 horse power), followed by its use in iron forges, foundries and wrought iron mills (360 horse power), and then for drawing wire (150 horse power). Ten years later in 1849, the total amount of steam power in use was only about 5,400 horse power. Toy workshops often shared the power of a small steam engine.[8] It is therefore clear that, up to 1830 at least, the availability of improved steam engines could have had little effect on industrial expansion in Birmingham.

The fact is that Birmingham had begun to develop as an industrial town well before the first consequences of technological change in the cotton industry began to kick in during the 1780s, and before the iron industry was transformed by Cort's puddling and rolling process in the 1790s. A number of factors contributed to this, the most important probably being the availability of iron ore and coal on the South Staffordshire and East

1. William Hutton, 1723-1815.

Worcestershire coalfield in the Black Country to the west. The nearest source of supply was at Wednesbury, just a few miles away from the city centre. Thus, according to Leland in 1538, 'a great part of the town is maintained by smiths who have their iron and sea-cole out of Staffordshire'.[9] This connection was greatly improved by the opening of the Birmingham canal in 1770. By this time the road to Wednesbury had become almost impassable in winter owing to the heavy weight of traffic.

Other factors contributed to the rise of Birmingham as an industrial centre well before the classic period of the Industrial Revolution beginning in the 1760s or 1770s. These are generally said to include the trading connections with London, the availability of good supplies of pure water, the presence of ample supplies of labour, and (an often favoured explanation) the fact that Birmingham was not incorporated until 1838, and therefore lacked a charter which would have imposed both a governing authority and gild restrictions on trade. Further, lack of incorporation meant that dissenters, with their known entrepreneurial skills, were not barred by the Clarendon Code of the 1660s from settling in the town. According to the town's first historian, William Hutton, this was a most important consideration: as he put it, 'a town without a charter is a town without a shackle.' However, although dissenters did figure prominently in the town's history both in Hutton's time and subsequently, other industrial towns such as Wolverhampton without a charter did not grow so fast; while some industrial towns in the Midlands such as Coventry had a charter but still had a significant number of dissenting settlers. So the 'town without a charter' argument is not entirely convincing. It might well be that *au fond* the centuries-old tradition of working in iron together with the available supplies of iron (some of it brought in not only from the Black Country but also from a distance on the river Severn, and then overland from Bewdley), plus the supplies of coal close at hand, constitute the basic explanations for the industrial growth of Birmingham.

By the mid-nineteenth century, Birmingham's reputation as the leading metalware industrial centre was well-established. Clearly enough, its expansion up to that time was, as we have seen, not based on any advanced use of steam power, but on an efficient hand technology of a traditional kind carried out for the most part in workshops and not in factories. A more detailed examination of the principal branches of industry in the 1850s will go far to confirm this view. We may start with the gun trade which, as already noted, was one of the oldest of Birmingham's industries.

The gun trade had grown during the eighteenth century, profiting not only from the demands for sporting guns at home, but also from the sale of guns abroad in the slave trade and the need for guns for military purposes. This last market expanded greatly with the outbreak of the wars against revolutionary France, and demand was especially strong during the Napoleonic wars from 1804 onwards. The numbers of guns made in Birmingham for the Board of Ordnance in the years 1804-15 was 1,743,382 – more than double the numbers made elsewhere in England in the same period. The entire production of guns of all kinds in these years was estimated in 1866 at nearly 5 million, although, more recently, estimates in 1982 put the figure (not counting slave guns) as high as 9,148,224.[10] This expansion in the gun trade led to the passing of a private act of parliament and the establishing of a public proof house in 1813 in Banbury Street near the Fazeley Canal which still stands today (its main entrance with its magnificent frieze above is clearly visible from the railway lines just south of New Street Station).

After the end of the French wars in 1815, production slumped badly, no arms being made at all for the government for at least ten years following 1817. However, by the mid-century, the trade was buoyant again: the average annual production of barrels proved (excluding arms for the government) between 1855 and 1864 was 327,781, which compares favourably with a similar period without a major war 1816-26, when the average annual figure was 127,337.[11] By 1851 there were 2,867 workers engaged in the Birmingham gun trade as compared with a total of 7,731 for England and Wales. It has also been claimed by this date that the Birmingham gun trade was the greatest supplier of arms in the world and that a large proportion of the arms used in the Crimean War, and the Kaffir War in Africa were made in Birmingham.[12]

By the mid-century, the gun trade had moved from its original site in the Digbeth area and had become concentrated for the most part in a small area near St Mary's, in a district bounded by Slaney Street, Shadwell Street, Loveday Street and Steelhouse Street. The only parts of the trade outside this area were the gun barrel makers (located in Aston, Deritend, Smethwick and West Bromwich), and the lockmakers (situated in Darlaston, Wednesbury, Willenhall and Wolverhampton). They still employed traditional craft techniques. The only technological advances in the first half of the nineteenth century were the production of gun barrels by rollers and the invention of the percussion lock. The first technique for the production of barrels by water- or steam-powered rollers is attributed to Henry Osborn, who patented his process in 1812 and 1817. The percussion lock replaced the flintlock by igniting a percussion cap. This led to the development of the breech-loading gun using a self-contained cartridge. The old muzzle-loading musket employing a ramrod gradually became obsolete; but although the first patent for a percussion lock dates from 1807, the War Office did not change to the new kind of lock until about 1839.[13] Meanwhile the basic techniques for the majority of gun-trade workers remained unchanged. Specialisation in the trade had by now been taken to a remarkable degree.

The first point to be made in this connection is that the so-called 'gun-maker' did not manufacture guns at all. His function was rather to market guns made up of parts produced by specialist workmen (the 'material men', working on sub-contract), the guns being assembled afterwards by other workmen (the 'fabricators' or 'setters-up'). The numbers of workers in each of these two main branches is remarkable: in 1982 an authority on the trade provided a list compiled from trade directories from the second quarter of the nineteenth century. This detailed seventeen types of material men and fourteen types of setters-up. In the 1860s a contemporary writer enumerated thirty-two different types of material men and sixteen types of setters-up.[14]

However, while some of the material men were obviously manufacturers of parts – such as gun-stock makers, and barrel-borers and filers – one or two, such as barrel-polishers, one would have expected to find among the setters-up. It seems likely that certain specialist trades were sometimes placed in one list, and sometimes in another. At all events, it is abundantly clear that the trade had its highly specialised aspects. Few women were employed in the trade, though some worked at the final polishing. On the other hand, many boys were employed, carrying guns and parts from one workshop to another; but curiously enough, in such a highly skilled trade, apprenticeship was not a prominent feature. A recent authority suggests that this is partly because skilled workers refused to train apprentices who might become future competitors in lean times, and partly because workers were paid piece rates and would not waste their time in training others (in fact, in other trades, qualified workers were often paid extra for supervising apprentices). Nevertheless, if apprenticeship was comparatively rare, it is obvious that a good deal of training on the job must have taken place for skills to be satisfactorily transferred and maintained.

To speak in general terms, the Birmingham gun industry of the mid-nineteenth century may be seen as an excellent example of a Birmingham industry based on metalware and still organised as a small-master economy. Its approach was wholly traditional, and up to the mid-nineteenth century it showed few signs of organisation on a larger scale in the interests of more efficient production. Indeed, the division of the work processes into so many different operations seems to show an old-fashioned clinging to jealously guarded traditional skills of a kind increasingly out of date. The establishment of the government-controlled British Small Arms factory in the 1850s at Enfield, north of London, utilising the new mass-production methods copied from America, was to cast a shadow over the gun trade in Birmingham in its traditional form.[15]

To turn now to the toy trade - a general term, as we have seen, covering the buckle, button, jewellery and pin trades. Of these, the buckle trade had faded virtually out of existence when the new fashion for shoe strings instead of buckles swept the country at the end of the eighteenth century. In 1791, the buckle makers in vain petitioned the Prince of Wales who ordered his followers to continue wearing buckles; and in 1792 a further petition to the Duke and Duchess of York again failed to turn the tide of fashion. Many bucklemakers simply went over to the button or brass trades.[16] As for the button trade, it prospered up to the 1830s, amd new types of button were made: the cloth-covered button with a flexible canvas shank (patented 1825), the fancy silk button (patented 1837) and the linen button (patented 1841).[17] By the 1830s, the fashion for many buttons on tail coats, breeches, and so on was beginning to wane, as the Victorian taste for sobriety in costume took more and more effect. By the mid-nineteenth century, the great days of the button trade were over, though the trade remained an important element in the economy of Birmingham, the most important products being metal and pearl buttons. By 1851, the number engaged in the trade was 4,980 - second only to the number engaged in the brass trade.

Another branch of the toy trade, the jewellery trade, concentrated in the St Paul's area of the town, expanded considerably after 1830. It produced a great variety of goods, ranging from small articles in gold and silver incorporating precious gems to articles of tableware and cheap imitations of expensive jewellery (the gilt toy trade). It was often said that anyone could set up for himself in this trade: all he needed was a bench, a leather apron, two or three pounds worth of tools (including a blow pipe), and for materials a few sovereigns and some ounces of copper and zinc.[18] An alternative version of this saying includes a copper kettle for the basic material, from which a Birmingham workman was said to be able to produce a hundred pounds' worth of jewellery, it being insinuated that the quality of the resulting product was not up to much. By 1851 there were 2,494 workers in the jewellery trade, together with a further 1,153 workers in gold and silver.[19]

The other branch of the toy trade which needs consideration is pin making, which seems to have been established by Samuel Ryland in the middle of the eighteenth century. He transferred the business to his nephew Thomas Phipson in 1785, and Thomas Phipson & Company were still the leading manufacturers in the first half of the nineteenth century – another tribute to Birmingham's contribution to the fashion industry. The pin industry is also famous for being selected by Adam Smith as an illustration of the application of the principle of the division of labour. It is said that the work of fifteen different workers went into the making of a single pin, and to its packaging. When visitors from London arrived to inspect the wonders of Birmingham's industry, they were always taken to see the organisation of the pin factories which employed many women and children. However, in 1824, a patent was taken out in this country by an American, Lemuel Wellman Wright, for a machine for making pins. In 1831 the first Birmingham patent for pin-making by machine was issued to David Ledsam and William Jones, the patent being for two machines, one for heading, the other for pointing.[20] It took some time for these machines to take over, of course, but by 1850 the handforging of pins was in decline.

By way of contrast, the brass industry in Birmingham expanded greatly from the mid-eighteenth century and throughout the first half of the nineteenth century. Up to 1740, articles were made of brass in the town although the raw material itself was not, but in 1740 brassworks were established in Birmingham for the production of brass sheets and ingots. Thereafter the industry became more specialised in its products: these included fittings for carriages and harness, cabinet brasswork of all kinds (candlesticks, door handles, curtain rings, castors, furniture hinges, locks, keys, screws and bolts), fittings for steam engines, and plumbing requisites. The increasing numbers of steam engines required not only brass cocks and taps, but fittings in the form of brass whistles, gauges and other accessories. The manufacture of brass coffin furniture became important. The spreading use of gas lighting brought a further demand for brass piping and fittings. Even before the outbreak of war against France in 1793, Birmingham was said to have the bulk of the trade in Europe in brass and copper goods.

After the French wars were over and peace-time European trade was resumed, the brass industry went from strength to strength, especially in the 1830s. Brass bedsteads became fashionable, while a new industrial use for brass from 1838 onwards was the production of seamless brass tubes, these being more suitable and reliable for use in boilers than brazed tubes, for example, in locomotive boilers. A new method of making brass (the crucible method) replaced the older cementation process. By the 1860s the brass industry had become the premier industry in Birmingham, the greatest centre of the brass and copper trades in the country. Some indication of its expansion can be seen in the increasing numbers of manufacturers and their works –[21]

	1800	*1830*	*1865*
Number of manufacturers	50	160	216
Number of works	50	280	421

Some of these works were of a considerable size. The seventeen brass houses averaged 115 hands each, while one exceptional works, Wingfields, employed just over a hundred in 1835 but had grown by 1860 to employ between 700 and 800. The majority of works were far smaller than this: the typical place of work in 1866 was a workshop employing twenty or thirty hands. By 1851 nearly half the workforce in the industry worked in cabinet brassfoundry and in making gas fittings and lamps; others were engaged in plumbers' brassfoundry, engineers' brassfoundry, naval brass-foundry (Muntz's metal, a new form of brass used for casting and working at high temperatures, had been invented earlier in the century for sheathing ships' bottoms), and general brassfoundry. Workers in the Birmingham brass industry were fortunate enough to be employed in an industry producing articles in particular demand in an expanding industrial society. At the mid-century, Birmingham led the world in the manufacture of brass. A contemporary observer, W.C. Aitkin, surveyed the importance of the industry in the 1860s in a memorable passage –[22]

> What Manchester is in cotton, Bradford in wool and Sheffield in steel, Birmingham is in brass; its articles of cabinet and general brassfoundry are to be found in every part of the world; its gas fittings in every city and town into which gas has been introduced... on the railways of every country, and on every sea its locomotive and marine engine solid brass tubes generate the vapour which impels the locomotive over the iron road, and propels the steam boat over the ocean wave... its yellow metal bolts, nails, and sheathing hold together and protect from decay 'wooden walls' of our own and other countries' ships - its 'Manillas' [coins] once made in tons, are the circulating medium of the natives of the Gold Coast - and its rings and ornaments of brass, sent out in immense quantities, are the chief decorations of the *belles* on the banks of the distant Zambesi.

Other minor industries must be mentioned. One is the manufacture of flint glass - it employed 1,117 workers in 1851. Two others are the industries specialising in the manufacture of papier mâché, and japanning. The former had grown up in the last quarter of the eighteenth century, and extended to the making of a variety of products, including roofs for coaches, bookcases, cabinets, tea trays, and even tables and chairs. These were usually given decorative finishes, including that of japanning, first made popular by the Birmingham printer, John Baskerville. The minting of coins was another industry in which the name of Matthew Boulton became prominent at the beginning of the nineteenth century. An apprentice of his, Edward Thomason, continued in this line of business, especially in tradesmen's tokens, and also in commemorative medallions, struck especially for foreign royalties and dignitaries.[23] Lastly, a new and prosperous industry originating in the 1830s was the manufacture of steel pens, the leading makers being Joseph Gillott and Josiah Mason. The pens of the latter bore the name of the firm for which they were made in massive quantities, Perry & Co. The same Josiah Mason was to be the founder of Mason College in 1880, which afterwards became the University of Birmingham in 1900, his trademark of the mermaid being retained as a well-known logos of the university.

What then are the main features of industry in Birmingham in 1850? Clearly it was highly diversified in nature, and rooted in the town's centuries-old skills in the working of metals, both ferrous and non-ferrous. The town had become the biggest centre in the kingdom for the manufacture of guns, brass work (especially the cabinet and lighting branches), jewellery (especially middle-class jewellery and trinkets), buttons, pens, screws and bedsteads. In 1843 it was said that there were as many as ninety-seven different trades, far more than in other towns, and as many as 2,100 separate firms (though this last figure is likely to be an understatement). In all these trades, metal working remained predominant.[24] The principal occupations listed in the census returns for 1851 are as follows –

Blacksmiths	1,091	Iron manufacture	2,015
Brassfounders	4,914	Other workers & dealers in	
Bricklayers	1,694	iron and steel	3,864
Button makers	4,980	Labourers	3,909
Carpenters, joiners	1,851	Painters, plumbers, glaziers	1,097
Cabinet makers	1,027	Messengers, porters	2,283
Cooks, housemaids, nurses	1,113	Milliners	3,597
Domestic servants (general)	8,359	Shoemakers	3,153
Glass manufacturers	1,117	Tailors	2,009
Other workers in gold & silver	1,153	Tool-makers	1,011
Gunsmiths	2,867	Washerwomen	1,965
Goldsmiths, silversmiths	2,494	Workers in mixed metals	3,778

From these figures it is clear that after domestic service the two largest occupations were those of brassfounders and button makers. To these must be added the gunsmiths, the workers in gold and silver, the iron workers, the workers and dealers in iron and steel, and the workers in mixed metals (varieties of brass and mixtures of copper, zinc and nickel). In addition, a proportion of the total for labourers were no doubt employed in the many branches of the metal industry. It can safely be said, therefore, that in the mid-nineteenth century Birmingham retained its position as the greatest town in the country for the fashioning of metals (or less elegantly, for metal bashing). Of course, not all the trades involved depended on fine craftmanship. On the contrary, some of the cheaper products had a dubious reputation for shoddy workmanship – mere 'Brummagen ware' - and there is the traditional joke (said to have its origin in the rival Black Country) about a hammer being a Birmingham screwdriver; though this is unfair to the better quality goods produced by many Birmingham skilled workers.

This raises again the interesting question of how skills were transmitted in the Birmingham industry of the time. In many cases, especially when the work involved was the simple operation of a press or stamp, no particular skill was necessary and what was needed could be taught easily on the job - just by 'sitting by Nelly'. Where some precise skills were required, some system of apprenticeship could apply. Yet Samuel Timmins, writing in the mid-nineteenth century, stated that in the previous centuries, there were no craft gilds, and that 'the system of apprenticeship was only partly known'.[25] If there were no craft gilds to uphold the apprenticeship system, then it is understandable that given the wide opportunities for juvenile employment, apprenticeship at a reduced wage between the ages of fourteen and twenty-one would not have been very popular. Further, it is often said that with so many metal trades in Birmingham, a worker in one trade could readily switch to another if his trade suffered depression; and a rigid system of apprenticeship would have impeded such transfers.

2. Memorial to Boulton, Watt and Murdock, Broad Street.

Timmins did not say that apprenticeship did not exist at all, however, but that it operated only to a limited degree. That the practice was declining in the mid-nineteenth century seems to be borne out by evidence given before the Children's Employment Commission in 1843, where one observer said that few were bound apprentice, and that there was even some hostility among manufacturers to the system. One witness in the brass industry said that he would not take in-door apprentices – they were too troublesome, and many boys did not want to become regular apprentices. Two other employers agreed with this: many apprentices were petty thieves 'being both troublesome and bad' - and getting worse every year. Another was of the opinion that 'The system of apprenticeship is quite changed. No respectable manufacturer will trouble himself about them... many parents will not bind their children, because they hope they will gain a man's wages before the time of their serving expires'.[26] Hostility (and probably prejudice) could hardly be more apparent.

Thus, evidence for the decline of apprenticeship appears to be quite strong, but this is somewhat puzzling, given the fact that there is plenty to show that apprenticeship was common enough in Birmingham in the eighteenth century.[27] In that century, advertisements appeared from time to time in *Aris's Gazette* for apprentices in the toy trade and for runaway apprentices. Moreover, the modern Index of Apprenticeships in Birmingham Central Library is of relevance here.[28] It is based on references to apprenticeships in local collections rather than to the indentures themselves, and so is by no means a comprehensive guide. Nevertheless, it records fourteen bound apprentice in the gun trade between 1840 and 1872, even though the modern authorities, Bailey & Nie, consider that apprenticeship was virtually absent from this trade.[29] As was suggested earlier in this chapter, the reasons for this given by these authors are not entirely convincing. Certainly apprenticeship continued in Birmingham at the mid-nineteenth century in highly skilled trades such as that of the goldsmiths - there were at least seven apprentices bound in this trade between 1862 and 1869.

Perhaps the answer to the problem is that apprenticeship was becoming more informal at this time in an expanding industrial city with so many trades. In the more specialised trades, such as that of the goldsmiths, there was probably a call for the traditional type of apprenticeship, but in other trades it was not uncommon for apprenticeship to be of a loose, informal kind, based on a verbal agreement between the workman and the father of the apprentice. This was very different from a formal document or indenture for a term of seven years drawn up before a magistrate. One employer witness in 1843, a brassfounder, said that he had only one apprentice, but that his men had many.[30] Premiums for such agreements between workmen and their assistants would obviously be low and the unwritten agreement was hardly likely to be enforceable in a court of law. Nevertheless, it could be a way for a well-meaning parent to obtain extra attention for his son in learning his trade without the expense and formality of the traditional apprenticeship.[31]

To turn now to the question of the size of industrial units in Birmingham at the mid-century: it will be recalled that at the beginning of this chapter it was observed that mechanisation in the form of steam-driven machinery housed in factories had not gone very far by 1850. This is certainly true of Birmingham. A commissioner reporting to the Children's Employment Commission in 1843 remarked that there were no factories in the town similar to those in the north of England. Instead, all over Birmingham there were workshops which varied in size from those employing three or four children and young persons, to others employing fifty, sixty and even a hundred.[32] Larger workplaces were also to be found, the largest apparently in the still important button trade. Turner & Sons were said to employ 500 (possibly including out-workers), Chatwin employed more than 200, and William Elliott, 253.[33] Radcliff's brass foundry has about 150 hands, while Rice Harris, owner of the Islington Glass Works, claimed to employ 540.[34] (This is a much larger number than was usual in the Stourbridge industry, the centre of flint glass manufacture, and must be somewhat suspect.)

In fact, industrial work units at the time were a striking mixture of the traditional workshop and of the larger workplace symbolic of the new industrial age. One visitor in 1844 commented on the size of the larger firms - Watt's works, it was said, employed about 400 workmen, Turner & Co had 'several hundred', Jennings & Bettridge, makers of papier mâché, had about 200 hands, while Phipson & Co, button makers, employed 'some hundreds of children'.[35] On the other hand, the French writer L. Faucher observed in 1856 that large enterprises had not developed as they had in the north, and that most master manufacturers employed only five or six workers.[36] Other sources in the 1850s also refer to the continued existence of large numbers of small masters - 'a singular and peculiar class in Birmingham' - and also to a class of garret masters, who were really 'an anomaly in the working world'.[37]

It seems clear that, at the mid-century, where the continued use of simple labour-saving hand machines such as the press and the stamp was still appropriate, they were still employed. This was the case even though the workshops had increased in size and might even share a steam engine with an adjacent workshop. Only in heavy industry such as the brass industry was the industrial unit relatively large since it needed to employ steam-powered rolling and grinding machinery.

The expansion of the traditional workshop system is an interesting subject. Timmins, writing in 1866, described the way in which he thought this took place:

> Beginning as a small master, often working in his own house with his wife and children to help him, the Birmingham workman has become a master, his trade has extended, his buildings have increased. He has used his house as a workshop, has annexed another, has built upon the garden or the yard, and consequently a large number of the manufactories are most irregular in size.

If this is an accurate picture of how the workshop system developed – and it clearly does not apply to the large purpose-built brass foundry – it would be instructive to enquire into how far the process had gone by the 1850s. Professor Allen reckoned that as late as 1860, work premises might be divided up into the large factory with 150 workers and above; the small factory, with from thirty or forty workers up to 150; the workshop, employing thirty or forty workers; and the workshop of the garret master, employing only his family and an occasional journeyman or apprentice. It was usually only for the largest workplace that premises were specially built. The small factory often simply consisted of a chain of converted dwelling houses, and the workshop and garret master were commonly dependent upon a factor for the supply of raw material and the marketing of their goods.[39]

To refer to the marketing of products is to be reminded of the importance of trade and the service industries in the Birmingham economy. The mid-century years were to see an increasing expansion of trading in Birmingham, something linked closely with industrial expansion, of course, and part of the national boom of the mid-century years. However, trade had experienced vicissitudes earlier in the century especially during the wars against France, and in the late 1830s and early 1840s (the so-called 'Hungry Forties'). Undoubtedly Birmingham profited from the local canal system earlier in the century, and the local economy received a further boost from the building of the Birmingham to Liverpool railway line in 1837, followed by the Birmingham to London line in 1838. When the national depression in trade lifted from 1843 onwards, these links made their contribution to local recovery. Older transport services were hit by the coming of the railways, such as the London coach services, while canal companies had to drop their charges to meet the new competition from transport by rail. For example, the cost of transporting a ton of hardware from Birmingham to London by canal was reduced from £3 in 1836 to £2 in 1842.[40]

How far the improvement in trade of the fifties was due to increased exports, and how far to increased domestic trade is difficult to say. Undoubtedly foreign trade had long been an important part of Birmingham commerce. Nearly a hundred years previously, Boulton & Fothergill, toymakers, had an extensive trade in Europe, Boulton remarking in 1767 that 'more than half the letters we receive are wrote in the German Language'; his partner Fothergill spent two years abroad visiting European customers.[41] In 1783 William Hutton claimed that the growth of foreign trade was a principal cause of Birmingham's economic development – 'To this modern conduct of Birmingham in sending her sons to the foreign market, I ascribe the chief cause of her rapid increase.'[42] Certainly trade was depressed during the war against France at the beginning of the century,[43] but Birmingham's foreign trade picked up again after 1815, especially with the boom in the brass industry, and in this connection it is worth recalling again W.C. Aitkin's proud boast quoted earlier in this chapter about the world supremacy in its different forms of Birmingham brass, on both land and sea.

As for the service trades, it is evident that large numbers of men, women and children were engaged in these trades. An estimate based on the Birmingham 1861 census returns is that about 40% of the working population were engaged in this way, that is, nearly 61,000 out of a working population of about 150,000. Further, the wholesale and retail trade occupied nearly 20,000 men and women, which is about a third of all those in the service trades and 13% of the total work force.[44] Since the national figure for trade, transport, public services and professions as a percentage of the total occupied population in 1861 has been estimated at 38%,[45] Birmingham had evidently kept up with other towns in this respect.

Among the service trades, the professions were of great importance in the commercial life of the town: in 1851 according to the census returns, there were 107 solicitors, 170 law clerks, 130 accountants and 1,073 commercial clerks. There were also 327 commercial travellers. The food trades were represented by 787 grocers, 799 butchers (for some reason or other, the census also records there were 310 butchers' wives), 141 fishmongers, and 258 cowkeepers and milk sellers. Many working men needed a hot meal at midday, and their wants were supplied by numerous cook shops, selling a plate of meat for 3d and 1d for potatoes or bread. There were as many as ninety-five small cook shops in the town in 1841, and publicans also supplied meals at the same prices.[46] Other foodstuffs were obtainable from so-called huckster shops at this time. According to the committee reporting to Chadwick's Sanitary Enquiry in 1841 –[47]

> Tea, coffee, sugar, butter, cheese, bacon (of which a great deal is consumed in this town) and other articles, the working class purchase in small quantities from the hucksters, who charge an enormous profit upon them, being as they state, compelled to do so to cover the losses which they frequently sustain for bad debts. Huckster dealing is a most extravagant mode of dealing: there were in this town in 1834, 717 of these shops, and the number has greatly increased since that time.

Certainly the working man in Birmingham liked his drink, and work on the numerous forges and furnaces was thirsty work. His wants were supplied in 1851 by 204 malsters, 717 brewers, and 718 licensed victuallers and beershop keepers (no doubt there were a number of unlicensed beershops, too, known in the Black Country as 'wobble shops'. Occasionally such shops might be prosecuted, but the police probably had better things to do than to keep close watch on them - there were only 353 police officers in the town, roughly one for every 660 of the population). Other occupations which catch the eye in the 1851 census returns are the surgeons (169) and druggists (233), the schoolmasters (149) and schoolmistresses (475), and the clothing trades. These last were numerous, but catered for the trade of the middle classes rather than the working classes, who often made do with second-hand clothing. The clothing trades included hatters

(115), tailors (1,619 men, 390 women), shoemakers (2,783 men, 822 women), dressmakers (352 men, 226 women), straw hat and bonnet makers (435), miliners (3,597), seamstresses (577), stay-makers (398), drapers (619) and hosiers (144). The largest category of all occupations was that of general domestic servant (711 men and 8,359 women), while in a separate category were placed cooks, housemaids and domestic nurses (1,113 in all). Lastly, at the bottom of the wage-earning scale were general labourers (3,909), messengers and porters (2,283), hawkers (355), charwomen (470) and washerwomen (1,965). One oddity is the category of 'persons connected with shows, games and sport': there were 721 men so classified.

Thus the economic life of Birmingham was vigorous and many-faceted in the mid-nineteenth century, with a strong tertiary sector. As we have seen, its development earlier in the century owed little to steam power before 1830. In one sense it would be possible to answer the question posed at the beginning of this chapter by suggesting that Birmingham was not the product of the Industrial Revolution at all, in that it had developed substantially as an industrial centre long before the tech-nological changes associated with that revolution took effect. Its multitude of small workshops demonstrate the fact that at the heart of its economy in 1850 there still existed a traditional small master economy; and it is worth while recalling that Boulton's famed Soho manufactory employing up to 1,000 workers in fact consisted of a number of small workshops and was based on much sub-contracting of work to smaller firms. However, this argument could be pushed too far, and fails to take account of the use of steam power in heavy industry such as the brass industry which was so prominent a feature of Birmingham industry in 1850, and which helps to account for the existence of larger works such as Wingfields.

So Birmingham industry flourished on the basis of traditional hand production in workshops, and large-scale production of metals in foundries and forges employing steam power – a combi-nation of the old and the new; and by the 1850s, of course, steam railways were proving a valuable new form of transport for both raw materials and finished goods. The larger-scale industries were essential in supplying metals, for example, to the toy trade and the gun trade. It should also be added that it was greatly to the benefit of Birmingham industry that not only did increasing national prosperity bring growing demands for consumer goods such as jewellery, but the vast urban expansion of the time brought massively increased markets for cabinet brass work, plumbing requirements of all kinds, gas fittings, and so on. Birmingham, it might be said, just happened to possess the industries (apart from the textile and extractive industries) which were most in demand during the great economic expansion which we conveniently characterise as the Industrial Revolution. No wonder then that the mid-century years were years of pros-perity for Birmingham.

However, if Birmingham fails to confirm to the commonly accepted norm of industrial devel-opment during the Industrial Revolution, how far did it escape the alleged immiseration of the workers that is often associated with the Revolution? How far was the social scene dominated by a ruthless class of industrialists indifferent to the sufferings of an exploited working class? We may now move on to examine the social scene in its broad outlines at the mid-nineteenth century, starting with the part played in society by the middle classes, and afterwards turning to the working and living conditions of the working classes.

In the first place, it must be said again that Birmingham was essentially a middle-class town where the leaders of society were industrialists and business men. There was no local aristocracy to dominate the social scene. There was no resident leisure class, and no-one lived in Birmingham purely for the pleasure of its gracious buildings and amenities - it was too dirty, noisy and smoky for that. Moreover, the town's leading citizens were not especially wealthy: an estimate of their fortunes in 1828 gave only fifteen worth over £100,000, twenty-six with £10,000, and 300 or so with £5,000,[48] and this out of a population in 1831 of 146,986. What united the Birmingham middle classes was a determination to stand up for the best commercial interests of their town. This is shown by the influence exerted by them through the town improvement commissioners and their efforts to improve the central thoroughfares and markets of the town; by their vigorous representations against the Orders in Council in 1812 which they alleged were having such a disastrous effect on their overseas trade; and above all, perhaps, by their taking a leading role in the struggle to achieve parliamentary reform in the early 1830s.

Indeed, it can be argued that the Birmingham Political Union, led by the Birmingham banker Thomas Attwood, played a major part in mobilising public opinion in favour of the passing of the great Reform Act, 1832. It is no wonder that Birmingham was regarded as a radical town (though curiously enough, Attwood himself was a Tory, whose main interest in reforming parliament was as a means of achieving currency reform). The Birmingham Political Union (BPU) was established as a political union of the middle and working classes, and its original programme actually included five of the six points of the People's Charter. Shortly after the passing of the Reform Act, Robert Owen opened his Equitable Labour Exchange in Birmingham in 1833, having enlisted the support of some of the leading Birmingham figures in the enterprise. He is on record as having planned to involve 'the Attwoods, the Scholefields, the Muntzes, the Jones and many others who had long been labouring in the public vineyard.'[49] The Equitable Labour Exchange soon collapsed, but the BPU was revived in 1837, aiming at further franchise reform, and Attwood actually introduced the first Chartist petition into the House of Commons in 1839. Subsequently middle-class support for Chartism declined following the Bull Ring riots in that year, and the increasing threat of Chartist violence. Even then, in 1841 a local Quaker business man, Joseph Sturge, sought to combine the cause of the repeal of the corn laws with further franchise reform (the 'New Move') in co-operation with Feargus O'Connor, the Chartist leader; but this effort also came to nothing.

Other prominent business figures in Birmingham were engaged in reforming activities. For example, William Hawkes Smith and William Pare were both committee members of the Equitable Labour Exchange and members of the Birmingham Co-operative Society. Pare was a tobacconist and later manufacturer, and a strong supporter of Robert Owen. When Owen set up his community project at Queenswood in Hampshire in 1839, Pare sold £500 worth of his railway shares to help finance the community, and moved himself and his family to Harmony Hall in Queenswood, where he served as governor for some years. In fact, he was far more active than Owen in the practical business of running the community. His communitarian beliefs were well-known: a campaign against him as Registrar of Births and Marriages in Birmingham was led by the Bishop of Exeter, and he was forced to resign on the general grounds that he was a socialist and unfit to serve in such an office. Subsequently Pare became a veteran supporter of the co-operative movement.[50]

After the passing of the Reform Act, 1832, Birmingham for the first time acquired parliamentary representation. Thomas Attwood and Joshua Scholefield, a leading manufacturer, became its first members of parliament (though Attwood never succeeded in getting the House to approve his plans for currency reform). However, the campaign to reform the national system of parliamentary representation led naturally to the reform of municipal authorities. These bodies were modernised by the Municipal Corporation Act, 1835. Birmingham, of course, previously had no corporation, and civic affairs were supervised by the town Commissioners whose powers had beeen conferred by a succession of private improvement acts, starting with the Lamp Act, 1769; but under the Municipal Corporation Act it was possible for unincorporated towns to acquire municipal status. Thus in 1838 Birmingham was granted a charter and corporation. Oddly enough, this was only after a lengthy controversy. Many ratepayers argued against incorporation on the grounds that the town commissioners already governed the town well enough, and they already had more power than the corporation would have under the 1835 act. Incorporation, it was argued, was an unnecessary expense.[51] The three leading officials in the new council were all prominent members of the BPU: William Scholefield was the first mayor, William Redford the first Town Clerk, and R.K. Douglas, editor of the *Birmingham Journal*, was Registrar of the Mayor's Court. In addition to the mayor, there were sixteen aldermen and forty-eight councillors.

From all this it is apparent that a number of Birmingham employers were actively interested in reform. How far did this influence relationships with their employees? In fact, contemporary observers from outside the town agreed that there was less class conflict in Birmingham than in some of the newer industrial towns such as Manchester. De Tocqueville, for example, visiting Manchester in 1835, remarked that 'separation of class [was] much greater in Manchester than in Birmingham'.[52] Asa Briggs, Trygve Tholfsen, and other modern historians have taken the same view.[53] One indication of the state of labour relations might be thought to be the amount of strike activity: the total of strikes for the years 1800-50 is 103, and for individuals prosecuted in the course of trade disputes the number is 135.[54] All depends on the nature and duration of particular strikes, of course, but an average of two strikes a year (and rather more per annum after 1820) in a town where the workforce trebled in the first half of the nineteenth century, and there were a quarter of a million inhabitants by 1871, does not seem remarkably large. There is no doubt that paternalistic attitudes persisted among employers during the first half of the nineteenth century.

This is to be seen in a variety of ways, and is often explained as one result of the number of small workshops in the town where employer and employee worked on the same bench, often side by side. There was also the possibility of advancement to the rank of employer, something much more possible in a workshop economy requiring little starting capital than in an economy dominated by large-scale industrial units. Nevertheless, paternalistic attitudes were not confined to small employers, but were displayed by a number of the largest employers giving evidence before the Children's Employment Commission in 1843. Thus William Elliott, a large button manufacturer employing about 250 hands, said that he had found that consideration and attention to the welfare and happiness of the workpeople produced the best results – 'decidedly thinks that the people are quite conscious of such attention, and grateful for it'. Mr John Bourne, proprietor of a cabinet brass foundry, claimed that in the thirty years he had been in business, by conciliatory

3. Thomas Attwood, 1783-1856.

conduct and kind treatment, the men became attached to their employer; many of his men had worked for him between fifteen and thirty years, and he employed a number of their children. James James, owner of a large screw manufactory, said that he had paid increasing attention to the intellectual and religious instruction of his workpeople, and always tried to promote rational amusements among them, for example, sending a party of men to travel on the Liverpool-Manchester Railway at its opening. Benjamin Jones declared that Mr James' workpeople were happy and contented, and that he was certain that Mr James was universally respected.[55]

Other examples can also be given of similar paternalistic attitudes, of the existence of sick clubs in the larger works, of workmen drinking toasts to employers and contributing to presents for special occasions (for example, the coming of age of the employer's son), attending works dinners and feasts, and going on trips and jaunts, especially 'gipsy parties' (outings to local beauty spots and places of interest). Of course, by today's standards, some of the evidence given by employers before the 1843 Commission seems unctuous and patronising, and the modern reader might well be inclined to question its sincerity; but Victorian earnestness did exist, and did influence at least some employers' outlook and conduct. This earnestness might be the result of and reinforced by the evangelical movement: Mr Bacchus, a leading glass manufacturer, encouraged his workers to attend church or chapel, and had contributed very liberally to the building of an adjacent church.[56]

There is plenty of other evidence to support the view that employers felt some moral obligation to their workers in mid-nineteenth century Birmingham. In one way this may be viewed as simple, old-fashioned paternalism, dating from the eighteenth century and earlier. Another way of looking at it is that it was a form of enlightened self-interest, since a contented workman would obviously work better than a discontented workman. A more cynical explanation might be that it was all a matter of social control though there is no evidence to show any deep-seated agreement or understanding among employers of this kind. Whatever the underlying motives might be, it is a basic fact that the paternalistic attitudes of many employers made for better class relationships than, for example, in Manchester.

These attitudes were based on tradition and, to some extent at least, religious belief. It has been observed that 'to discuss paternalism [in Birmingham] in the 1850s as though it was purely a device by employers to manage their workers would be to ignore the force of both tradition and religious conviction'.[57] It was real and it existed. For their part, the working classes took it more or less for granted, though they might resent visits (and the accompanying pamphlets) by church missioners, or efforts by a too earnest employer to get them off drink. On the whole, they accepted the social hierarchy of the time as part of the natural order of things. They might be critical of their employers, and certainly could go on strike from time to time, but many were conservative in outlook and voted Conservative in the general elections of 1868 and 1874, after the franchise had been extended to male working-class householders in the towns. Paternalism was certainly alive and well in mid-nineteenth century Birmingham.

What then of working conditions? In 1833, John Blews, a small manufacturer of locks and iron candlesticks, gave evidence that 'there was a general rule in Birmingham laid down that we work but ten hours' – that is, twelve hours less two hours off for meals. This was confirmed in 1843 by the Children's Employment Commissioner, R.D. Grainger, whose evidence was that the hours –[58]

… are generally moderate in Birmingham, the common hours being 12, out of which 2 are generally deducted for meals, so the actual time of labour is 10 hours: this may be considered the rule. In some manufactories 13 hours are the regular time… on the whole, it may be stated, that the hours of labour are probably shorter and less fatiguing than in any other large manufacturing town in the kingdom.

It must also be pointed out that St Monday was still often kept at the mid-century, though it was subject to more and more criticism. It was observed even in some of the larger works in the 1860s. A commissioner of the Children's Employment Commission (1862), Mr J.E. White, remarked that 'individual efforts are, as a rule, powerless to abolish this wasteful and injurious habit'. He also said that one employer in 1864 had only about forty or fifty workers in on a Monday out of a total workforce of 300-400, and that on a Monday few works were fully or even partially employed; in one large foundry the casters were getting to work for the first time in the week towards midday on Tuesday.[59] In addition to the day off on Monday, the larger firms also closed for a week or fortnight at Christmas for stocktaking, and one or two days were also given off at Easter and at Whitsuntide. The same time off was also allowed at some of the fairs and wakes still in evidence at the mid-century; their number had recently been increased rather than decreased in Birmingham.

How far the expansion of industry in Birmingham saw more hours being worked is hard to say, given that in Boulton's time in the eighteenth century the average working day seems to have been of about twelve hours (or even longer) in duration. In any case, it is especially difficult to estimate hours worked in the average workshop, given the keeping of St Monday, the leisurely pace of work at the beginning of the week and the very lengthy working day by the weekend: what counted in the smaller establishments, at least, was the production of so many finished goods for delivery to the factor, and not the working of uniform hours. Then there is short-time working to take into account, due to the non-delivery of raw materials, and the ebb and flow of demand for the product. Certainly no evidence has survived of working-class complaints against efforts by Birmingham employers to increase working hours in the first half of the nineteenth century, and although it is clearly dangerous to argue from lack of evidence, this absence of complaint appears to confirm that working hours in Birmingham did not increase significantly during the classic period of the Industrial Revolution.

It may be, of course, and it seems not unlikely, that in the larger workplaces, such as the foundries, the use of steam power might have brought a greater regularity of work processes and a harsher work discipline. This is certainly possible, but even then, steam power was not being used by 1850 on a massive scale, and the production methods used in foundry work were very different from the universal use of steam power in the large textile factories of the north. The reliance on simple hand machinery in Birmingham workshops died hard, and had a profound influence on the weekly pattern of work: one historian of Birmingham industry has even suggested that in both the domestic workshop and the majority of factories the workers often tried to concentrate the week's work into the last three days of the week.[60] This may be perhaps to go too far, although more recent left-wing arguments to show that a new discipline might be introduced into workshops on the basis of improved tools and/or a more systematic exploitation of labour have not been very convincing.[61]

However, there is one aspect of employment in Birmingham which drew criticism from a visiting commissioner in 1843, and that was the widespread use of women and children in the workshops. It was said that women were employed on work which was too heavy for them. Although children were not usually ill-treated, and started work at nine or ten, there were nevertheless two pin factories (those of Phipson's and Palmers & Holt) where the treatment of the children 'was strikingly opposed, to the general good usage of children in Birmingham'.[62] In Phipson's, women used a stick to wake up children who slowed down and became sleepy in the evening, while at Palmers & Holts, some male supervisors were especially violent in beating the children. These children in the pin factories came from the poorest and most wretched of parents, Mr Phipson himself describing pin-heading as 'the refuge for the destitute'. According to the commissioner, a Mr Grainger, 'In the whole of my enquiries, I have met with no class more urgently requiring legislative protection than the unhappy pin-headers'.[63]

The other criticism made by Grainger was of the working environment. Many of the workshops were in very old buildings which were dilapidated, ruinous or even dangerous, cold and damp, with broken windows. Such workshops were suffocatingly hot in summer (and also at night when the gas was lit) and very cold in winter. The privies in the yard were often in a foul condition, and frequently criticised by witnesses for not having separate compartments or any segregation of the sexes. Accidents in the workshops were common enough, the use of hand machines leading to sprains and contusions, wounds and fractures, and where metal was heated, burns and scalds. Of course, the bad state of some workshops is understandable enough, given the fact that by 1850 industry in Birmingham had been expanding for over a hundred years. It is no wonder that some of the older premises, and indeed the notorious garret workshops under the roof, were in such a poor condition. More modern buildings, built more recently, were much more satisfactory.[64]

Lastly, a brief survey of living accommodation for the working classes in Birmingham about 1850: a good general impression may be gained from the three national enquiries into local sanitary conditions which were carried out in the early 1840s. In 1840 the *Report of the Health of Towns Select Committee* (p. xii) considered that Birmingham was in a better state than some other industrial towns. In their words –

> The great town of Birmingham… appears to form rather a favourable contrast, in several particulars, with the state of other large towns… the general custom of each family living in a separate dwelling is conducive to comfort and cleanliness, and the good state of the town, and the dry and absorbive nature of the soil, are very great natural advantages.

In short, there were no cellar dwellings, the water supply was very good, it was a very healthy town, the 'abodes of the poor' were much better than in Liverpool, Manchester and London, and though there were many back-to-back houses, they were not necessarily inferior to other houses. *Chadwick's Report*, 1842, confirmed these findings, again observing that back-to-back houses were not necessarily bad, but laying much greater emphasis on the poor state of some of the older courts, which were narrow, ill-ventilated, filthy and badly drained, with disgusting privies. This second report agreed with the 1840 report in condemning the lodging houses as great sources of disease.[65] The third of the 1840s reports (the *First Report of the Commissioners of Inquiry into the State of Large Towns and Populous Districts*, 1844) adds little to the earlier reports except to stress the bad state of the older courts. Finally, in 1849, a report by Sir Robert Rawlinson on sanitary conditions in the town yet again emphasised the unsatisfactory state of the older courts: there were about 2,000 close courts undrained, many being unpaved, and the privies described as 'a frequent source of nuisance'.[66]

The broad picture which emerges is thus of a relatively healthy town with numerous back-to-back houses, the better-quality housing with higher rents being available to better-paid workers, the worst housing with the cheapest rents being in the older insanitary courts. Mortality rates in the early 1840s averaged at 2.7%, only 1% higher than that of Bath, and lower than the rates for Hull (3), Liverpool (3.5) and Manchester (3.2).[67] The greatest danger to health was likely to have been the earth closets, which, according to Rawlinson, were shared in most cases by four households; they were badly neglected and usually in a foul condition. However, it is worth remembering that even in Edgbaston, the most favoured middle-class residential area, there was still no deep underground drainage. According to Mr R.T. Cadbury, chairman of the Improvement Commissioners –[68]

> In the Hagley Road the gutters are receptacles of drains and filth till they become in the most putrid state, reeking with the contents of water closets in the finest neighbourhood of Birmingham.

Not only this, but there were many cesspits on premises in the Hagley Road. In 1849 a party of workmen engaged for £2 to empty one cesspit here found the smell so abominable that they demanded an additional £1, then a further £1 and a pint of brandy every hour.[69]

Lastly, even a preliminary sketch of working-class society in Birmingham about 1850 would be incomplete without some reference to education and religious observance. Given the fact that child employment was so widespread in Birmingham, it is not surprising that children's attendance at school was somewhat limited. Literacy rates were not high. In 1846, 29% of bridegrooms were still making their mark and unable to sign their names in Birmingham registers, while 47% of brides similarly could not sign. However, this was not very far different from the national figures for literacy in 1851 published by the Registrar General in the Census Returns. They estimated that 30.7% of men, and 45.2% of the women were illiterate. Clearly, literacy among working children would vary from family to family, dependent on how important the parents thought it to be. A spot check on literacy in Palmer & Holt's pin factory in 1843, where children came from very poor homes, revealed that among children aged seven to twelve, 67% of the boys and 58% of the girls could not read, while 81% of the boys and all of the girls were unable to write at all.[70]

4. Birmingham Town Hall, 1834.

Provision for working-class education was still restricted in Birmingham at the mid-century. Church schools had grown in number since their inception in 1809, while between 1837 and 1852 four new elementary schools had been founded by the King Edward Foundation for the sons of the superior working classes. There were still more private schools in the form of dame schools and common day schools than there were church schools, charity schools, or those of the King Edward Foundation. Working-class education had yet to become compulsory or free: both the church schools and the private schools charged a few pence a week, and many parents preferred their children to be earning a wage rather than paying for their attendance at school.

If children did attend school, it was usually for only a short period, perhaps up to two years, before they began work. Consequently, the numbers of boys and girls at school in Birmingham in 1850 were not impressive. Nationally, one in 8.36 attended a day school in 1851, while in Birmingham the figure was 11.02.[71] It should also be mentioned that the Sunday School Movement had established 56 Sunday Schools in Birmingham by 1838, and by 1841 some 35% of working-class children were attending them.[72] They taught reading the Bible, of course, thus increasing reading skills, but less than half of the schools taught writing as well. Since the Sunday School day on average lasted only four hours, including prayers and singing, it was hardly a substitute for full-time schooling.[73]

As for religious observance, it is well-known that the results of the national survey of church and chapel attendance in 1851 caused the Victorians great concern; roughly only about half of those free to go to a place of worship on Census Sunday actually did so, and the attendance in the larger industrial towns was even lower than this, causing the compiler of the Religious Census, Horace Mann, to comment gloomily that 'the masses of our working population... are never or but seldom seen in our religious congregations'. The overall figure for attendance in Birmingham was 31.1% (Wolverhampton, 53.1%; Dudley, 55.3%). What proportion of attenders were working class can only be guessed at. One recent calculation, which admittedly is highly speculative, puts the figure at 24% of the working population at maximum, and at 12% at minimum.[74]

It is not difficult to adduce reasons for these low figures. It must have been easy for some immigrants into the town to lose the habit of church attendance in their native villages. Pew rents might be another obstacle - more than half the total sittings were still subject to them, even among the Primitive Methodists, who in any case had only three chapels (elsewhere in the West Midlands the Primitive Methodists had a much greater appeal to the working classes). Then again, lack of a suitable best suit or dress could be a barrier, bearing in mind that there was the general feeling that church was for the better-off, who occupied the rented pews. Some churches held separate services for working people, sometimes in a tent pitched in a working-class area, and this must have increased the feeling of social segregation. Nevertheless, it would be unwise to consider the working classes of Birmingham at the mid-century to be a relatively heathen if not godless part of the community. A third of their children attended Sunday School. Some certainly were pupils at church schools, and even those who were not exposed to the teachings of the church or chapel might well have said their bed-time prayers at their mother's knee. So some scraps of Biblical knowledge, however muddled or incoherent, might still have been transmitted to Birmingham working-class children at this time, even those whose parents rarely if ever attended church or chapel.

It is time to draw some conclusions. At the beginning of this chapter, the question was asked, how far was Birmingham a product of the Industrial Revolution? On the evidence presented in the previous pages, the answer must be that it was an important industrial town *before* the coming of the Industrial Revolution, and contributed greatly to it but not in the ways too often thought to be characteristic of that revolution. Thus, industrial expansion in Birmingham was not dominated by new labour-saving machinery or by steam power, though the latter became important after 1830. Further, there are few signs that it was accompanied by increasing class divisions or class struggle. In particular, working hours remained very much the same, the traditional St Monday being retained at least up to the mid-nineteenth century, while holidays and local wakes were similarly unchanged. There was certainly a growth of larger workplaces, of which the large brass works were characteristic, but not of large and crowded factories of the kind found in the cotton districts.

The one aspect of the Industrial Revolution in the textile industry which became notorious and was also to be found in Birmingham was the ill-treatment of children. This does not seem to have been widespread in the town, but was observed and commented on by visiting commissioners in at least two pin factories. As for living conditions, certainly Birmingham had its overcrowded and insanitary areas, especially in the old courts, but its health statistics were rather better than those in other industrial towns. It was a relatively healthy place, in spite of the atmospheric pollution and the insanitary and foul earth closets. The urban squalor and degradation so vividly described by Engels as typical in Manchester in 1844 were less apparent in Birmingham, though of course all industrial towns suffered to some degree from overcrowding and congestion as a result of the massive influx of population. In some places in Birmingham the famous guinea gardens – plots of an eighth and sometimes a sixteenth of an acre – lingered on, even in the central areas.

This introductory sketch of the economic and social scene has had to concentrate on essentials, and in the interests of brevity has omitted some aspects of the life of the town such as leisure activities which will appear in subsequent chapters. The political scene has only been lightly touched upon, and will certainly reappear later: Birmingham played an important part in the struggle over the Reform Bill, and was to become nationally famous again in the 1870s not only as a model of efficient local government, but also as the home territory of the national leader of the campaign for tariff reform and colonial preference. Nevertheless, the basic features are clear enough. Having survived some years of depression in the early 1840s, by 1850 Birmingham was on the verge of a period of further expansion and increasing prosperity. The period of the 1850s and 1860s was to see a remarkable growth in the national economy in which Birmingham played a full part. Economic development in the second half of the nineteenth century and up to 1914 will therefore form the subject of the following chapter.

CHAPTER TWO

ECONOMIC CHANGE

In the preceding introductory chapter, much emphasis was laid on the fact that Birmingham in the mid-nineteenth century was very much a manufacturing town. Only recently had it acquired its own corporation, and at the time there were still those who thought the improvement commissioners had sufficiently adequate powers to make a locally elected council both otiose and unnecessary. Only in 1889 did the town become officially a city, though it had none of the features usually associated with ancient foundations - no medieval castle or walls, and no medieval cathedral (St Philips, originally a parish church, dates from the eighteenth century). Even though by the 1870s Birmingham was beginning to take a pride in being well-governed, its mayor was a leading manufacturer and business man, Joseph Chamberlain. So it seems appropriate that this chapter should concentrate on economic conditions in Birmingham between 1850 and 1914, since industry, trade and the service sector constituted the life-blood of so many of its inhabitants throughout this period, as indeed it already had been doing when William Hutton made his first visit to Birmingham in the previous century.[1]

How did the economy of Birmingham fare during the second half of the nineteenth century and the first few years of the following century? In very general terms, it participated in the continued national expansion of industry and of trade during the period. British industry as a whole experienced two decades of considerable prosperity in the 1850s and 1860s, usually regarded as a time of actual boom conditions,[2] the one major qualification being the slump in the cotton industry due to the interruption in the supplies of cotton from America during the Civil War in the early 1860s. Certainly 1870 and 1871 were years of great prosperity (they were also years of war between two formidable trade rivals, France and Germany), but the following twenty years or so were somewhat different. Indeed, the Victorians were sufficently alarmed at the fall in prices and the reduction in profits to coin the somewhat misleading term, 'The Great Depression' for the period 1873 to 1896.[3]

Subsequently trade picked up again, though there was an increasing awareness that industrial competitors such as the USA and Germany were threatening Britain's supremacy in overseas trade (both countries were well ahead of Britain in steel production by 1913), while American tariffs in the 1890s were excluding some British goods. The result was a campaign for tariff reform and colonial preference in the early 1900s led by Joseph Chamberlain, now a national figure and Colonial Secretary up to September 1903 in the Conservative government led by Arthur Balfour. The First World War broke out in August 1914, thus ending a period in which Britain, as the first industrial nation, found her industrial supremacy increasingly challenged. The reality of this was to become very apparent after the war. However, it is worth mentioning at this stage that new elements were developing in British industry before 1914 - the rise of new industries such as the cycle, motor car and electrical industries which were to play a vital part subsequently in the Midlands in compensating for the relative decline of the staple industries of iron, coal and shipping.

Against this background, we may examine the fortunes of Birmingham manufacturing between 1850 and 1875. The principal industries remained as before: the brass trade in all its varieties, the gun trade, buttons and jewellery. The brass trade continued to flourish and indeed expand, with the sustained demand for brass bedsteads and the introduction of brass paraffin lamps. The number of factories in the tube trade doubled between 1868 and 1873.[4] Jewellery also expanded, helped by the discoveries of gold in California and Australia in 1849-51, and by national prosperity in Britain. Electro-plating also flourished, and so did the manufacture of umbrellas: Birmingham supplied nearly all the country's umbrella fittings.[5] Buttons, on the other hand, began a slow decline as the industry was faced by foreign competition and by a shortage of pearl shell due to the failure of South American supplies.[6]

The gun trade experienced mixed fortunes. It was to be transformed by the introduction of factory production. Up to the 1850s, with the exception of a few trades, principally in heavy industry and in the pen trade, the traditional tools of the stamp, press, lathe and drawbench were all extensively used in Birmingham workshops, but as mere accessories to manual skill, which was the determining factor. L. Faucher, in his *Studies in England* (1856) put it as follows:[7]

> A Birmingham... le travail est purement manuel. On emploie les machines comme un accessoire de la fabrication; mais tout dépend de l'adresse et de l'intelligence de l'ouvrier.

But after the outbreak of the Crimean War in 1854, and following the visit of a government commission to the great American gun factory at Springfield in 1853, the British Government decided to set up a large gun manufactory at Enfield, north of London, using American machinery. In alarm, sixteen Birmingham firms organised a rival firm with a factory at Small Heath in 1861 – the Birmingham Small Arms Co. Ltd. When the Franco-Prussian War began in 1870, the gun trade naturally flourished and a new firm was set up, the National Arms and Ammunition Company, which established four factories for the production of the new Martini Henry rifles, and for the manufacture of the brass, ammunition and machinery required.[8] These developments meant that henceforth the gun trade was divided into the old gun trade, producing sporting guns in their traditional workshops, and the factory-based trade producing military guns by mass-production methods. The factory trade obviously prospered in times of war, in the early 1870s, but thereafter languished when peace returned.

If the industrial scene is surveyed before the onset of the Great Depression, then it is clear that on the whole, Birmingham industry continued to prosper and expand in the 1850s and 1860s. Indeed, in common with the rest of the country's industry, the early years of the 1870s were especially prosperous. Asa Briggs goes so far as to refer to the 'roaring boom of 1870-73'.[9] Of course, the trade cycle had produced something of a mini-boom nationally in 1864-65, followed by a financial crisis in 1866. After this, trade was relatively flat until a recovery came in the years 1869-70, blossoming into the splendour of 1870-73; so progress was uneven, as might be expected, but there is no mistaking the prosperity of the early 1870s.

In some ways, the old-style Birmingham industry based on the small business operating in the traditional workshop reached its zenith in these years, and as we shall see later, they were the years of civic confidence in which Joseph Chamberlain carried out his striking municipal reforms. Yet even then there were signs of approaching change. In addition to the changes in the gun trade just described, newer and larger firms were beginning to emerge. Elkington's, the largest firm in electro-plating, continued to expand, and so did the Tangye Works at Soho, founded 1864, providing supplies for railways such as tubes for boilers, nuts and screws for rails, and accessories for rolling stock. They also made hydraulic machinery. The Metropolitan Carriage and Waggon Company employed as many as 1,200 workers at Saltley in 1862. Kynoch's manufactured percussion caps in Great Hampton Street, afterwards moving to Witton, and ultimately becoming the Metals Division of Imperial Chemicals Industries.[10] Increasingly then, larger enterprises were appearing, but their numbers at this stage must not be exaggerated. By 1870 there were probably fewer than twenty firms employing more than 500 workers. These included Joseph Gillott's and J. Mason's pen factories, Robert Wingfield's brass and engineering works (employing 800 hands in 1862), Tangye's works, Elkington's (employing 500 in 1850 and more than 1,600 in 1880), and some button firms also employed between 200 and 500.[11] However, the larger firms were still heavily outnumbered by the myriad smaller enterprises.

After 1873 Birmingham fell increasingly under the shadow of the Great Depression, as it was called at the time. It used to be said that there were so many trades in Birmingham, that if one or more was depressed, a worker could transfer without difficulty to another trade which was less depressed; but it has been pointed out that most trades were specialised, so that the ease of transfer from one trade to another can be exaggerated. At all events, by 1875 the national depression of prices and profits began to have repercussions in Birmingham.[12] The small arms factories were slack, and so was the brass trade. By 1876 the depression had spread to the greater part of local industry, prices had fallen, unemployment increased and the export trade was greatly diminished.[13]

If attention is concentrated on the earlier period of the Great Depression up to 1886, it seems that jewellery was the most depressed of all the local industries, at least according to the Chief Inspector of Factories and Workshops. There was some loss of demand for the higher-grade gold wares in the years 1876-80, and by 1885-86 there were changes of fashion, and silver jewellery became more favoured as the price of silver fell; and there was increasing competition from America. Nevertheless, numbers in the trade kept up well – they advanced from nearly 10,000 in 1871 to over 14,000 in 1881.[14]

The brass trade could not avoid being affected by the fall in prices, but continued to expand moderately. Unemployment was limited: it grew in 1878-79, but then fell again after two years. There was some depression again in 1885-86, but on the whole buoyancy was maintained because there was as yet little foreign competition, and the price of copper nearly halved between 1875 and 1885. The production of brass bedsteads still increased. The output locally was about 5,000 a week in 1865, rising to 20,000 in 1886.[15]

The fortunes of the gun trade were somewhat different. It has already been mentioned that the military trade had become monopolised by factory production, while the cheaper type of sporting guns and muskets were more and more manufactured in Belgium. High-class sporting guns made in Birmingham were still sold on the American market, but were affected by American tariffs. As for the military section, the British Small Arms Company was unable to pay dividends for several years, and in 1880 began to make bicycles. The National Arms and Ammunition Company wound up in 1882 and its four factories sold. There was some improvement in demand from 1885 when the threat from Russia on the north-west frontiers of India increased, and more arms were needed for the Indian army. Nevertheless, Allen calls the whole period 'disastrous' for the gun trade, except for the manufacture of revolvers and ammunition.[16]

Buttons also suffered some decline, especially pearl buttons, due mostly to competition from abroad, especially from Germany. Only the metal button section was relatively unaffected. The glass industry was faced with greater competition from Belgium, especially Belgian tumblers and wine glasses (the tableware firms of Stourbridge also complained of this). There was increased competition from Germany here too. As a result, some Birmingham glass manufacturers switched to lamp chimney shades.[17] As for other industries, tin plate and hollowware suffered from foreign competition, and some firms established themselves at Lye and Wollescote near Stourbridge, in the Black Country, where labour was cheaper. The production of pen nibs remained steady, and although wire manufacture was now centred in Warrington and Middlesbrough, and Belgium was also exporting wire, some branches remained active, such as pin and screw production. The food and drinks industries also grew - by 1886 Cadbury's employed 500, and newer and larger breweries were being built.[18]

Certain significant changes were already to be discerned in Birmingham during this phase of the Great Depression. The first was the increasing use of female labour in place of men. This was certainly part of the price-cutting procedures introduced by employers, but probably owed something also to the restrictions on the employment of children resulting from the factory and workshop acts of 1867, together with increasing attendance at school. The second change relates to the modes of production: more modern machinery was coming into use, expecially the power press, and more gas engines were being employed. Thirdly, there was some increase in the size of the work unit, as has already been noted, even though the brass small master remained prominent in the handicraft brass and button trades. Lastly, there was an increasing awareness among Birmingham manufacturers of the need to fight foreign competition, especially from Belgium and Germany. They were particularly concerned at foreign tariff barriers erected against them, and also at the handicap suffered by Birmingham manufacturers of the heavy transport costs from central England to the coastal ports (earlier on, there was some anxiety on the subject of preferential rates given by some railway companies to favoured customers, but these had been made illegal).

These matters of foreign tariffs and of inland transport costs were among the subjects raised by the Council of the Birmingham Chamber of Commerce in their evidence before the Royal Commission on the Depression in Trade in 1885. Most significantly, although the Council had earlier spoken strongly in favour of free trade, in 1885 it advocated the formation of 'a trading union between Great Britain and the colonies', and the placing of import duties on certain classes of foreign goods.[19] No longer were the colonies regarded, as Disraeli had put it, as 'those millstones round our neck', but with the scramble for Africa and the consequent extension of the Empire, they were seen more and more as valuable trading outlets. At this stage of his career, Chamberlain was still a free trader, but he was later to become a leading campaigner for tariff reform and imperial preference. It must be said that a section of the Chamber of Commerce protested at the suggestion of imposing home tariff barriers against foreign imports, and at a subsequent meeting, by a small majority, the Council's 1885 proposal was rejected. Nevertheless, the views expressed by the Chamber of Commerce before the Royal Commission are a strong indication of the feelings of Birmingham manufacturers on the need to combat foreign competition, and of a growing support for imperial preference.

After 1886, and indeed from the putative end of the Great Depression in 1896 right up to the outbreak of war in 1914, the older industries of Birmingham experienced mixed fortunes. The two leading industries continued to be jewellery and brass. Jewellery recovered from its earlier decline, and the gold branch once again prospered. The numbers employed in the trade rose further from about 15,000 in 1886 to 30,000 in 1914. Brass also expanded, the numbers in this industry rising from 20,000 or 22,000 in 1886 to nearly 32,000 in 1911. Although older sections such as those producing gas fittings and cabinet work remained relatively static, there was now additional demand from firms producing electrical equipment and from the motor industry. There was also a greater demand for more elaborate shop fittings. The pen industry still grew, having almost a monopoly of the world's steel nib supply, 75% of output being exported. The production of rolling stock also increased, as foreign demand was still strong. Hollowware was prosperous up to around 1900, when it was hit by a wave of imported German enamelled steel ware.[20]

As for declining industries, buttons further lost importance, due to continued changes in fashion, stronger foreign competition, and exclusion from American markets by tariff walls. Only the metal and uniform-button sectors flourished, the result of government orders. The old gun trade was also diminished in size, being confined to sporting guns. The military branch did rather better, at least up to and including the period of the Boer war (1899-1902). Overall, the Birmingham gun trade employed less than half the number that had been employed in the trade fifty years previously, although the ammunition trade had expanded.[21] The actual figures of production show that although British gunmakers retained control of the home market, much of the export market had passed to Liège in Belgium by the end of the century. Liège had a larger labour force, and both labour and raw materials were cheaper. Whereas in 1866 Birmingham had exported between 100,000 and 150,000 African guns, in 1891 out of a total of 561,000 barrels proved, 176,000 were African barrels, all exported to Liège for setting up.[22] By 1900, Birmingham commercial proofs numbered only 390,268, a real decline having set in since 1891. Liège commercial barrel proofs in 1900 had risen to the far greater figure of 2,319,689.[23] Birmingham had become a customer of the Liège gun trade, though Liège still purchased many of its breech castings and gun furniture from Birmingham.[24]

So much for the fortunes of the long-established industries of Birmingham: we have now to consider the new industries which were very important in providing alternative means of employment (and were to be vital in maintaining the relative prosperity of Birmingham during the slump between the wars). The first is the manufacture of bicycles. It expanded greatly in the 1890s, and employed more than any other trade in the area save for brass and jewellery. By 1911, Birmingham and Aston employed 9,350 men and women - over 40% of all cycle workers in the Midlands region.[25]

Next, of increasing importance, was the motor car industry. This had begun in Coventry, but then developed in Birmingham, employing 5,400 hands by 1911. It also provided work for large numbers of small firms in the area which supplied parts and accessories such as metal tubes, sheet metal, wire, screws, locks, glass and lighting equipment. Another important accessory made locally was the new pneumatic tyre, patented by Dunlop in 1888.[26] A third new industry was the electrical industry. The Birmingham Electricity Supply Company was established as early as 1889, and this provided the city's first power station. The Company was taken over by the Corporation in 1900. Soon firms were set up for the production of dynamoes and motors, together with electric light fittings, switches, wire and so on. They included the General Electric Company factory opened at Witton in 1901. The total of electrical units supplied by the Birmingham power station rose from 3 million in 1901 to 63 million in 1911.[27] Other expanding industries included paper bag and box making, together with office furniture, while Cadbury's, having moved to Bournville in 1879, had expanded greatly, so that by 1914 the firm employed some 6,000 workers, with exports worth half a million pounds.[28]

However, according to Allen, the most striking change in industry from 1890 onwards was the transformation of the engineering industry. By 1914 it ranked as the most important industry in the area.[29] The 1890s saw the beginning of a new machine era. It was the end of the centuries-old dominance of the hand-operated press, stamp, and lathe. The change was based on the replacement of wrought iron by new forms of steel which permitted the employmentof high-speed, power-driven machine tools. There was an increased demand in the motor industry, and especially in the electrical industry, for small precision-made machine parts. Hence the increased use of power presses and other machine tools, and also of gas engines to supply power. The old treadle-operated lathe became obsolete. Power presses replaced hand presses; drilling machines replaced punches; heavier steam and hydraulic stamps were employed; and planing, milling and boring machines were widely used. The new steels allowed more accurate machining than wrought iron so that it was inevitable that they should replace iron not only in the construction of machine tools but also in the production of machine parts.[30]

Developments of this kind undoubtedly transformed sections of Birmingham industry and, as might be expected, were to be seen especially in the newer industries just described. By 1914, according to Dr Smith, 'the machine was in the ascendant over hand labour', though she adds a cautionary note that this was not necessarily so in the majority of firms in every trade.[31] Caution is certainly necessary here. It is all too easy to exaggerate the spread of mechanisation in Birmingham industry before 1914, given the size of some of the largest establishments. Dr Smith herself points out that mass production and standardisation had not gone very far by 1914 except in the small arms factories, tyres, cycles, engineering, and among some of the more progressive firms. Indeed, the number of workshops, which by definition did not employ power, actually increased from 3,872 in 1895 to 4,868 in 1910.[32] Even between the wars the size of the average firm was still relatively small in Birmingham (see Chapter Eight).

Nevertheless, the need to face foreign competition placed a greater emphasis than ever before on lowering costs, and this could be achieved not only by mechanisation and by the economies of scale, but also by moving to newer, cheaper sites on the periphery of the city to the south, east and north. By the end of the century, workers could travel greater distances to work by utilising bus and tram services, or simply by cycling to work. An encouragement also to large-scale enterprise was the development of the public limited liability company. Their growth was particularly noticeable in the 1890s, and was associated with the new industries, especially cycles, cycle fittings, tubes and tyres.

Size of Largest Firms in Birmingham by 1914

Name	Nos Employed
Cadbury's	6,000
Dunlop's	4,000
Austin Motor Works	2,000
Nettlefolds	3,000
Buttons	2,000
Elkingtons	2,000
Perry & Co.	1,500
Metro Rwy Carriage	1,100
Brown, Marshall & Co.	1,100

How big then were the largest Birmingham firms by 1914? (See table above)[33] The real giants were not numerous - they probably numbered less than ten. Largest of all was Cadbury's, who had moved from Bridge Street in 1879 and were now established in extensive and spacious premises in Bournville. In addition, the family had built a whole new village close by, much influenced by the Garden City idea, with trees, open spaces and gardens as prominent features. However, the estate was not intended exclusively for occupation by Cadbury employees. By 1914 the business had become world-famous, not only for its original product of cocoa, but also for its different varieties of chocolate; as already noted, its export sales were about £500,000, and it employed 6,000 workers.[34] Second in size was probably Dunlop's, a newcomer to the area. The first Dunlop factory was built not in Birmingham, but in Dublin. By 1914, the Birmingham factory was employing some 4,000.[35] In addition to these two very large employers, there were several firms not very far behind in size. Among them was the newly established motor works at Longbridge, which opened in 1905. The factory covered some two and a half acres. It produced its first car in 1906, and in 1910 a small car was built which became famous, the Austin Seven or Baby Austin. By 1914 the company was turning out 1,500 cars a year, and employing 2,000 workers.[36] Nettlefolds, the leading manufacturer of screws, was still expanding, with a workforce of up to 3,000. Buttons Ltd, formed by the amalgamation of four local firms, henceforth dominated the button trade, employing about 2,000 workers. Elkington's, the electro-platers, had 2,000 workers as early as 1887, while the two railway carriage works, the Metropolitan Railway Carriage Co., and Brown, Marshall & Co., each employed about 1,100 workers at Saltley in 1884. The largest pen manufacturer, Perry & Co., had 1,500 on their pay roll in 1891.[37]

In addition to these large firms, there were numerous smaller firms with labour forces under 1000 but still employing some hundreds by 1914. For example, in the machine tool industry, the average firm employed between 300 and 400 by 1914. One firm, James Archdale & Co., had 450 workers in 1889 and 600 in 1910.[38] Even in the declining glass trade, one firm, that of O.C. Hawkes, makers of mirror and ornamemtal glass, employed 300 in 1878 and 800 in 1899.[39] Thus, there is no doubt that the size of firms generally expanded in Birmingham in the nearly thirty years following the end of the Great Depression. Yet at the same time, it is very noticeable that some of the largest firms were in the newer industries – food manufacture, the motor and electrical industries (Allen mentions one firm in the electrical trade employing nearly 2,000, but does not name it;[40] at a guess, it could have been Joseph Lucas & Co.).

With the exception of Cadbury's, these firms grew naturally in a city with a long tradition of manufacturing, especially in metal, while the success of Cadbury's is to be seen in the context of an increase in real wages and in consumer consumption at the end of the nineteenth century. Cocoa had become a cheap and popular bedtime drink. However, it would be quite wrong to suppose that smaller firms had almost died out by 1914. This is not so at all; and the figures given earlier for the increased number of workshops illustrates the point very well. In fact, there were still very many small firms in Birmingham, for example, in the jewellery and traditional gun trades. It has been said that by 1914, the majority of firms were still Victorian in method and scale.[41] Asa Briggs has quoted the industrialist Norman Chamberlain's belief that as late as 1914, the majority of masters in Birmingham were probably still 'small men'.[42] It is clear, then, that though some Birmingham firms grew to a formidable size, larger than those of some of the Manchester cotton proprietors, for example, their growth was accompanied by masses of smaller enterprises, some of them of a transient nature, of course, others becoming well-established and forming a part of the industrial scene between the wars. This point will be made again in a subsequent chapter when the size of firms in the inter-war period comes under review.

Were any distinctive changes noticeable in the organisation of the larger and more progressive industrial firms? Several internal changes require comment, in addition to the increasing use of power machine tools. At long last the system of sub-contracting to groups of workers led by charge hands who paid their own teams began to die out. It was a way of organising labour very common in, for example, iron works and in coal mines in the Midlands. Increasingly all classes of workers were paid individually by the works office. Further, St Monday which was already on the wane was replaced by a full day's work on Monday, and by half-day working on a Saturday, thus making possible the growth of Saturday afternoon attendance at sporting functions. Another aspect of change was to be seen as one of the results of the coming of limited liability; shareholders expected efficient management and greater control of work processes by executive directors and managers through the office rather than by the shop floor, where the charge hands dictated the pace of work. However, this must not be taken too far: even when a family firm became a limited liability company, paternalism might still have a part to play. Members of the family might still take an active role in day-to-day administration. This was so in the Quaker firm of Cadbury's where leading members of the family might still exercise executive functions; while at Longbridge, Herbert Austin, who was a trained engineer, went round the workshops himself and was not above demonstrating the proper use of a file to an apprentice.[43]

So far as external relations are concerned, there was a decline in the role of the factor, a kind of middleman who might either organise the various stages of production as in the traditional gun trade, or might simply supply raw material and/or market the finished goods. By the end of the nineteenth century, most manufacturers had enough capital to do without him, though once more there were exceptions among the smaller firms. There was a similar decline in the role of the merchant, since the largest firms employed their own overseas agents, though the merchant might still be of service when specialised knowledge of a foreign country was required, as in trade with South America.[44] A further change in external relations can be seen nationally in the industrial combination movement, and examples of this occurred in Birmingham industry. However, there were only a few vertical combinations in the area, the largest being that of Guest, Keen and Nettlefold. Nettlefolds were very large screw manufacturers with premises in Smethwick, and they had already carried out numerous minor mergers in the Midlands and South Wales. In 1900 in South Wales, Guest & Co. and another Welsh firm, the Dowlais Iron Company, merged with the patent Nut and Bolt Company of Birmingham and West Bromwich. In 1902 these three firms then joined with Nettlefolds to form Guest, Keen & Nettlefold, with a.capital of £4.5 million. The new firm acquired further companies in the Midlands and South Wales before 1914.[45]

In the nature of things, horizontal combinations were far more common than vertical combines - one authority goes so far as to say there were hundreds of smaller amalgamations[46] - the most important large-scale merger being that of H & J Stewarts & Menzies of Scotland with Lloyd & Lloyd of Birmingham, the result being the formation of Stewarts & Lloyds of Birmingham in 1902, with a capital of £1.75 million. Other large combines included the Edie Manufacturing Company which absorbed the BSA Company, while Kynochs expanded to take in works in Stirchley making shells, together with other brass works. Mergers also took place in the button trade, which was depressed at the beginning of the twentieth century; the three leading firms merged, bought up two others, closed several factories and concentrated production on the most efficient plants. In the bedstead trade, there were two mergers, one of six firms, the other of four. The merger movement seems to have begun in the late 1890s, climaxing in 1902, then slackening in the last years of prosperity before the war.[47] Its causes were various: sometimes it was the result of the search for wider markets or for the economies of scale, for the elimination of trading rivals or even the need to rationalise production in a declining market.

Combination was, of course, a national phenomenon at the end of the nineteenth century, and its basic driving force was competition, both internal and external. The external competition faced by Birmingham manufacturers, as we have seen, came from the USA, Germany and Belgium, where tariff barriers presented real problems. Foreign tariffs allowed Britain's industrial rivals to form their own combines which could divide up their own home markets, making for further difficulties for British exporters; and this itself encouraged the growth of combination at home. All in all, Birmingham industrialists could not escape from the need to improve production and maintain profits in the period between the ending of the Great Depression and the outbreak of the Great War in 1914. In spite of the great tradition of individual enterprise in Birmingham, the tide of economic change made it inevitable that industrial combination should manifest itself, even though it was relatively limited in scale before the war.

One aspect of all this was the development of price associations by which employers sought to limit cut-throat competition among themselves. In Birmingham there developed the so-called Alliance system which had some currency in the 1890s. The first alliance was in the bedstead trade in 1891. It was based on the idea that firms in the alliance would sell at agreed prices and would restrict employment to trade union members (the 'closed shop'). The system thus owed much to close co-operation with the trade unions concerned. At one time it was estimated that as many as 500 employers and more than 20,000 workers were covered by the Birmingham Alliance system, but none of the alliances lasted for very long. Although price associations became common enough, the problem always remained of what to do about the rogue manufacturer who simply ignored the association and undercut the prices of his competitors. Often due to this problem, most associations had only a limited life. The bedstead alliance seems to have broken down by 1901 not so much for this reason, but because of hostility among furniture retailers to the monopoly in the supply of brass bedsteads held by the alliance. As a result, the retailers switched to wooden bedsteads.[48]

Of course, all this expansion of industry in Birmingham was accompanied by a corresponding expansion in the service sector. Manufacturing industry can hardly grow, for example, without the services of commerce to sell its products. It is interesting to compare the occupational structure of the city in 1911 with occupations in 1851, a comparison which emphasises the great growth of service industries locally; they were growing nationally, of course. Business was becoming more complex and requiring, for example, more managers, clerks and sales representatives. By 1914 the up-to-date office had acquired typewriters and telephones. Again, as industry developed in new areas at a distance from Birmingham city centre (the main areas were to the north-west, beyond Ladywood; to the south and south-west around Selly Oak, Stirchley and Bournville; to the south-east around Small Heath; and to the north-east in the Erdington area), so further demands were made on the building trades, and on the need not only to house, but to feed, clothe and transport workers to their place of employment.[49] All these changes can be illustrated by reference to the major occupations in 1911, and in particular to changes in the service sector since the mid-nineteenth century. Of course, it must always be borne in mind that the population of Birmingham grew from 233,000 in 1851 to 526,000 (in round terms) in 1911 (this is ignoring areas finally incorporated in the Greater Birmingham Plan, 1911). This is an increase of about 125%, so that some increase in occupational totals must be expected. Nevertheless, some very significant changes in a number of occupations took place (see table opposite).

To start with the commercial clerks, their number rose dramatically from 1,073 in 1851 to 9,587 in 1911 - about a ninefold increase.[50] Commercial travellers numbered 327 in 1851 and

Service Occupations in Birmingham in 1851 and in 1911

Occupation	1851	1911
Commercial clerks	1,073	9,587
Commercial travellers	327	1,531
Dealers in money (insurance)		1,693
Insurance dealers (life, house, ship)		731
Insurance agents		689
Accountants	130	
Merchants, agents, accountants		2,523
Bricklayers	1,694	3,260
Bricklayers' labourers		1,651
Painters, glaziers, decorators		2,859
Navvies and paviours		1,224
Domestic service (indoor)	8,359	9,680
Tailors (male)	1,619	1,651
Tailors (female)	390	1,989
Dressmakers	226	2,938
Milliners	3,597	728
Butchers	799	1,747
Grocers	787	2,261
Bakers	595	1,735
Bread, biscuit and cake makers		1,190
Malsters, brewers, lic. victuallers	1,639	4,385
Schoolmasters	149	664
Schoolmistresses	475	1,634
Motor car drivers		208
Tram service (men)		976
Tram service (women)		23
Railways (men)		5,619
Railways (women)		48
Gas, water, electricity supply		1,688
At gas works		1,412
Sanitary services		327
Engine drivers, stokers, firemen		1,093
Newsboys and newspaper vendors		294
Charwomen	470	2,728

Sources: Census Returns, 1851, 1911

1,531 in 1911. Dealers in money, with reference to insurance, get a separate entry in the 1911 census returns, and were 1,693 in number (those specialising in life, house or ship insurance numbered 731, and a further separate category of insurance agents amounted to 689; evidently insurance was an expanding business in 1911). There were 130 accountants in 1851. Unfortunately, and surprisingly, there is no separate listing for them in 1911, and they are lumped in with merchants and agents to give a total of 2,523. Since both the Institute of Chartered Accountants and the Society of Incorporated Accountants and Auditors had been established in the second half of the nineteenth century, and the profession of accountant had acquired an enhanced professional standing, it is likely that there was a substantial number of members of these bodies in Birmingham by 1911. The fact that Commercial Occupations are grouped together under their own heading in the Census Returns is a reminder of the increased importance with which commerce was viewed at the time.

As for housing, the expansion of Birmingham meant that building workers were numerous in 1911. Bricklayers numbered only 1,694 in 1851. In 1911 their number had risen to 3,260, with an additional figure for their labourers of 1,651. In addition, painters, decorators and glaziers numbered 2,859, while navvies (labourers) and paviours (who laid paving stones) together came to 1,224. Domestic service was still a major occupation, though interesting enough, the number does not show an increase commensurate with the rise in population. In 1851, indoor domestic servants totalled 8,359: in 1911 this figure had risen to only 9,680. It is generally held that domestic service was becoming more expensive towards the end of the century, and this may be one reason why there was such a limited increase in the Birmingham numbers.

In recent years, historians have laid emphasis on the growth of consumerism in the last quarter of the nineteenth century as real wages rose. This may help to account for the marked increase in the numbers engaged in the clothing trades: although the total of male tailors changed little between 1851 and 1911, the number of women engaged in the trade rose remarkably from 390 to 1,989, possibly because they could be employed cheaply in the factory production of cheap menswear using the new Singer sewing machine. The number of male dressmakers declined from 354 to 11, but female dressmakers shot up from 226 to 2,927 in 1911. All this may be the result of changes in classification, since milliners declined sharply from 3,597 in 1851 to only 728 in 1911. The 1911 figure seems very small in a female population of roughly a quarter of a million. As for the food trades, butchers increased in numbers from 799 to 1,747 in 1911, grocers from 787 to 2,261, and bakers from 595 to 1,735 (there were in addition 1,190 bread, biscuit and cake makers in 1911). For the drink trade, it is difficult to make comparisons, because of different modes of classification, but in 1851 malsters, brewers and licensed victuallers totalled 1,639; in 1911 workers in the drink trade totalled 4,385.

Lastly, the 1911 Census gives figures for new service trades which are understandably absent from the 1851 survey. Thus, motor car drivers (not domestic) numbered 208. Larger numbers were engaged in the new tram service: 976 men and 23 women. One large transport group was engaged on the railways - 5,619 men and 48 women (actually, there were 119 railway engine drivers and stokers, and 143 railway labourers mentioned in the 1851 Census, so they were not entirely omitted then). Another group was made up of those engaged in gas, water and electricity supply, and those in the sanitary service: in the first group there were 1,688, together with another 1,412 at the gas works themselves, while there were 327 in the sanitary services (were they sewer men? Or public lavatory attendants? We are not told). Apart from those employed on the railways, there was another group of engine drivers, stokers and firemen (they were described as 'not railway, marine, or agriculture') who totalled 1,093. Lastly, by the end of the nineteenth century, the advent of cheap newspapers for an increasingly literate public had led to the appearance on the city streets of the newsboy and the vendor of newspapers. There were 294 of them in Birmingham in 1911.

It hardly needs to be said that occupational figures derived from census returns have their shortcomings. One major problem undoubtedly is that of the changes in classification which can take place between one census and the next, especially over a period of sixty years. This difficulty has been amply illustrated in the preceding paragraphs. There are other problems relating to the precise nature of some classifications: for example, does the 1911 figure for laundry workers (92 men, 1,628 women) include washerwomen (1,965 in 1851)? On another point, why is there such an extraordinary rise in the number of charwomen from 470 in 1851 to 2,728 in 1911? Is the 1851 figure simply wrong? Or was it cheaper to employ a charwoman in 1911 than a daily servant? Or could more women afford a charlady who could not before? There were certainly more offices to clean in 1911, of course. Nevertheless, it is clear that the picture as a whole is of an increase in service occupations which commonly goes beyond the 125% increase in the population mentioned earlier. Such an increase is only to be expected in view of the national trends of the time. Service industries (or the tertiary sector) were beginning to occupy a larger proportion of the national economy until at the present day in employment terms they far exceed the numbers employed in manufacturing. At the end of the nineteenth century signs of this change were already manifest in Birmingham.

However, the question arises, was there any particular reason why this should be especially noticeable in Birmingham before the Great War? It is difficult to say, but it could be that the creation of new industrial sites on land available at a distance from the city centre was a contributory cause. Not only did this create new jobs, but it also necessitated the extension of existing transport services, especially by tram and by bicycle. Those workers seeking accommodation near their place of work in the new areas had new housing provided for them by speculative builders, either rented or, in some cases, purchased by mortgage. The need to incorporate these outlying areas had not escaped the attention of the city council. In 1911 their efforts climaxed in the Greater Birmingham Scheme which greatly enlarged the city so that in area it became three times the size of Glasgow and twice the size of Manchester, Liverpool or Belfast. Greater Birmingham henceforth measured thirteen miles at the extreme points on the map from Rubery in the south to Oscott in the north.[51]

However, the specific causes of the expansion of the service sector of Birmingham industry must remain a matter for speculation. The simple fact is that the service industries did expand impressively in the second half of the nineteenth century, and it would clearly be wrong to trace the development of manufacturing industry without reference to them. As always, manufacturing and the service sector grew together in a symbiotic relationship, each feeding and encour-

aging growth in the other.[52] Of course, the blue-collar worker on the shop floor has always tradi-
tionally regarded the white-collar worker as having a softer time, working shorter hours and
keeping his hands clean; life in the workshop or factory has always been regarded as more robust
than work in the office.[53] Nevertheless, the sales staff and office workers have always been vital
elements in the success of any business, and were certainly so in the Birmingham economy of
the early twentieth century.

One last aspect of industrial growth requires further consideration: this is the issue of tariff
reform, touched on earlier in this chapter. In the first half of the nineteenth century,
Birmingham had an important influence on national events in spearheading the reform
agitation of the 1830s. It was to do so again from the 1880s onwards on the subject of tariff
reform. We have already seen that in 1885 the Council of the Chamber of Commerce was
actively considering the subject. Belief in the sanctity of free trade had previously been very
strong in the mid-nineteenth century, and Gladstone had completed the task begun by
Huskisson and Peel in reducing import duties and confining them to a very small number of
imports. Nevertheless, by the 1870s, Birmingham business men became increasingly restive at
the extent of foreign tariffs raised against their exports. First they founded the Birmingham
Reciprocity League for equal terms of trade between Britain and her foreign competitors, then
in 1881 the Fair Trade League was established for a similar purpose.[54] Thus, 'fair trade' was
advocated as a substitute for free trade, which it was thought had served its purpose. According
to Bismarck, free trade was the weapon of the strongest nation, but Britain could no longer
claim supremacy in world trade. Curiously, in the 1880s Chamberlain was still a supporter of
free trade, and in 1887 actually refused election as chairman of the Birmingham Chamber of
Commerce because the Chamber had recently adopted a resolution in favour of fair trade.
Signs of change were to come in the 1890s: in 1895, Chamberlain, who had split from the
Liberals over the issue of Home Rule for Ireland, accepted office as Colonial Secretary in a
Conservative government led by Lord Salisbury. Already he was beginning to refer to the
colonies as 'undeveloped estates'. In March,1896 he called for an Imperial Zollverein (customs
union). Chamberlain remained colonial secretary throughout the Boer War (1899-1902), and
transferred the notorious concentration camps (in which Boer women and children were held)
to his own control and had them speedily reformed.[55] In September 1903 he resigned from
office in order to pursue a campaign for tariff reform.

This campaign was based essentially on free trade within the Empire, or (to put it
another way) on Imperial Preference - that is, to trade freely with the colonies while
imposing duties on selected incoming foreign goods. The Tariff Reform League was set up
to keep the public informed on the subject, while a Tariff Reform Commission composed
of Chamberlain's supporters issued several reports proposing a threefold system of tariffs.
Chamberlain's advocacy of tariff reform proved a godsend to his political opponents, the
Liberal Party. They had been divided over the issue of the Boer War; now they could close
ranks and unite in the cause of free trade. In particular, they claimed that tariff reform
would mean taxation of foreign foodstuffs. This would result in the price of food going
up. One of the most effective Liberal posters in the general election of January 1906

showed two loaves, one big (Liberal), the other small (Conservative), and the voter was invited to choose accordingly.

In vain Chamberlain claimed that although tariff reform might result in some adjustment of food prices, this would be heavily outweighed by the encouragement given to industry and to the improvement in employment. As he saw it, tariff reform meant work for all. Undoubtedly the majority of Birmingham business men thought similarly; tariff reform seemed to be in their best interests, and also ultimately in the best interests of their workers. Unfortunately for these employers, many working-class voters thought otherwise, upset by the prospect of a rise in the cost of living. In vain, too, were the efforts of Balfour, the Conservative Prime Minister, who had succeeded his uncle, Lord Salisbury, as premier, following the Khaki Election of 1900, to provide compromise solutions to the tariff reform problem. What had begun as a campaign to unify the Empire, and as protection for the sake of the Empire, slid into protection for its own sake. As such it had the support of many British manufacturers, but not of many working-class voters, frightened by the possible imposition of food taxes (the 'big loaf' and the 'little loaf'). They were not convinced that tariffs would mean more jobs. Unluckily for Chamberlain, unemployment decreased in 1905 when trade picked up. Things were made worse for the government when a scandal erupted over its decision to permit the importing into South Africa of 27,000 Chinese labourers to help reopen the mines on the Rand, where white labour was scarce and expensive. The resulting 'Chinese slavery' was much resented by many of the British working classes, and as an electoral issue it proved as damaging as the scare over tariff reform. Moreover, Canada, Australia and New Zealand had helped to win the Boer War, and all of them strongly opposed the importing of cheap foreign labour as a matter of principle, and regarded it as an affront to their feelings. If anything, 'Chinese slavery' did the Empire real harm.[56]

The results of all this were that the Conservatives suffered a crushing defeat in the general election of January 1906, the Liberals securing a clear majority over all other parties of 84 seats. The Conservatives won only 157 seats, though of these, Chamberlain's supporters held 106 seats, and Balfour's supporters held 32. Balfour himself lost his seat. Free trade was thus triumphant, and tariff reform laid low. Chamberlain himself was unrepentant, and had saved all his seven Birmingham seats. He stood by his policy, and remained immensely popular in Birmingham, where his seventieth birthday was celebrated with great enthusiasm in July 1906. Shortly after he suffered a severe stroke which incapacitated him and he was virtually forced into retirement. He died in July 1914. Tariff reform made no further progress, and Birmingham went without its benefits (real or imagined) in the period which remained before the outbreak of the Great War in August 1914. It was not until the financial crisis of 1931-32 that free trade was at last abandoned as government policy, and a system of import duties and imperial prefer- ence was introduced (there had been some minor adjustments to the free trade policy during the war and subsequently). The major Imports Duties Bill, 1932 was introduced by the new Chancellor of the Exchequer: by an irony of fate, he was Neville Chamberlain, son of Joseph Chamberlain. Whether Birmingham industry would really have profited from a policy of tariff reform before 1914 is a moot question. According to A.J.P. Taylor, in its great days, it had been as much, if not more, a battle over political power as over economic; tariff reform sprang from the sentiment of imperialism, and was defeated by Liberal idealism. By 1932, no great principle was at stake. The idea of Protection had long been accepted.[57]

In conclusion, and to sum up, it may be said that Birmingham industry experienced great prosperity in the middle decades of the nineteenth century, and succeeded very well in weathering the storms of the so-called Great Depression. Indeed, Birmingham adjusted better than the Black Country, where the exhaustion of local supplies of coal and iron ore and the development of new areas of steel manufacture away from the Black Country brought real difficulties. Birmingham could always bring in supplies from a distance, and could diversify its industrial structure, as it did with the development of the newer industries of bicycles, motor cars and motor cycles, and the electrical industry. These would be vital to its economic welfare between the wars.

Again, industrial practices were modernised with changes in the working week (the ending of St Monday, and half-day working on Saturdays); with the decline of sub-contracting and of factoring, the increasing adoption of powered machine tools and the growth of the engineering industry. Like industry elsewhere, Birmingham industry was influenced by the combination movement, both vertical and horizontal, by price associations and by limited liability. For a time, Birmingham business men and industrialists were prominent on the national scene, just as they had been in the reform agitation of the 1830s, but this time over tariff reform and imperial preference. In this regard they proved less successful. Joseph Chamberlain was not to receive the triumphant accolade accorded Thomas Attwood by the inhabitants of Birmingham when the great Reform Bill was passed in 1832. It was left to Chamberlain's son Neville to introduce tariff reform at a time of heavy unemployment in 1932 when the issue had ceased to be controversial. Even then, Neville Chamberlain is hardly remembered for this, but rather remains in the popular memory as the author of the ill-fated Munich Agreement with Adolf Hitler in September 1938. Unfortunately, Birmingham business acumen proved no match for Hitlerian megalomania.

However, Birmingham industry had come a long way between 1850 and 1914. When war broke out in 1914, its metal industries in particular were well-equipped to make an immense contribution to the war effort, and its labour force was well-organised and disciplined to provide the maximum production required to meet the unprecedented demands of total war. Moreover, the pre-war growth of the new industries in Birmingham were to be of great benefit after the war when the staple industries of textiles, iron, and coal in other regions were to decline and suffer heavy unemployment throughout the inter-war years.

CHAPTER THREE

THE CIVIC GOSPEL, AND AFTER

In the last chapter, it was very largely the economic life of the people of Birmingham in the second half of the nineteenth century which was discussed; and at first sight it might seem a little strange at this point to switch to changes in the local government of the borough. In fact, to ignore this aspect of change in the community would be to miss out developments of profound significance in the life of the town, developments which were to have important social consequences not only for the inhabitants of Birmingham, but also for other towns and cities as well. These changes began in the 1860s and were most striking in the 1870s. By the beginning of the next decade, they were attracting world-wide attention. In 1890, J. Ralph, writing in *Harper's Monthly Magazine*, famously claimed that Birmingham was 'the Best Governed City in the World'. Moreover, Ralph declared that above all else, Birmingham was 'a business city, run by business men on business principles'.[1] This was praise indeed, coming as it did from an American observer, well-aware of his own country's rapid rise to world economic power, a power famed for its business efficiency. By this time Birmingham's business leaders had made the city (it achieved the status of city in 1889) a model of a self-governing community for other towns to copy, not only in this country but also abroad. How did this come about? And how far was Ralph's description of Birmingham really justified?

Curiously enough, the town which had shown such radical initiatives in the forming of the Birmingham Political Union in the 1830s was hardly a model of local self-government in the 1850s and the early 1860s. The reason was that when the town was incorporated in 1839 (as noted in Chapter One), the local Improvement Commissioners already had considerable powers, given to them by a succession of local acts, to improve the markets, roads, lighting and other amenities in the town.[2] These powers were extensive enough to make many ratepayers critical of the creation of a new, separate municipal authority. Moreover, disputes arose as to the extent of the powers of the new borough council. Not until 1852 were the powers of the Improvement Commissioners transferred to the town council. By then the traditional local government practice of spending the minimum on services in order to save the ratepayers money was becoming well-established in Birmingham. This was by no means unusual. At a time when householders were burdened by a variety of taxes - for example, poor rates, highway rates, burial board rates - it seemed natural enough to keep general rates as low as possible; only a few more enlightened larger towns, such as Liverpool, Leeds and Glasgow, were beginning to see the need for more comprehensive municipal services. Birmingham was not at first among such towns. When the Birmingham Improvement Act, 1851 vested all the powers of the Improvement Commissioners in the town council (together with certain additional powers) the years began of what Asa Briggs has called the worst period in Birmingham local government. This may be to judge these early years of the infant borough council too harshly,

5. Joseph Chamberlain, 1836-1914.

and in the light of the vigorous reforming policies adopted by the council under the Chamberlain regime later on; but certainly the record of the council between 1852 and the later 1860s is hardly distinguished.

Another reason for this perhaps is that the new town council failed to attract leaders of the quality of the earlier radicals such as Attwood and Scholefield, and the council became dominated by what one observer called 'the unprogressive tradesmen class - many of them worthy in their way, but of limited ideas. In their businesses they were not accustomed to deal with big transactions and high figures...'[3] Large-scale spending therefore filled them with alarm. However, smallmindedness was not their only fault; they were also prone to quarrelling over petty matters and to factionalism which led to the council being shunned by the urban élite.

The most prominent figure on the council during the 1850s was Joseph Allday, a Tory radical and editor of a somewhat scurrilous weekly, the *Argus*. He was a council member for almost the whole of the 1850s, from 1849 to 1859 (he died in 1861). His policy was simple enough: he believed that all forms of reform were expensive, and that the less spent by the council the better. His own followers were known as the Economy Party, while he dubbed his opponents the Extravagent Party. Examples of his belief in economy are not hard to find. Under his guidance, the council refused to appoint a Medical Officer of Health (Liverpool already had one) or a stipendary magistrate. The costs of the town gaol were cut, a project for a public bath was rejected and in 1855 a new improvement bill was thrown out. All kinds of public expenditure were cut, for example, the cost of maintaining the roads fell from £23,280 in 1855 to £15,835 in 1856; no additional street lamps were provided; drainage and sewerage facilities were cut; and a proposal to provide additional police was rejected.[4] When the improvement bill was rejected in 1855, the public works and finance committees resigned, whereupon Allday became chairman of both new committees. Between 1853 and 1858, expenditure on public works fell by a third.[5]

Some improvement was to be seen from 1859 onwards, and Thomas Avery replaced Allday as leader of the council. However, he was also a great believer in economy, and used public meetings of ratepayers to influence decisions of the council; he was quite prepared to collaborate with the Poor Law Guardians to prevent the council from taking advantage of the Municipal Mortgage Act,1860, which would have permitted greater borrowing powers (and incidentally would have by-passed the town meetings of ratepayers).[6] Still, some advances were made; for example, a new Improvement Act, 1861, did permit further loans for improvements, and a number of small improvements were carried out without putting up the rates. New initiatives were shown in the provision of baths and washhouses in 1862, the opening of the Central Lending Library in 1865, and of the Central Reference Library in 1866. Four district libraries were also opened in 1866.[7] Nevertheless, welcome as these improvements were as evidence of a new spirit of enterprise, the tone of Avery's policies is shown in his address to the British Association meeting in Birmingham in 1865. Having referred to the town's public debt which had apparently increased noticeably owing to the rapid execution of public works and improvements, he went on to suggest that:[8]

6. Highbury, residence of Joseph Chamberlain.

... it would have been desirable to have omitted some of the least important of these undertakings and to have extended the others over a longer period of time, and that for the future they should either be suspended altogether or proceeded with more slowly and deliberately.

Perhaps a turning point was reached when, in 1869, Avery strongly advocated full municipal control of the town's water supply - 'it is surely the duty of a wise local government to endeavour to surround the humbler classes of the population with its benevolent and protecting care'.[9] By this time the doctrine of the Civic Gospel was becoming more widely known. Its origins seem to lie in changes in middle-class thinking in Birmingham about the responsibilities of urban government. These changes are commonly linked with the increasing influence of nonconformist and especially Unitarian ministers in the town. It happened that Unitarianism was strong in Birmingham in the mid-century years, and Unitarian and other nonconformist ministers were the first to proclaim the Civic Gospel. The greatest among them was probably George Dawson, who was originally a baptist minister at the Mount Zion Chapel in 1844, but broke with the baptists to open his own church, the Church of the Saviour in 1847.[10] Many of his opinions were influenced by Unitarian beliefs derived from James Martineau of Liverpool. Certainly Dawson's views became widely influential - he was an inspiring speaker (according to Charles Kingsley, 'he was the greatest talker in England'). Dawson's views were based on religious idealism and a firm conviction that local government must assume wider responsibilities for the welfare of the local community. Dawson may well be considered the leader of the Civic Gospel movement. His beliefs were clearly expressed in a striking address delivered at the opening of the public library in 1865:[11]

A great town exists to discharge towards the people of that town, the duties that a great
nation exists to discharge towards the people of that nation - that a town exists here by
the grace of God, that a great town is a solemn organisation through which should flow,
and in which should be shaped, all the highest, loftiest and truest ends of man's intellectual and moral nature.

In other words, just as parliament was responsible for the well-being of the nation as a
whole, a town council should be responsible for the welfare of all within and subject to its
authority. Such ideas were shared by other nonconformist ministers – Charles Vince, Dawson's
successor at Mount Zion, a much loved man; H.W. Crosskey, minister of the Unitarian
Church of the Messiah in 1869 (a church attended by Joseph Chamberlain, his brother Arthur,
his brother-in-law William Kendrick, and R.F. Martineau); and Robert William Dale, minister
at Carr's Lane Congregational Church from 1854 to 1895.

It could be asked, of course, why such men ministering to their flocks should have had such
influence over middle-class opinion, given the fact that attendance at church or chapel in
Birmingham in 1851 was below the national average, and in spite of the strength of Dissent, the
Anglican percentage of churchgoers exceeded that of dissenting attenders.[12] There are a number
of possible answers to this question. In the first place, Unitarianism was a creed which emphasised practical Christianity - eighteenth-century evangelicalism with its emphasis on the sacred
word of the Bible was not enough. Unitarianism strongly supported good works, and well-
organised good works at that. Dale went so far as to proclaim that for Christians engaged in
practical Christianity, the eleventh commandment was that 'thou should keep a balance sheet'.

Secondly, it is easy to understand how business interests should be attracted by such
beliefs, and it is significant that the Unitarian Church of the Messiah had among its regular
attenders (as we have seen) such leading business men as Joseph Chamberlain, his brother
Arthur (a brass manufacturer), and the Kendricks, large-scale hollowware manufacturers.
Moreover, there were close family links between many Unitarian families. These family
relationships were important in getting things done: Briggs goes so far as to say that many
important decisions in city life were taken by a small knot of nonconformist families, many
of them living in the middle-class residential suburb of Edgbaston, so that the Civic Gospel
became a personal affair.[13] It should also be mentioned that among the nonconformist sects
other than Unitarianism, Methodism was relatively weak, but Quakerism quite strong;
seven of Birmingham's nineteenth-century mayors were Quakers, and between 1866 and
1873, five new Quaker councillors were elected.[14] Thirdly and lastly, the economic climate
in the late 1860s and early 1870s was increasingly favourable to business interests, culmi-
nating in a positive boom. Business men, often now with managerial experience in the
larger firms of the time, were more and more attracted to positions in local government.
Here was another opportunity to display organisational skills. It is no wonder that later in
his parliamentary career, in 1892, Joseph Chamberlain observed in an American magazine
that 'the leading idea of the English system of municipal government' might be said to be
that of a joint-stock or co-operative enterprise in which every citizen is a shareholder, and

7. Main Hall, Highbury, 1890s.

of which the dividends are received in the improved health and the increase in the comfort and happiness of the community.[15]

So much for the conventional views of the subject of the origins and nature of the Civic Gospel. Is there anything further to be said on this? Revisionist views have not got very far on the Civic Gospel, though one obvious line of attack could be the extent of self-interest which made business men active members of the council and believers in what E.P. Hennock prefers to call 'the municipal gospel'.[16] However, an investigation some years ago into business enterprise and local government in Birmingham in the second half of the nineteenth century concludes that though the active presence of business men as council members was everywhere apparent, there is no evidence of corruption.[17] Another, very recent, investigation has sought to demonstrate 'the more free and open character of Birmingham politics prior to the Chamberlain era'. Whatever may be said about the nature of Chamberlainite reform and the Birmingham caucus, it is not easy to show clear examples of local radicalism in the pre-Chamberlain period, especially in the period of the Old Woodman Council, even though there are signs of changing attitudes during the Avery regime.[18] A less difficult line of argument which might be pursued with greater advantage is that whatever the achievements of the Civic Gospel under Chamberlain's leadership, the spate of reforms he initiated were long overdue; Birmingham was notoriously behind other towns and backwards in municipal development. The Civic Gospel therefore merely repaired omissions rather than made innovations. It was not wholly original, though admittedly never before had it been so clearly stated or thought through.[19] This seems a fair enough comment, though it does leave untouched the major achievements in themselves of Chamberlain's mayoralty. To see these reforms in due perspective does not diminish their fundamental importance, which is undeniable. We may now turn to consider these in some detail.

8. Drawing Romm, Highbury, 1890s.

Joseph Chamberlain came from a comfortable middle-class home in London, and as a young man was sent to Birmingham to look after his father's investment in the firm of Nettlefold (Chamberlain's uncle) who had bought the patent rights in an American screw-making machine.[20] In this firm Chamberlain became the accountant and commercial manager, specialising in sales and marketing. In what became the well-known firm of Nettlefold & Chamberlain, his greatest achievement was the successful expansion of sales overseas. By the 1870s, the firm was one of the largest in Birmingham, employing more than 2,500 workers; though by this time, Chamberlain had become involved in national politics as chairman of the executive committee of the Birmingham-based National Education League, set up in 1869, and in the same year he was elected Liberal councillor for St Paul's ward in Birmingham. In 1873 he was elected mayor - a remarkable achievement. In the following year, he and his family sold their half of the partnership in Nettlefold & Chamberlain to the Nettlefolds for £600,000. Chamberlain was now able to devote more of his time to local politics. He retired from business on 27 June 1874, twenty years to the day since he had joined the firm. The workers and their families, some 2,000 in all, were treated to a special excursion by train to the Crystal Palace, where they sat down to a large-scale celebratory dinner. From then on, Chamberlain's life was given up to political work, at first in Birmingham, then later at Westminister. It is often too readily assumed that Chamberlain cut his political teeth in local politics, later moving on to national politics. Strictly speaking, it is really the other way round: he had first begun in national politics with the National Education League, and this had drawn him into municipal politics.

Chamberlain served three years as mayor, 1873 to 1876. He was re-elected three times, but resigned when he gained a seat in parliament, being elected unopposed as MP for Birmingham in 1876. His three years as mayor were momentous years for the people of Birmingham.

Towards the end of his mayoralty Chamberlain became increasingly popular and influential, the result of a number of important and progressive acts of municipalisation, the practical consequences of his belief in the principles of the Civic Gospel.[21] The first was the taking-over by the council of the local gas supplies. In itself, this was no great innovation: by 1870 there were already 49 municipal gas undertakings in England and Wales. What was novel was the speed and efficiency with which the project was carried through under Chamberlain's leadership, and (very important) the resulting profits. It involved the taking-over of the Birmingham Gas, Light, and Coke Company (founded in 1819 with a share capital of £300,000) and of the Birmingham and Staffordshire Gas Light Company (established 1825, with a share capital of £600,000). The borough debt was raised from half a million pounds to two and a half million pounds (something unthinkable under the Old Woodman regime), but profits on sales of gas began to flow in - £34,000 in the first year.

Chamberlain next turned his attention to Birmingham's water supplies, provided for the most part by the Birmingham Water Works Company, founded in 1826. The quality of the company's water was very poor: Chamberlain even alleged that the town's inhabitants were compelled to drink water as bad as sewage before clarification. This was a more serious matter than the purchase of the gas companies, which had been a matter of money and profit for the borough; water supplies were a matter of the health of the people. According to Chamberlain, 'The power of life and death should not be left in the hands of a commercial company, but should be conducted by the representatives of the people'.[22] Following on a large-scale sanitary survey in 1874-5, the Birmingham Water Works Company was taken over by the municipality. By August 1875 both the gas and water bills had been given the royal assent. Also in 1875 there was set up the Birmingham, Tame, and Rea District Drainage Board, following much controversy concerning the piping of raw sewage into the river Tame at Saltley. A special Sewage Enquiry Committee was appointed and a lengthy report issued, which recommended the disposal of some 14,000 open middens and ashpits. The new Drainage Board provided an integrated drainage system over a wide area well beyond the town's own boundaries.[23] Meanwhile, a Medical Officer of Health was appointed in 1872 (an appointment made compulsory by the Public Health Act of that year), and the first borough Health Committee was formed in 1875. By 1875, more than 3,000 contaminated wells used by 6,000 people had been closed down. The beneficial effects of these reforms could be seen in the improved death rates in Birmingham: in 1871-75, the death rate averaged 25.2. In the period 1880 to 1885, the rate dropped to 20.7.

By 1875 and still under Chamberlain's leadership, Birmingham's municipal progressiveness was beginning to gain a reputation for the town as a centre of municipal collectivism, or as some liked to call it subsequently, 'gas and water socialism'. But there was more to come. In the same year the Birmingham Improvement Scheme was introduced.[24] This was to be Chamberlain's crowning achievement as mayor. The scheme was to involve the clearance of ninety-three acres of slum property to the east of New Street, and the construction of a new road containing business premises and shops, Corporation Street. The scheme was made possible by the powers conferred on local authorities by Cross's Artisans Dwellings Act, 1875. The estimated cost of the scheme was £550,000, and to meet this cost the Corporation was able to borrow at 3.5% repayable over fifty years, when after this time the property would belong to the Corporation. Joseph Chamberlain estimated the annual cost at £12,000. There is no doubt that the area to be cleared contained some of the worst slum property in central Birmingham. According to William White, the chairman of the Improvement Committee, describing his own ward, St Mary's Ward –[25]

> Little else is to be seen but bowing roofs, tottering chimneys, tumbledown and often disused shopping, heaps of bricks, broken windows, rough pavements damp and sloppy... acre after acre... completely given over to misery and squalor.

This then was Chamberlain's last great improvement in Birmingham, and long before Corporation Street was completed he had left the Council on becoming an MP. This was in 1876, when he replaced (unopposed) George Dixon, who had retired (it should be noted that Chamberlain had stood for parliament once before in Sheffield in 1874, but had been unsuccessful; there was no question of his failing to be elected this time). Chamberlain was justifiably proud of what he had achieved in Birmingham. Just before he entered the House of Commons, he summed up what he had accomplished in an often quoted passage in a letter to a friend - 'I think I have now almost completed my municipal programme, and may sing *nunc dimittis*. The town will be parked, paved, assized, marketed, gas-and-watered, and improved - all as a result of three years' active work'. In fact, not all of these undoubted advances were made when he was actually mayor; Birmingham already had three parks when he first became mayor (though Cannon Hill Park was acquired in 1873), and the town did not become an assize town till 1884. Nevertheless, his accomplishments as mayor were outstanding.

However, all was not achieved entirely through the force of a single dynamic personality. Good organisation also played its part, and manifested itself first among Birmingham Liberals in connection with parliamentary elections and also with elections to the Birmingham School Board. As a result of the 1867 Reform Act, Birmingham acquired a third parliamentary seat although voters had only two votes. A good deal of tactical voting was therefore required to secure the return of Liberal candidates, and this was achieved by careful party organisation. A similar organisation of votes also became necessary for success in the School Board elections. When the Birmingham Liberal Association was reorganised in 1868, William Harris took charge of voting tactics. This was really the beginning of the famous Birmingham 'caucus' (defined blandly by the Concise Oxford Dictionary as 'a group of people with shared concerns within a larger organisation'). Later, the term was used in a derogatory sense by Disraeli to describe the National Liberal Federation, set up by Chamberlain and his followers in 1877 - the implied reference being to the notoriously corrupt electoral organisations in the USA (the Democratic Party Tammany Hall group in New York is an outstanding example). In fact, there was nothing corrupt about the Birmingham caucus, but it did represent a notable advance in the mobilisation of voting power. Chamberlain himself defended the work of the caucus as 'democratic'.[26] Certainly it helped to keep him in power, and to maintain his popularity. This showed itself yet again when he was re-elected as mayor for his third term in 1875 by fifty-eight of the sixty-four members of the town council. By the beginning of 1876, he saw himself as possessing 'almost despotic authority'.[27]

9. St Philip's Cathedral.

However, there is a downside to Chamberlain's civic achievements, positive though they undoubtedly were. It is not merely that the gas and water undertakings were not novelties in local government but merely represented a catching-up with reforms already made by other local authorities; there is also the point that the Improvement Plan was designed not only to clear slum properties but also to provide a handsome new street, lined with impressive shops with offices above. There was therefore a strong commercial element in the whole scheme; slums were to be replaced by business premises which would pay high rates. Work did not start on the main thoroughfare till 1878, and the annual cost of the scheme came to double the £12,000 predicted by Chamberlain; and profits on the scheme were not made until 1892. Some of the slum properties were refurbished, but rents were increased as a result. Nearly half the houses in the condemned areas were demolished, but little was done at first to rehouse those who had lost their homes. Only sixty-two houses were built on the site of the demolished slums.[28] To sum up: Chamberlain's motives were undoubtedly worthy in wishing to lower the very high death rates in the central slum areas, and he spoke strongly to the council on this point:[29]

> The town must pay for this state of things in meal or in malt. We must pay in our health, or with our money. Which is the better - to keep our money, and lose our health, or to keep our health, without which money and life itself are practically valueless?

But very little was done before 1914 to provide alternative accommodation for dispossessed tenants. It was believed very strongly that this must be left to private enterprise. The council was prepared to let plots to builders at less than market prices, but this was as far as they would go. The most direct result of the Improvement Scheme was therefore the creation of a wide new street full of quality shops with office premises above, a handsome street indeed, but without a working-class dwelling in sight. Meanwhile, at the north end of New Street, the open space between the new Council House and the Town Hall was turned into Chamberlain Square, and a fountain erected to commemorate Chamberlain's taking over for the town of the water company.

We may now turn to municipal progress in the post-Chamberlain era. This remained steady, but somewhat less spectacular after Chamberlain's departure. The new Council House was opened adjacent to the Town Hall in 1879, too late for Chamberlain to have occupied the Mayor's Parlour which looked out across the square named after him. Its architect was H.R. Yeoville Thompson, and the fresco adorning the front of the building represented Britannia awarding the Birmingham manufacturers; other sculptural groups representing literature, art and science in their relation to industry. In the Council Chamber itself there are also frescoes emblematic of Birmingham industry.[30] Thus, fit and proper acknowledgement was made of the foundation of Birmingham's prosperity. The influence of industry and commerce are to be seen clearly enough in the composition of the council in the remaining years of the nineteenth century and up to 1914.

Naturally enough, the size of the council increased with the growth of the population within the town's boundaries, especially after the implementation of the Greater Birmingham Plan, 1911. Thus, the full council in 1869 consisted of forty-eight councillors and sixteen aldermen – sixty-four members in all. The Greater Birmingham Council of 1911 was nearly double this size – ninety councillors and thrity aldermen. Its powers had increased after it had acquired county borough status in 1888, its status was enhanced by becoming a city by royal decree in 1889, and the title of Lord Mayor was acquired in 1896. At the heart of the council's operations lay an elaborate system of committees – thirteen of them in 1869 and twenty-one in 1914. In the latter year they fell into four groups – seven committees dealing with public health; seven for the implementing of various acts of parliament; four were trading committees; and (the most important) there were three committees covering Finance, General Purposes and Estates. Birmingham Council became a model for civic administration, and indeed, according to Asa Briggs, the successful development of the committee system was by far the most important feature of the constitutional history of Birmingham between 1865 and 1914.[31]

Yet the committee system did not develop by chance. It was the logical outcome of a city run (as Ralph put it in 1890) by business men on business principles. The composition of the council in 1914 speaks for itself:[32]

Manufacturers	42	Working men	10
Merchants	5	Builders	5
Lawyers	14	Farmers	2
Other professional men	13	Women	2
Retailers	15	Miscellaneous	12

A council with over two-thirds of its membership drawn from industry, commerce and the law knew what it wanted from its local government officials, and it got it.[33] Of course, it must be said that no great figure emerged to lead the council after Chamberlain's departure into national politics

10. Church of the Messiah, Broad Street, 1865.

- something commented on in the *Birmingham Mail* in 1906 - but great names from industry such as Sir George Kenrick (Lord Mayor, 1908) and Ernest Martineau (Lord Mayor, 1912-13) were still prominent. There is really no indication that the calibre of the council had declined by 1914, though financial restraints resulted in less adventurous policies, as, for example, in 1907, when a plan for a proposed new road from Paradise Street to Broad Street was rejected by the council.

Nevertheless, the period after 1876 was not without some major and significant changes. Of these, the Elan Valley Water Supply project was one of the most important. By the 1880s, the City had fourteen resevoirs, with a capacity of nearly 630 million gallons, but it was still not enough for an ever-growing conurbation. New water supplies were becoming essential, and it was decided to bring them from the Elan Valley in the depths of Wales - not an entirely novel idea, since Liverpool was already obtaining its water from the Principality. The project was on a vast scale, the catchment area covering 70 square miles, and it involved piping water to Birmingham over a distance of 73 miles. It was authorised by Act of Parliament in 1892. Soon a colony of workers sprang up in this remote area of Wales, a kind of hutted encampment. The whole undertaking was formally opened by King Edward VII and Queen Alexandria on a visit to the site in July 1904. The works included six massive resevoirs, while south of the City at Frankley a receiving resevoir was built, together with filters, a pumping station, new trunk mains and so on. Soon the city was consuming daily some 23 million gallons of water.[34]

A second major advance in municipal services came with the municipal take-over of the city's electricity supply. Towards the end of the nineteenth century, the Electricity Supply Company was making good profits. The precedents for municipal ownership were clear, and a Bill was introduced into parliament in 1899 for that purpose. A new large power station was erected in Summer Lane in 1906, and an additional power station was built in Nechells in 1915.

By this time the demand for electrical supplies had increased considerably. Originally the most important customer for electricity had been the tramway companies, but industry was using more and more electric power, especially after the outbreak of war in 1914.

However, the most striking change in the structure of local government in Birmingham before 1914 was the implementation of the Greater Birmingham Plan, 1911, already alluded to earlier in this chapter. Inevitably, as the city grew, from time to time it incorporated local authorities on the periphery. In 1891, for example, Saltley, Balsall Heath and Little Bromwich were absorbed, followed by Quinton (including Harborne) in 1909. Finally, in 1911, Handsworth, Aston, Erdington, Yardley, King's Norton and Northfield all came in, and the annexations were confirmed in a Parliamentary Bill in the same year.[35] The result of these repeated extensions of the city boundaries was a massive increase in the official population of the City of Birmingham: it rose from 401,000 in 1881 to 840,000 in 1911.[36] Of course, this led to a great increase in the responsibilities of the City Council. At the same time, it was now evident that it was the largest organ of local government in the country after London. It could now truly boast of being the Second City in the kingdom, exceeding in population Manchester, Liverpool and Glasgow. It was still a great manufacturing and commercial centre, of course, but by 1914 it had acquired all the administrative functions and cultural amenities appropiate to a city of such prominence.

Such functions and amenities included all the advances already noted, such as having its own assize court, the new law courts, county borough status and the title of Lord Mayor.[37] The Central Library was burned down in a great fire in 1879, and only a thousand books were saved out of the 50,000 books in the Reference Library (though 15,000 books out of the 17,000 books in the Lending Library survived). The books which had been destroyed were replaced, and a new library was opened by John Bright on 1 June 1882. Meanwhile the Arts Gallery opened in 1885, situated in the premises of the Gas Company (it attracted more than 15 million visitors in the period 1886-1910); and work started on a new gallery of art, the Feeney Galleries, in 1912. As recorded previously, the first municipal parks were opened in the 1850s, then Cannon Hill Park was acquired in 1873, and another five parks by 1914. The corporation also took over large open areas at Rednal Hill in 1889, Bilberry Hill (1889), and Beacon Hill. Smaller recreational grounds were also opened at various places within the city, and in 1906, J.S. Nettlefold founded the Birmingham Playgrounds, Open Spaces and Playing Fields Association.[38]

Other cultural advances made in the second half of the nineteenth century include the establishment of the Midlands Institute in 1854 (the Queen's College, a small theological college, had been opened earlier in 1843), and the founding of Mason College in 1880 by Sir Josiah Mason.[39] In 1896, the college in Edmund Street became a university college with Joseph Chamberlain as its president. Moves were then made to turn the college into a full university, Chamberlain giving the project his strong support. Indeed, thanks to his energetic and enthusiastic leadership, early plans for the new institution to be part of a larger partnership of university colleges were replaced by the notion of an independent university for Birmingham with its own charter, standing on a new site in Edgbaston (the site of the present university campus). Chamberlain was thus successful in creating an entirely new and independent university, the first civic university in the country. His achievements were given strong support by the business community in the city. Unlike the universities of Oxford and Cambridge, it was founded with the aim of giving educational opportunities to those with talent to reach the highest levels of culture. It deserves to be remembered as Chamberlain's final and supreme gift to the city of his adoption before the stroke in 1906 which put an end to his political career.[40]

Another important educational advance but on a different plane was the setting up of the new system of local elementary schools made necessary by Foster's Education Act, 1870.[41] These were schools administered by the Birmingham School Board and paid for out of local school rates in the remaining years of the nineteenth century and up to 1902, when a further Education Act abolished the school boards and transferred their powers and the schools themselves to local authorities such as the Birmingham Corporation. These schools will be described and discussed in Chapter Six, but they were clearly an important part of local government services in Birmingham, especially after 1880 when elementary education became compulsory, and free after 1891. The board schools were in addition, of course, to the existing voluntary schools run by the church societies. Another, more specialised type of school established by the council was the Technical School, opened in Suffolk Street, with its three branch schools.[42] Thus, elementary education became of increasing concern to the city authorities after 1870, but secondary education remained for the most part firmly in the hands of the King Edward Education Foundation before 1914.[43]

One other aspect of council activity needs to be considered, and this is local transport. By the mid-century the major railway stations serving the national network had already been built: Snow Hill was opened in 1852 (and re-built in 1870), and New Street Station was opened in 1854. The first major improvement in local transport came with the introduction of horse-drawn trams in 1872. Further progress was delayed in the following years by disputes over the mode of traction - should it be by steam or by cable? In 1873 a local line, Hockley to Colmore Row, was built by the council, then leased out to local companies. A number of tram companies was then founded, the council adopting the same procedure of building lines, then leasing them out to private companies.

The trams were propelled by steam, and were hardly very attractive or pleasant to use. The American writer J. Ralph was very critical of them, calling them 'hideous, cumbrous, and dangerous', and said that no American city would tolerate them. An experiment with cable traction and a stationary engine from Hockley Hill to Colmore Row proved a failure. Then in 1890 self-contained electic cars employing accumulators were tried on the Bristol Road, but they kept running out of power, leaving passengers stranded. In 1896, two Canadian tramway experts, Ross and Mackenzie, offered to take over the entire existing system, but after protracted negotiations their proposals fell through. Finally in 1889 the Council decided to run the lines itself, when the leases fell in. By the General Powers Bill of 1903, the Corporation was enabled to go ahead in December 1903, and in the following month the first municipal tramcars were in service between Bull Street and the city boundary in Aston Road. By January 1907, all steam trams had been withdrawn, and replaced by electric trams powered from overhead wires. By July 1911 the Corporation had complete control over all the City's tramways. In its first three years of ownership, it ran 300 tramcars over 34 miles of track in the City, making profits of more

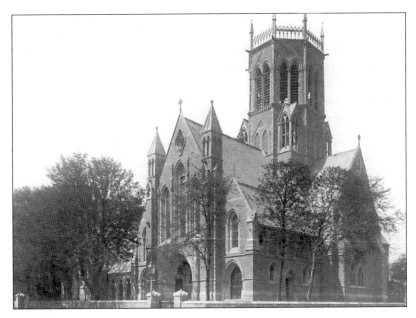

11. Church of the Redeemer.

than £75,000 for the relief of the rates. This tramway service was supplemented in 1913 just before the outbreak of the First World War by the purchase by the Council of ten omnibuses.[44]

So what benefits to the people of Birmingham had been brought to them by municipal policy in the period 1850 to 1914? How far in particular had the Council gone, in Avery's words of 1869, to 'surround the humbler classes of the population with its benevolent and protecting care'? Certainly substantal progress had been made. The supply of cheap gas, the great improvement in the provision of pure and plentiful water supplies, and the beginnings of the demolition of the central slums all contributed to the fall in death rates by 1914 (as will be noted in the next chapter). Cultural amenities were greatly enhanced by the opening of the lending and reference libraries and of the art gallery. In addition, there was a substantial increase in the number of public parks and open spaces, and an extension of the tramway system under municipal control improved public access not only to the parks, of course, but to places of work and to the city centre. At the same time, the work of improving the city's highways and lighting them went on steadily, together with the vital sanitary reform of installing or improving deep drainage and providing water closets (again, see the next chapter). The availability of elementary education was also greatly increased by the building of the board schools, which were taken over by the corporation in 1902. All this adds up to an impressive list of municipal reforms, and to a striking illustration of the Civic Gospel in action.

Does this mean then that Ralph's description of Birmingham as the best governed city in the world was really justified? Clearly, there is much evidence of local government activity in the last quarter of the nineteenth century, but this in itself does not validate Ralph's claim. In the second half of the nineteenth century, all the great industrial cities were engaged in making life rather more civilised for their inhabitants. National legislation, especially in the field of public health, combined with local ratepayer power made this inevitable. London itself was ruled by a progressive London County Council, set up after the County Councils Act, 1888, and with increased powers after 1899. Its record of municipal housing before 1914 was far superior to that of Birmingham. It would really take a very lengthy and sustained comparison of the organisation and achievements of the major cities of the time both in this country and elsewhere to substantiate Ralph's sweeping assertion.

However, it seems fair to say that much that is commendable was achieved. To put it all into perspective, two major points must still be emphasised: the first is that, as indicated earlier, Birmingham under Chamberlain was merely catching up with the progress already being made in other towns and cities. Before Chamberlain, it had really lagged behind in civic advances; and even when it did catch up and in some respects surpass other cities, there was still a lack of any real planning in the city. The new Council House was positioned somewhat awkwardly in relation to the older Town Hall. This was perhaps unavoidable, but it was often observed that roads leading into the city centre led nowhere, being soon swallowed up in a maze of smaller streets. In spite of the much later reorganisation of the street system after the Second World War, few efforts were made to provide an impressive central square. This had to wait till near the end of the twentieth century. Manchester, Liverpool and Leeds may all be considered to have done better than this before 1914.[45]

The second major point to be made is that although Chamberlain's Improvement Plan did result in a new and impressive business thoroughfare – a wide boulevard of shops and offices, lined with trees, as we have seen – it did little to rehouse the inhabitants of the slums which had been cleared. The Council was firmly opposed to municipal building, preferring to leave house building to private enterprise. It did, however, build twenty-two houses in Ryder Street in 1890, and eighty-two houses in nearly Lawrence Street; but a proposal to build a further 116 houses on sites cleared in Woodcock Street and Milk Street was dropped. The only other scheme was for four two-story blocks of sixty-four two-bedroom flats with shared sculleries in Milk Street, this project being completed in 1901.[46] This was as far as the Council was prepared to go, other than the improvement of existing dwellings, and the opening up of some of the squalid courts by demolishing one side of the court so as to admit a freer circulation of air. The London County Council went much further than this, beginning a policy of building flats centrally and of small garden suburbs further out in south London, for example, in Tooting and Norbury. Liverpool was the first to undertake municipal building as early as 1869, and by 1912 the Council there had built 2,322 dwellings, more than 11,000 properties had been renovated and 5,500 houses demolished.[47] By way of contrast, a Special Committee set up by Birmingham Council in July 1913 with Joseph Chamberlain's son Neville as chairman, reported that there was a housing shortage in the City. As many as 200,000 inhabitants were housed in 43,366 back-to-backs (there were only 2,881 back-to-back houses remaining in Liverpool, and none at all in Manchester). More than 42,000 properties in Birmingham had no separate water supplies, no sinks and no drains. More than 58,000 occupiers had no separate lavatories. Only 1,396 houses were built in 1914 by private enterprise, although an estimated 2,000 were required. In the face of all this, the Council's policy of limiting action to merely repairing houses was clearly inadequate.[48]

12. St Chad's Roman Catholic Cathedral, 1841.

13. Birmingham Council House, 1879.

It is clear then that the failure to provide adequate accomodation for tenants dispossessed by the Improvement Plan, or subsequently for those still living in the central slums, constitute something of a blemish on the Corporation's civic record. The Civic Gospel failed to operate adequately in this area, because business interests did not think it proper to compete with private enterprise in building homes for the people. Of course, they were not alone or exceptional in this belief. As long ago as 1884 the matter came up in the House of Lords when Lord Wemyss asked, 'If they [local authorities] build houses, would they furnish them? Would they put fire in the grate or food in the cupboard? And if not, on this principle, why not?' Wemyss was the chairman of the Liberty and Property Defence League, founded 1882, and he spoke for many of the propertied class.[49] So it is not surprising that the business men on the Council took the view they did. As we shall see in a subsequent chapter, the even greater housing shortage of the 1920s forced them to a change in policy. Before 1914, however, as Asa Briggs has observed, Birmingham did not develop an enlightened working-class housing policy on the basis of the Improvement Scheme; and the Housing of the Working Classes Act,1890, which permitted building by local authorities, had few results in the city.[50]

In conclusion, whatever its shortcomings, the Civic Gospel had a marked impact on local government policies in Birmingham, taking effect, it might be argued, even before the Chamberlainite mayoralty. In no other city were its beliefs so clearly and repeatedly affirmed, and it certainly influenced informed national opinion on the duties of local government bodies. It is true, of course, that some of the loftier expectations of its believers - for example, the idea that cities should rival the architectural beauties of Italian cities such as Florence - were never fulfilled in Birmingham. In fact, an odd mixture of architectural styles was employed after 1870, much of it a kind of Italian Rennaissance together with Gothic Revival. Certainly there was no uniformity of style, as there was no rational planning in the layout of the city. It has been said that Birmingham was 'a city of bits and pieces', and the one feature commonly encountered in the city was the extensive use of terracotta, more widely used than elsewhere in England. According to one authority on terracotta, the late Dr Michael Stratton, terracotta became 'the architectural symbol of the civic gospel'.[51] This may be to take the pervasive influence of the civic gospel a little too far, but it is an interesting comment.

In the final analysis, it was Chamberlain who took the first major steps to put the Civic Gospel into effect. He must be given credit for both preaching and practising the gospel. Of course, his later career after he had left Birmingham ran into political sands, but his achievements before he entered parliament were outstanding, and he was understandably proud of them. His remarks in this connection on being appointed president of the Board of Trade in 1880 are well known: he said that unless he could secure for the nation the same social improvements as had already been secured in Birmingham 'it will have been a sorry exchange to give up the Town Council for the Cabinet'.[52] There is no doubt that the most substantial and positive achievements of his whole career were in Birmingham, crowned ultimately by his part in the creation of the University of Birmingham.[53] The famous Clock Tower in Chancellor's Court at the University is a lasting memorial to his efforts. Indeed, it is fitting that *The Times* should have paid tribute to this aspect of his career in its obituary published on 7 July 1914 –

> He preached... and practised a pride in Birmingham such as the Greeks in classical times and the Italians in the Middle Ages felt in their cities. He built up the idea of a self-sufficient community with stately and beneficiant public institutions and a dignified public life – not dependent on London for picture galleries, museums and libraries, or on Oxford or Cambridge for the best educational facilities, but in all things complete in itself.

Of course, the Civic Gospel and its implementation in Birmingham was not the achievement of one man alone – many contributed to its fulfilment, lesser lights who supported Chamberlain and followed in his footsteps. Whatever qualification may be made to the way it was carried out in practice, the fact remains that the Civic Gospel achieved national and even international renown. Yet its story often merely forms part of the history of local government as it evolved in the second half of the nineteenth century.[55] Since it is the purpose of this book to lay emphasis on the economic and social history of Birmingham, efforts have been made in this chapter to stress its contribution to the well-being of the people of Birmingham. It is clear that the Civic Gospel contributed greatly to the welfare of the city's inhabitants. It was more than the provision of municipal gas and pure water, but (as we have seen) extended to municipal paving and lighting, public libraries and parks, the museum and art gallery, improved public transport and the acquisition of the board schools. These are the practical results of the Civic Gospel, the only qualification necessary being that the board schools were adminstered by a School Board separate from the local government structure until the schools were taken over by the Corporation following the Education Act, 1902. The one notable failure of the Civic Gospel (and one shared by many other cities and towns) was the reluctance to embark on a programme of municipal building; but this was to be remedied in the inter-war years, as we shall see later, when large-scale government financial assistance became available to all municipal authorities to meet the urgent, post-war need for working-class housing.

CHAPTER FOUR

LIFE AT WORK

The majority of the inhabitants of Birmingham in the second half of the nineteenth century spent most of their waking hours at work. Not for them long years of retirement or the holidays abroad which are taken for granted today. Whereas in previous centuries they might be described as the 'lower orders', the 'lower classes', the 'common people' or even 'the mob', by the early nineteenth century the expression 'the working classes' was increasingly used. It was appropiate enough: the great masses who lived in the new industrial towns were certainly workers, and work dominated their lives. This and the following chapter will therefore be devoted to an investigation into the nature of life at work in Birmingham, and then to the home environment.

During the second half of the nineteenth century, life at work nationally was to undergo significant changes. Domestic industry of the traditional kind based on the home slowly disappeared. Workshop industry was still of importance, but as we saw in Chapter Two, larger workplaces and large-scale factories became common. Working hours were reduced, partly because of government legislation, and partly as a result of collective agreements negotiated by the trade union movement, which was of increasing importance. The working week gained a new uniformity as St Monday faded away, and Saturday half-day working became more and more the norm. Child labour vanished in time from the workplace as hours of juvenile labour were restricted by law; and with the coming of compulsory education in 1880, child labour was forbidden before the age of twelve. More female labour was also employed.

How did these national trends affect life at work in Birmingham? In the first place, if the national picture is examined in a little more detail, the working day underwent only minor changes in the 1850s, with more significant changes, notably in the building trades, in the 1860s.[1] In 1870-74, however, which were years of unparalleled prosperity, there took place a general reduction of hours, especially in the unionised trades.[2] By 1875 the normal working week was from 54 to 56.5 hours; the nine-hour day was replacing the ten-hour day. Thereafter in the 1880s and 1890s the trade unions pressed for a further reduction by statute to the eight-hour day, the Amalgamated Society of Engineers staging a protracted (but unsuccessful) strike in 1897 over the issue. Meanwhile, the movement for a shorter working day on Saturdays had made progress. In 1850 the Factory Act had made textile mills close at 2 p.m. on a Saturday, while the building trades in London had long been pressing their employers for this change. By the 1870s the battle appears to have been won. According to the Royal Commission on the Working of the Factory and Workshops Acts, 1876, the Saturday half-holiday had become all but universal.[3]

Against this background it can be seen that Birmingham followed the national trend quite closely. Although St Monday still caused concern among even large-scale employers (one told the Commission on the Employment of Children, 1862, that he lay awake at night, thinking of ways of circumventing his men and getting them to work on Mondays), it was no problem by

14. Crooked Lane, industrial premises, 1886.

the mid-1870s.[4] St Monday had become a relic of the old days when workers had idled at the beginning of the week and worked long hours at the end. Its passing was compensated for by the early cessation of work on Saturday, and also the reduction of hours in the early 1870s. No doubt the disappearance of the charge hand with his own team of workers, noted in Chapter Two, is also of relevance here; more efficient management centred on the office could hardly counternance indefinitely either the payment of teams by butties or the easy-going nature of voluntary attendance on Mondays. So St Monday gradually faded away in the Birmingham area, though it lingered on in the Black Country right up to the outbreak of the Great War in 1914.[5]

The other great change in the Birmingham working week was the substantial reduction in the hours worked per week, a change which mirrored the national reductions mentioned earlier. The national figures for the working week in the principal Birmingham trades of ironfounders, brass-workers, engineers and boilermakers in the second half of the nineteenth century are as follows:[6]

Reductions in hours of labour: mean of returns given of hours per week

	1850	1870	1890
Ironfounders	60.4	57.8	53.9
Brassworkers	59.5	55.6	53.6
Engineers	59.3	58.0	53.7
Boilermakers	60.0	57.6	53.7

These figures show a remarkable fall in the number of hours worked in the forty-year period surveyed – in round terms, a reduction of about six hours a week. The ten-hour day of the mid-nineteenth century had been replaced in many trades by the end of the century by the nine-hour day. Moreover, pressure was exerted by the unions from the 1880s onwards for a statutory reduction for all trades to the eight-hour day. This was encouraged by the success of the London gas stokers in gaining an eight-hour day in 1889. This was also achieved in Birmingham by the municipal gas stokers in October of the same year,[7] by civil service workers in the 1890s, and by the miners in 1908. Kynochs led the field among Birmingham employers in granting the eight-hour day in 1894. Following the publication of Rowntree's Survey of Poverty in York in 1901, the same firm took the remarkable step of granting all its employees in 1903 a minimum living wage of 22s per week, by which 200 to 300 employed by the firm gained an increase in wages.[8] In 1909 the Trades Boards Act (also known as the Sweated Industries Act) provided for the setting-up of joint boards of workers and employers in certain sweated industries, such as chain-making in the Black Country, to negotiate over working hours and conditions. Thus the major national changes in the pattern of the working week towards a reduction in hours and half-day working on Saturdays was followed faithfully in Birmingham.

There was also another and important dimension to the reduction in working hours, and this was the fall in the cost of living, especially from the 1870s onwards. Cheap wheat began to be imported from America in the early 1870s, while the first really successful cargo of frozen beef and mutton from Melbourne arrived in London in 1880. There were further imports of pork from the USA, beef from the Argentine and lamb from New Zealand. At the same time taxes on food were gradually reduced, especially on tea, on which the tax was lowered from 1s 10d a pound to 4d a pound in 1880. All this resulted in the retail price of food in the typical workman's budget falling by 30% between 1877 and 1897.[9] Thus, in addition to shorter working hours, the Birmingham worker also benefitted from a rise in real wages. It is no wonder that some historians have seen the last quarter of the nineteenth century as a period which witnessed the rise of a consumer society. One of them gives the following figures for the increase in real incomes during the second half of the century –[10]

	Income per person	
	At current prices (£)	*In real terms (1801=100)*
1851	25	113
1901	44	240

Of course, qualifications have to be made to this rosy picture. The averages given above can hardly apply to the lowest ranks of the working classes, the residuum, the denizens of the slums. For those in more regular employment, with the development of a more uniform working week and the disappearance of the small working unit led by a charge hand, work discipline would in all probability have tightened up. This is likely to have been particularly noticeable in the larger establishments in the newer industries such as the electrical industry, the cycle industry, the manufacture of tyres and the motor industry. As manufacture developed at a distance from the older industrial sites in the city centre, the working day was actually lengthened for some by the need to travel to work by bus or tram. Then again, some workers were thrown out of work during the Great Depression, though the new industries helped to provide more jobs.

We have no unemployment figures for Birmingham during the Depression, but national trade unions with branches in Birmingham suffered heavily in the worst years. For example, the societies of ironfounders and boilermakers had less than 1% of their members unemployed in 1872-73, but more than 20% unemployed in 1879. Similarly, the National Union of Ironworkers had 35,000 members in 1873; in 1879, membership was down to 1,400. Further, the investigations into the extent of poverty in London by Charles Booth, and in York by Rowntree highlighted the extent of urban poverty towards the end of the Victorian period. All this needs to be taken into account. There is also the question of how far the replacement of the older, hand-operated machine tools by powered machine tools such as the power press introduced a new element of strain. In some cases, this could have been so; in others, it could have actually reduced the amount of physical labour required (though power presses were notoriously dangerous to use). Yet in spite of all these caveats, it seems undeniable that there was a substantial reduction in the number of hours worked, and an equally significant increase in real wages in Birmingham in the last quarter of the nineteenth century.

We may now turn to another striking change in labour conditions in Birmingham which occurred in the second half of the nineteenth century. This is the virtual ending of child labour. It will be recalled that at the mid-century, the employment of young children in industry was widespread; work became general at the age of nine or ten, and about 2,000 children under the age of ten were employed in the area.[11] On the whole, children do not appear to have been treated badly at work, though the Children's Employment Commissioners in 1842 did point out exceptions to the rule in

15. Lavender sellers in the Bull Ring, 1901.

two named pin factories. Nothing further was done to regulate working hours and conditions for children other than those in the textile and allied industries until after the second Children's Employment Commission of the early 1860s had issued their reports. Then, in 1867, two very important acts were passed. The first, the Factories Act, 1867, extended the existing factory legislation to all places of work employing more than fifty persons, limited the weekly hours of children aged between eight and thirteen to thirty hours, and provided for fifteen hours schooling a week. Only part-time work and no night work were permitted in these places below the age of thirteen. Young persons between thirteen and eighteen and women were also limited to ten hours a day. The second act, the Workshops Act, 1867, defined a workshop, and laid it down that no child under eight should be employed; employment between eight and thirteen was again to be part-time, while young persons and women were limited to ten and a half hours daily, with schooling for the children of up to ten hours a week. These two acts had a profound effect on the employment of children in Birmingham, even though it took a considerable time for them to be implemented. This is especially true of the Workshops Act, where the mistake was made at first of entrusting the enforcement of the act to local inspectors, who lacked authority and could be subject to local influence by employers. In 1871 the factory inspectors took over the work of inspecting workshops.

For the first time then, the employment of children in Birmingham in both factories and workshops was subject to regulation, with the consequence that there was a severe shortage of child labour; in some trades, twice as many boys and girls were required as previously because of the restrictions on hours. Moreover, these restrictions came at a time when more and more children were being sent to school rather than out to work. It is true that school attendance was patchy and did not last long. It was not compulsory, and the lure of another wage-earner in the family was hard to resist in many working-class families.[12] Nevertheless, the relative prosperity of the time meant that more parents could afford to keep their children at school for longer periods. In 1870 Forster's Education Act set up additional elementary schools ('board' schools), paid for out of a locally-levied school rate, and run by boards of ratepayers. Such boards were given the option of making attendance compulsory in their localities. In 1876 Lord Sandon's Act advised parents that it was their duty to send their children to school. This act was followed by another education act in 1880 which made attendance compulsory up to the age of twelve (with certain provisions for early leaving between ten and twelve). By Lord Salisbury's Act, 1891, elementary education was in effect made free, while in 1899 the official school leaving age was put up to twelve without exemption.[13]

Thus in the course of a little over thirty years, a dramatic change took place in the labour market. Children had been removed from both factories and workshops by the combined effects of first the factory and workshop legislation, and then the education acts. Initially, of course, there was a period of some confusion, and of a shortage of labour. According to one inspector, half-time boys were 'practically expelled' from the forges because they could not work at night; but the difficulties were overcome in time, especially in the boom conditions of the early 1870s, while the increased use of steam power and of power-operated machine tools was encouraged. By 1900 elementary education was provided up to the age of fourteen, although one group of school children were permitted legally to be at work from the age of twelve onwards – the so-called 'part-timers'. In 1894 their numbers were estimated at 170,686,

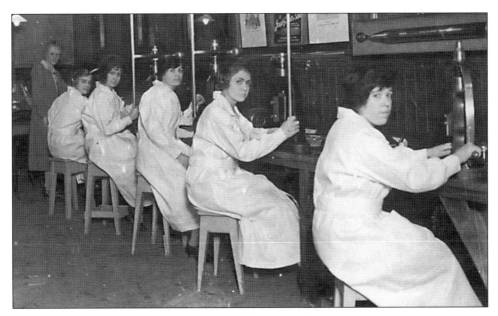

16. Workers at Gillott's Pens, 1926.

the vast majority being in Lancashire, Yorkshire and Cheshire, where they were employed in the textile mills. In Lancashire at this date these numbers represented about two out of three older children, but in Staffordshire (which included the Black Country, of course) only one in fourteen.[14] To judge from the Staffordshire figures, Birmingham is not likely to have been a great employer of part-timers. Of course, even in the 1890s, some illegal employment of children went on. As the Fifth Report of the Royal Commission on Labour put it –[15]

> It appears that boys are frequently employed under age, and when the inspector comes round, are hidden, so that the infraction of the law is seldom discovered. The extent of this evil varies, however, very largely in different localities.

By the end of the century then, the employment of children full-time in Birmingham which had been so common fifty years before had almost come to an end. However, out of school work appears to have continued on a considerable scale. Boys and girls were cheaper to employ than adults. Many boys were employed as errand boys, messingers, delivery boys and van boys. There was particular concern about boys working as van boys, who later went into dead-end jobs as general labourers. This was common enough in London and also in Birmingham, where the problem was investigated by Arnold Freeman.[16] One notorious instance of excessive hours worked after school was provided by the use of lather boys in barbers' shops. It was alleged that these boys worked extraordinarily long hours – five hours every evening with fifteen hours on Saturdays and six or eight on Sundays.[17] In Birmingham, the boys were said to work similarly long hours, it even being claimed that two lather boys had died from overwork, the first a boy of eleven, the other a boy of twelve 'done to death in the same way in Digbeth'.[18]

Reports of such ill-treatment may well be exaggerated, but there is no doubt that juvenile labour both before and after school hours was still to be found in Birmingham before 1914. This is not surprising in view of the extent of child labour a half-century before. In January 1914, a survey of elementary school children in Birmingham reported that 2,585 children were working 10-20 hours a week, 2,145 working 20-30 hours, and (though it is hard to believe) 1,725 working 30-40 hours per week.[19] Even comparatively recently, part-time employment of Birmingham school children was quite common.[20] Another important change in the workforce in Birmingham in the period between 1861 and 1911 was the increased employment of women. G.C.Allen provides us with a useful table here –[21]

Percentage of females to total amount of employment

Industry	1861	1891	1911
Brass and non-ferrous metals	24	22	27
Buttons	58	63	77
Saddlery and harness	28	28	33
Other leather goods	-	-	67
Pens	94	92	90
Tinplate ware	18	22	37
Cycle	-	6	25
Electrical appatatus	-	3	18
Jewellery (excluding electro-platers)	28	26	35
Brush	22	49	58
Paperbag and box	-	95	94
Bedstead	-	26	25

Here it is apparent that the predominance of female labour in the manufacture of pens and of paper bags and boxes, was maintained, though there were significant increases in buttons, brass and non-ferrous metals, and in tin-plate ware, in cycles, electrical apparatus and brushes. The most obvious explanation of these increases is that adult female labour was a good substitute for the loss of child labour, and was still much cheaper than male labour (women's wages were about half that of men's). Another reason is that women's manual dexterity made them especially suitable in such new trades as the cycle and electrical industries (they were also far less unionised than men). Lastly, a marginal factor but not unimportant, is that the working-class family was growing distinctly smaller by 1914. Married women were producing only half the number of children born in the mid-century years, and so were available for a return to work at an earlier age than before.[22] The movement towards the employment of more women in Birmingham industry is interesting and important, but it was still on only a small scale. Although the employment of women before marriage was acceptable enough at the time, after marriage it was still considered that women's proper place was in the home as wife and mother.[23]

References have been made so far in this chapter to trade unions, but in view of what has been said in Chapter One about the comparatively peaceful nature of labour relations in Birmingham at the mid-nineteenth century, it would not be expected that trade union activity would be very extensive at this time. This is true enough; the trade union movement had not spread very widely in Birmingham by 1850, and like the national movement, it was confined very largely to the skilled craftsmen who could afford the subscriptions necessary to pay for out-of-work benefits and strike pay. However, with the improvement in trade in the 1850s, trade unionism moved into a new phase which the Webbs, the pioneer historians of the movement, described as the period of new model unionism.[24] The reference was to the Amalgamated Society of Engineers (the ASE), founded 1851, destined to become one of the most powerful unions of the second half of the century. In fact, features of the ASE which the Webbs thought deserved the title of 'New Model' were scarcely new at all. It is true that the ASE was a nationwide organisation, but efforts had been made before in the 1830s to set up national bodies of trade unions, but they had failed. Again, although the ASE was something of a model for other craft unions, there continued to exist for many years numerous small craft unions which were purely either local or regional. Moreover, the Webbs gave the impression that henceforth trade unions were to be peaceful organisations, unwilling to go on strike, as compared with their earlier, turbulent history. Yet the ASE called a widespread strike in 1854. Nevertheless, the Webbs were right in emphasising the importance of the establishing of the ASE in 1851, in that craft unions of its type both nationally and in Birmingham were to play increasingly significant roles in the history of labour during the ensuring years of prosperity.

This is seen in the setting up of the London Trades Council in 1860 by a group of leading trade unions. Its purpose was to discuss issues of more than local interest, such as affairs in parliament, labour legislation and even foreign policy as it affected workers abroad. William Allen, secretary of the ASE, said that the business of the London Trades Council was 'to look after parliamentary affairs'. Similar bodies were founded by 1860 in Glasgow, Sheffield, Liverpool and Edinburgh. In 1866 it was Birmingham's turn to establish a trades council. A meeting was called by Roger Bateson, national treasurer of the General Union of Carpenters and Joiners, which met on 22 May 1866, attended by twenty-five delegates, representing 4,814 members. The Council which resulted held its first official meeting in July 1866. A new and influential body had come into existence in Birmingham.[25]

The precise reasons for the founding of the Birmingham Trades Council are said to be two local incidents. The first was the discontent in the building trade caused by the employers' insistence on the 'Discharge Note', a certificate from a previous employer. The second was the sending to prison under the Master and Servant Acts of one William Carroll who had told his employers that his fellow workers would not work with non-unionists.[26] These two local events might well have been instrumental in the setting up of the council, but it seems likely that a trades council would have been instituted sometime in the 1860s in any case.

It is interesting to note that, just as in London, it was the older well-established craft unions in Birmingham which took the initiative in forming the trades council. The original body represented thirteen trades in all – six separate trades of woodworkers (carpenters, joiners, cabinet makers, wood turners, mill sawyers and lath benders), shoemakers, tailors, painters and basket makers, fire-iron makers and coachmakers. These were by no means the sum total of trade unions in Birmingham: according to the London Trades Council there were forty-three union bodies in Birmingham. As might be expected, the aims of the Birmingham Trades Council were somewhat more localised than those of the London body. They were said to be 'to watch over the social and political rights of the workers, and generally to further the benefits of trade unionism'.[27] Only three years after the founding of the Trades Council, in 1869 it acted as host to the second meeting of the national Trades Union Congress. This Birmingham meeting lasted six days, and was attended by forty-seven delegates (thirteen from Birmingham), representing in all a quarter of a million members. A number of prominent figures in the national trade union movement attended the Congress. They included George Odger (secretary of the London Trades Council), George Potter (editor of the radical *Beehive* paper), Thomas Burt (soon to be one of the first two working men MPs) and George Holyoake (the local life-long radical, one-time Chartist lecturer and later a leading supporter of the co-operative movement and its historian).[28]

The 1870s were to see a significant expansion of the trade union movement in Birmingham, though still confined to the established craft unions. This expansion was especially evident in the boom years of the early 1870s, when substantial reductions in the working day were achieved. In 1871 the first branch of the Amalgamated Society of Railway Servants was established in Birmingham, and in 1872 the important Union of Brassworkers was set up, with William John Davis as secretary. In the same year the bakers struck for £1 a week minimum, while the filesmiths, bricklayers and masons, electro-plate workers and fire-iron forgers all obtained advances in pay.[29] Yet it cannot be said that this activity was any indication of an increased militancy among Birmingham trade unionists (it was instead the consequence of unparalleled local prosperity) and indeed the movement nationally was trying hard to dispel the unfavourable impressions made by the Sheffield outrages, 1866, and by the *Hornby v. Close* decision in 1867.[30] A Royal Commission into trade unions was appointed in 1867, and leading trade unionists testified before it as to the essentially pacific nature of unionism, and the unions' belief in peaceful picketing. Their efforts were rewarded by the Trade Union Act, 1871, which confirmed the legal status of trade unions; but the Criminal Law Amendment Act, 1871, made picketing illegal. In the same year the TUC set up a Parliamentary Committee, designed to keep pressure on members of parliament to give fair treatment to the trade unions.[31] In 1875 and 1876 Disraeli's Tory government passed two Acts which together made picketing legal again. At last the trade unions appeared to have gained an unequivocal declaration that trade unions were legal, while the legality of picketing (an essential element in the functioning of trade unions, of course) had also at last been firmly established.

By the mid-1870s then, the trade union movement nationally had regained the ground temporarily lost at the end of the previous decade, and indeed the TUC Parliamentary Committee considered the 'work of emancipation' to be 'full and complete'. Its secretary, George Howell, even thought this Committee had served its original purpose, and could be disbanded. The prosperity of the early 1870s certainly helped the movement to expand: by 1872 the TUC claimed it represented 375,000 members. By 1874 this figure had grown to 1,191,922. In Birmingham, trade unionism continued to grow, though still confined for the most part to skilled and semi-skilled workers. The political scene was dominated by the Liberals, and especially by Joseph Chamberlain, mayor of Birmingham, 1873-76. He was a great believer in conciliation and arbitration in trade disputes, and his influence over local trade union thinking was considerable. As we have seen, labour relations in

Birmingham had always been far more peaceful than in other large industrial centres, so that Chamberlainite doctrines were readily acceptable to the unions, including his earlier beliefs in free trade; in 1881 the Trades Council passed a resolution in favour of free trade, although by this time the Chamber of Commerce had begun to discuss imperial preference. This identification of trade union beliefs with traditional ideas of co-operation with employers in Birmingham as espoused by Chamberlain - in effect, an alliance with the masters - has led the historian of the Birmingham Trades Council to describe the 1870s and 1880s as the era of 'Cloth-capped Chamberlainism'.[32] Chamberlain himself was chairman for a time of the Midlands Iron and Steel Wages Board which operated on a sliding scale of prices and wage rates.

During the 1870s and 1880s there was one important development in the trade union movement nationally which had repercussions in Birmingham. This was the widening of the scope of unionism to include some of the unskilled and semi-skilled trades, a change which is often referred to as 'new unionism'. The new unions which came into being are commonly distinguished from the older craft unions in that their members could not afford the subscriptions which permitted the out-of-work benefits of the wealthier craft unions. The limited funds of the new unions were used rather to support strikes. Further, the new unions were often led by more aggressive, socialist-minded leaders, more inclined to use the strike weapon than the older, more conservative craft unions. New unionism achieved national recognition with the well-known London match girls strike led by Annie Besant in 1888, and then the famous London Docks Strike in 1889 (the strike for the 'docker's tanner'), organised by Ben Tillett, supported by leading socialists such as Tom Mann, John Burns, Eleanor Marx and Annie Besant. Nevertheless, it would be wrong to give the impression that the new unions were taking over the trade union movement as a whole. By 1900, their numbers were still less than a tenth of the total trade union membership. Moreover, not all of them were led by socialists, or were confined to the unskilled, and some even provided traditional friendly society benefits. Nevertheless, they did supply a newer element of militancy, and an injection of socialist ideas which were opposed to the liberal doctrines held by many older unionists of the time.[33]

How did all this affect trade unionism in Birmingham, where the unions were so well-known for conciliatory attitudes? Certainly a good deal of union activity was to be seen in the late 1880s and early 1890s. In 1886, the ASE joined the Birmingham Trades Council, led by J.T. Tanner, a strong advocate of the eight-hour day. In the next year, the builders struck successfully against a reduction in rates of pay, while the railway workers also came out on strike, but rather less successfully, 1,066 out of 3,600 on strike actually being dismissed. In 1889, as we have seen, the Corporation granted the Eight Hour Day to the Birmingham gas stokers. By 1890, during a period of trade recovery in Birmingham, advances were gained by builders' labourers, by cabinet makers and by iron-plate workers. Meanwhile, in 1889 the Bedstead Workers Association was founded with 400 members. In December 1889 the bedstead workers came out on strike, and the brass workers stopped work in sympathy. The dispute went to arbitration, and a remarkable 15% advance on piece rates was achieved. Clearly, trade unionism was active and spreading in Birmingham in these years. The results can be seen in the numbers of societies affiliating to the Birmingham Trades Council in 1893 as compared with 1885—[34]

17. Easy Row, business premises, 1932.

	Societies affiliated	Branches	Delegates
1885	25	25	64
1893	56	66	86

However, it must be reiterated that this does not mean that the trade union movement in Birmingham was becoming more militant. On the contrary, the Alliance system, (first mentioned in Chapter Two) was uniquely confined to Birmingham, and shows how strongly conciliatory attitudes persisted in the local trade union movement. The Bedstead Alliance owed much initially to W. Mills, a manufacturer, and to W.J. Davis, secretary to the Brassworkers Union since 1872, with a break from 1883 to 1889 when he was a factory inspector. Davis had great influence with both sides of the trade. In 1893 the Bedstead Alliance was focused on an agreement between the union and the employers to the effect that only union workmen should be employed in the trade, the men agreeing to work only for Alliance employers. Both sides undertook that they would take action against any employer attempting to undercut either prices or wages. Wages were to be related to selling prices: for every 10% rise in prices, wages would go up 5%, irrespective of increases in the price of raw materials. Other alliances were also set up in other trades. It was estimated that some 500 masters and more than 20,000 workers were at one time covered by them. The Bedstead Alliance broke up in the early twentieth century, though it was reconstructed in 1912. Its major aim was to secure benefits for both sides of the contract – better profits for manufacturers, and better wages for workpeople.[35] The spirit of the alliance system was summed-up very well by W.J. Davis in 1900 –[36]

> We represent a community of interest. The employers find the capital, business capacity
> and enterprise, and should have the lion's share of the profit. We find the technical skill
> and muscle which the product requires. Therefore you must apportion fairly the profit
> between Capital and Labour.

Davis himself was elected to the town council in 1880 - the first trade unionist to be so elected. He stood as a Labour candidate, but took the Liberal whip.[37] In this way he was the counterpart in local government of those trade unionists who stood for parliament in the general election of 1874 and after, and similarly voted with the Liberals. There were eleven of these Lib-Labs MPs in 1889. Their numbers precluded them from having any great influence on the government of the day, and indeed in 1894 Joseph Chamberlain, who had left the Liberal party in 1886 over the issue of Home Rule, referred to them contemptuously as 'mere fetchers and carriers of the Gladstonian party'.[38] In the 'khaki election' of 1900, they actually lost four seats. It was becoming apparent to reformers on the left that the way forward for Labour was not in collaboration with the Liberal Party, but as a separate political body. When Davis and Eli Bloor (of the glassmakers union) stood for election as Lib-Labs in the general election of 1892, they were both defeated.

Certainly belief in the need for separate representation for Labour was increasingly expressed by the younger socialist unions, and a branch of the Marxist Social Democratic Federation was founded in Birmingham in November 1886 by Tom Mann, a member of the ASE, who fought municipal elections in Birmingham, but with little success.[39] In 1893 the Independent Labour Party was founded in Bradford by Keir Hardie, but it made little or no headway in electing independent Labour candidates to parliament. Finally in 1900 the TUC, much concerned at a recent spate of legal decisions in the courts hostile to trade unionism, at last decided to set up a Labour Representation Committee to make arrangements for the election of labour candidates. They were to be a distinct group, pledged to support legislation in the direct interest of labour. This committee was in effect the beginnings of the present-day Labour Party.

Yet even then, the Birmingham Trades Council Election Committee still clung to the Lib-Lab approach, supporting J.V. Stevens, secretary of the tinplate workers, as a Liberal candidate in the Birmingham East constituency in the 1900 general election (he lost to the Conservative candidate).[40] By early 1901, however, the Trades Council had changed its policy to one of active support for the newly-formed LRC. By March 1901 only eight trades councils had affiliated to the LRC, but Birmingham was the largest among them. In July 1901 the Birmingham Trades Council organised a conference at which the secretary of the LRC, J. Ramsay MacDonald, encouraged the eighty delegates to affiliate to the LRC. In February of the following year, 1902, the Trades Council made arrangements for the annual conference of the Labour Representation Committee which was held in the Central Hall.[41] By then the LRC's fortunes had received a substantial boost as a result of the Taff Vale Railway Case (1901) which had put union funds in jeopardy whenever a strike was called and the employers had suffered loss of profits. It has become even more urgent to strengthen separate labour representation in parliament. The Birmingham Trades Council sent delegates to London to protest to their local MPs against what they conceived to be a totally mistaken decision in the Taff Vale case.[42] In the general election of 1906, the LRC secured as many as twenty-nine seats (one other MP joining their ranks shortly after). In addition, twenty-four Lib-Labs were elected. The LRC now changed its name to the Labour Party, and set up a new body of its own MPs, the Parliamentary Labour Party. In this way, trade unionism in Birmingham, and more specifically the Birmingham Trades Council, had played an important part in helping to create the Labour Party, having abandoned its earlier support of Lib-Labism.

In surveying the history of trade unionism in Birmingham from the mid-nineteenth century to 1914, certain features stand out prominently. Undoubtedly the first is the desire for conciliation and arbitration in trade disputes whenever possible. The social origins of this are to be found in the predominantly small master economy of the earlier period, and the direct relationships between employers and their employees in the workshops. These relationships were not always amicable, of course, and strikes did take place from time to time, but the existence of the Alliance system confirms that co-operation between capital and labour was marked in Birmingham, perhaps more so than in any other large industrial centre. The point may be illustrated further by reference to the history of two prominent Birmingham unions, the first being that of the National Society of Amalgamated Brass Workers, and the second the Tinplate Workers Society. The brassworkers had over 7,000 members at the beginning of the twentieth century. As we have seen, its secretary, W.J. Davis (afterwards secretary and historian of the TUC) always aimed at a system which would secure a lasting friendship between employers and workmen. A Brass Trades Manufacturing Council was established to represent both sides of the industry and a Conciliation Board set up. According to Davis, it had always been his object in life 'to minimise the number of disputes with which I have been concerned'.[43] As for the tinplate workers, a price list for government work was set up by the Society and the Employers Association. When government tenders were invited, both sides would agree on prices selected from the list. Any firm paying less than the wages fixed by agreement between the Society and the employers would be reported by the union to the appropiate government authority.[44] The special relationship existing in many cases is well summed up in the Birmingham Trades Council Report for 1898 –[45]

> There has been an entire absence of any serious labour disputes, a spirit of conciliation having prevailed, which has enabled organised workmen to meet organised employers; and thus by reasoning and reciprocity, decisions have been carried out which have maintained an honourable peace, beneficial to workmen, employers, and the community.

Of course, this provides only a snapshot of conditions in Birmingham in 1898. Strikes did occur between 1898 and 1914, especially in the period just before the coming of the Great War in 1914 when they were particularly numerous. For example, in 1910 the bakers in Birmingham went on strike, while in 1911 there was the first national railway strike and a strike at the BSA works. In 1912 there was a strike at Avery's, and in 1913 a local railway strike and a strike at the Handsworth Carriage Works (this last was ended by the intervention of Bishop Gore of Birmingham).[46] However, strikes were a national phenomenon at this time, the number of days lost nationally through strikes reaching unprecedentally high levels - in 1911, 10.16 million days, and in 1912, 40.89 million days. A major cause of all this unrest seems to have been a rise in prices and a consequent decline in real wages between 1900 and 1910, together with boom conditions after 1908. Strike activity in Birmingham just before the First World War must therefore be seen against the national background, and according to Briggs, the views of the Trades Council quoted above continued with few qualifications to mirror labour relations in Birmingham before the war. The strikes do not indicate any sudden and permanent deterioration of these relationships, and indeed they tailed off after 1913.

Secondly, one strength of the trade union movement in Birmingham was the existence of many skilled trades which earned good wages and made possible trade union subscriptions which permitted a high level of out-of-work and sickness benefit. For members of the older craft unions their societies thus acted as friendly societies when off sick or out of work, even providing small pensions and funeral benefits. One notable example of this kind of union was the Flint Glass Workers Union with its rigidly controlled apprenticeship system, sickness and out-of-work benefits, and superannuation benefits.[47] For those whose unions were unable to support them in this way, there were in Birmingham numerous friendly societies who could give help, at the cost of a few pence per week (of course, some unionists earning good money could subscribe additionally to friendly societies apart from their own union, or might simply join burial clubs). At the mid-nineteenth century, Birmingham was well-supplied with friendly societies of this kind, and Rawlinson's Report to the General Board of Health in 1849 lists 213 registered societies in the town, of which 159 met in inns, public houses, or beershops. These societies had at least 30,000 members, and there were many more in small, unregistered societies. Rawlinson names some of the societies – for example, the Sick Man's Friendly Society, Abstainers' Gift, Society of Total Abstinence and the Rational Sick and Burial Society. Some had even more fanciful names, such as the Honourable Knights of the Wood, the Royal Dragoons and the True Blue Society. Rawlinson was somewhat critical of their convivial activities, especially their annual processions, as a waste of members' money –[48]

> Vast sums of money are expended by these clubs on unmeaning, gaudy and childish show. Once a year, usually in Whitsun week, they hold processions. More money is spent in processions, in loss of labour and in attendant expenses, than would pay the rent charge of a full supply of water, and perfect sewerage.

However, the government was well-aware that self help through friendly societies was of considerable help in keeping down the poor rates. It is sometimes thought that if a man was thrown out of work in Victorian times, unless he had considerable savings, he would be forced to go into the workhouse, or at least apply for out-door relief, if it was available locally. Not so: if his earnings permitted, he would be a member of a friendly society and could draw benefit, at least for a while.

In the second half of the nineteenth century, the friendly society movement continued to grow, though at a decreasing rate as the trade unions increased their activities. The national membership figures for the great affiliated societies which had begun to flourish in the 1830s demonstrate this clearly enough:[49]

	1872	*1888*	*1899*
Manchester Unity of Oddfellows	427,000	597,000	713,000
Ancient Order of Foresters	394,000	572,000	666,000
Salford Unity of Rechabites	9,000	60,000	136,000

The small local societies in Birmingham did not die out entirely, though they became of less importance. Many Trades Council officials in the 1890s were also officials in the national organisations. For example, the president of the Council in 1889-91, A.R. Jephcott, was Grand Master of the National Independent Order of Oddfellows in 1896. C.G. Cooke, president 1892-95, undertook secretarial work for friendly societies and was secretary of a lodge of the Manchester Unity. S.G. Middleton, Secretary of the Council, 1895-98, was a District Ranger of the Foresters.[50] Joseph Chamberlain himself paid tribute to the strength and influence of the national bodies in 1895 when giving evidence before the Royal Commission on the Aged Poor –[51]

> They are in touch with the thrifty-minded section of the working class. Their criticism of any scheme would be very damaging: their opposition might be fatal. They have very great parliamentary influence and I should myself think twice before attempting to proceed in face of hostility from so important and dangerous a quarter.

It has been estimated that by the end of the nineteenth century about half the adult males in the country were members of friendly societies ranging from the great affiliated societies to humble burial societies. This is a far greater number than were members of trade unions.

However, the friendly society activity for which Birmingham was best-known in the nineteenth century took the form of building societies. They dated back to the eighteenth century and commonly took the form of terminating societies – that is, societies set up to buy a small area of land, build a limited number of houses and then be wound up. Later, the modern type of permanent building societies was established and became common in the second half of the century. Their members were necessarily men in skilled trades, for labourers and other unskilled workers could not afford the regular payments required. Nevertheless, the Birmingham building societies throw an interesting light on one aspect of working-class life of the time, and in particular of provision for security in old age when work was no longer possible.

The extent of the building society movement in Birmingham in the 1870s is revealed by evidence given before the Royal Commission on Friendly Societies, 1870. According to a spokesman for the Birmingham building societies, nearly all the members were working men 'certainly 95 out of every 100'.[52] There were 13,000 houses in the town, he said, belonging to working men. Further, he claimed there were 'streets more than a mile long, in which absolutely every house belongs to the working classes of Birmingham - Albert Road, Victoria Road, Gladstone Road, Cobden Street, Bright Terrace, and so on... Bright Terrace has 28 houses in it, and they are all very nice houses'.

To judge from these names, they were all recently-erected streets. The building societies worked in conjunction with land societies, which bought the land and divided it into plots. The purchaser of a plot then obtained an advance from the building society to erect his house. One Birmingham

18. Municipal Technical Gun Trade School, 1915.

witness emphasised the good social habits resulting from house ownership. He was asked, 'You mean that such habits are increased by the possession by persons in that class of life of their own houses?'

> 'Yes, they save their money and instead of spending it in the public house, they spend it upon property. They go home at night and cultivate their gardens, or read the newspaper to their wives, instead of being in public houses. We are the greatest social reformers of the day...'[53]

This is a pleasant if perhaps somewhat rose-tinted picture of sober working-class life, with the husband reading to his no doubt attentive wife. The figures given for the numbers of working-class-owned houses also seem high. Of course, only well-paid workers could afford regular repayments. When asked the average wage of members of Birmingham building societies, the witness replied that the average wage was about 30s a week:[54]

> But there are others again, the clerks and respectable mechanics, who get their £100 or £120 a year. There are such members with us, but taking it altogether, the average would perhaps be from 27/- or 28/- to 30/- a week.

Again, this emphasises the fact that only the better-off workman could afford to own his own house, since the ordinary labourer's wages might well be less than a pound a week.

Nevertheless, by 1900 the workman in steady employment in Birmingham would generally have some safeguards against sickness and absence from work resulting from his union membership (if it offered friendly society benefits), or from membership of one of the affiliated societies, or even if his wages were low, from paying into one of the large industrial insurance companies (such as the Prudential Insurance Company or the Hearts of Oak) for funeral benefits. Giving the deceased a 'proper send-off' was of great importance in working-class families. This was the situation in 1906, when the Liberals won the general election of that year and formed what was to become a famous reforming ministry.

The legislation passed by the Liberals certainly had an effect on the working lives of the working classes as a whole.[55] It was directed at the poverty caused by old age, at the loss of earnings caused by ill health and unemployment, at low wages in sweated industries and at the difficulties of finding a job when unemployed. Thus, old age pensions were introduced in 1908, compulsory insurance against ill health brought in in 1911 for the working classes as a whole, 2.5 million workers also compulsorily insured against unemployment, the Sweated Industries Act, 1909, was passed and labour exchanges were introduced. All of these measures affected the working classes in Birmingham, though curiously enough, not all were at all popular with them. The great National Insurance Act, 1911, was actually disliked by the trade unions who opposed compulsory contributions, and supported it only reluctantly after the payment of salaries to MPs was instituted in 1911 (trade unions' financial support of Labour Party MPs had been effectively ended for the time being by yet another adverse legal judgement, the Osborne Judgement, 1909, which ruled that it was illegal for trade unions to use their funds for political purposes).

The period before the coming of war in 1914 saw a great strengthening of the trade union movement. This was mainly because the national insurance scheme was administered by so-called 'approved' societies, the name given to selected insurance companies and friendly societies, including those trade unions which offered friendly society benefits. The result was that many workers, finding themselves obliged to join such a society, became members of a trade union. The membership of trade unions therefore rose dramatically, from about 3.13 million in 1911 to 4.14 million in 1914. An additional reason for this great increase of about a million was that many unskilled workers who benefitted from the relatively full employment of the immediate pre-war days came into the unions for the first time. A good example of this is the Workers Union, founded 1898, with a membership of 5,000 in 1910, and a claimed membership of 91,000 by December 1913. By 1914, the numbers of skilled and unskilled trade unionists were almost equal; in the 1890s the new unionists had been outnumbered by skilled members by about ten to one.[56]

What would a man, who had begun work as a boy in the 1860s and had given up working just before the Great War, have made of the changes at work during his lifetime? In the first place (if his memory was up to it) he was very likely to remark on the way the working day in Birmingham had changed. It was shorter, and the working week began first thing on Monday, instead of sometime on Tuesday. Further, the working week ended at midday on Saturday, in most cases. He might or might not be aware that the reduction in the working day was the result partly of the factory and workshop acts, and partly by the pressure exerted by the trade unions, which by 1914 were to be found in most trades, rather than solely in the skilled trades dominated by an aristocracy of labour.

As for the working environment, this too had changed. In the mid-nineteenth century, the small domestic workshop was still very common, sometimes situated literally under the proprietor's roof, as was the case of the garret workshop. Bigger firms certainly existed, but they were in a minority. During the suceeding half century, larger enterprises developed, as we have seen, so that the largest works were among the biggest in the country. The average worker's working environment would therefore depend on whether he or she was employed in one of the industrial giants or in a smaller workplace. It has already been suggested that work discipline was likely to have become more vigorous in the largest works, but it is not easy to find hard evidence on this subject. Unskilled work was always likely to be more boring and monotonous than skilled work, but, according to one authority, young boys at least seemed able to find time for football in Birmingham in the dinner hour, and for gossip when work was slack. Many boys were said to change their job frequently just before the War, so unskilled work was presumably not hard to find. At eighteen the majority of such boys faced dismissal when their age qualified them for an adult wage.[57]

All this applied to boys who had left school, and our elderly retired worker would have been able to testify that during his lifetime both boys and girls had disappeared from the place of work as the factory and workshop acts were enforced, and schooling became compulsory. Another change was that more women were being employed during the last quarter of the nineteenth century, and of course, the use of power-driven machinery became more widespread, as has been noted. Some historians believe that this led to de-skilling, that is to say, to the replacing of traditional craft skills by simple machine-minding techniques; but although this did happen to some extent in some trades, such as engineering, the new machines had to be serviced and maintained, and machine operators had to possess certain skills to perform efficiently.[58]

This raises the subject of apprenticeship and its survival in Birmingham in this period. Although, as was seen in Chapter One, there was some hostility among employers in Birmingham to apprenticeship in the 1840s, it certainly survived later in the century in some trades. In engineering, it was strongly supported by the Amalgamated Society of Engineers, in whose interest it was to maintain the system; the ASE argued that any machine replacing craft work must be operated by a skilled man at the full craft rate.[59] The Tin Plate Workers Society, who had merged with a similar body in Wolverhampton in 1875, also supported the apprenticeship system.[60] According to Dr Charles More, in the early years of the twentieth century, apprentices still formed the greater part of the recruits to engineering, fitting, turning and pattern making, and also to moulding and smithing. In building and woodworking, carpenters and joiners, wet coopers and some cabinet makers, as well as some bricklayers, masons and painters, were all apprenticed. The largest numbers of apprentices in 1906 were in building (100,200) and in engineering (94,000). All in all in 1906, it seems that 21% of all working males between fifteen and nineteen were apprenticed.[61] If these figures are anywhere near correct, then it would appear likely that apprenticeship was still important in a number of leading trades in Birmingham in 1914.

So much for changes in the workplace: but what about life in periods of sickness or unemployment? Again, our retired worker would be able to confirm the importance of keeping clear of the poor law authorities and the workhouse, and here again the important role of the friendly society, or of the union if it provided friendly society benefits, must be emphasised. As we have seen, friendly societies had a long and distinguished history in Birmingham, and they continued to be important right up to 1914. However, many of them assumed a new role as administrative agents for the new national insurance scheme introduced by the 1911 National Insurance Act, a function which they shared with the powerful insurance companies. Since all the working classes earning less than £130 a year were compulsorily insured under the terms of that act, membership of a friendly society as such became less important. On the other hand, the benefits available under the 1911 Act were very limited, and applied only to the insured worker, and not to his family, whose doctor's bills had still to be paid (as were the bills for hospital treatment, unless it had been given in a poor law infirmary). There was therefore still a good case to be made for friendly society membership, irrespective of the legal requirement to subscribe to the national insurance scheme. It must not be forgotten, too, that the 1911 Act also provided an unemployment benefit scheme, but it applied to only a limited number of trades, known to be subject to periodic bouts of unemployment. Its rates of benefit were also lower than those of sickness benefit.

To return to local conditions: one of the undoubted scourges of working-class life was unemployment, and this was when some additional income from whatever source became vital. Absence of local statistics for the unemployed in Birmingham makes it impossible to generalise confidently on this subject, but it is clear enough that in the period covered in this chapter there were two major periods of unemployment. The first was during the Great Depression, and the second the years from 1906 to 1909. As regards the first, there is little more to be said, although the difficulties of some of the principal trade unions for the metal trades makes it clear that the times were hard for some workers. As for the second period, J.V. Stevens estimated in 1906 that about 10,000 were out of work (6% of male workers). Further evidence of distress is provided by the activities of the City Distress Committee and of the City Aid Committee, which opened several branches round the city. A joint appeal by the Lord Mayor and the Bishop of Birmingham raised £7,800 for distress relief, and work for the unemployed was made available in the city parks. By the end of 1908, 2,000 men had registered with the Distress Committee, and 6,645 in the winter of 1908-09. By 1909-10, however, the worst was over.[62]

All in all, life at work in Birmingham had undergone significant changes by 1914. Peremptory dismissal was still a possibility, of course, and no doubt occurred from time to time. Nevertheless, it was probably somewhat less likely than it had been sixty years earlier. Perhaps the most important reason for this was the rise to national importance of the trade union movement and its pervasive influence. Wage rates and conditions of labour were now fixed nationally in a number of trades. National strikes were either threatened or actually took place in the years preceding the outbreak of war in 1914, and senior members of the government actually intervened to restore peace. Efforts of this kind were unprecedented, and even went to the extent of the government's negotiating with the miners through a committee consisting of the prime minister and five other ministers.[63] Clearly, trade unions were now a power in the land, a force to be reckoned with, and Arthur Balfour, leader of the Conservative opposition in the House of Commons, was not alone in expressing his disquiet in a speech in 1912 –[64]

> The power they have got, if used to the utmost, is under our existing law, almost limitless, and there is no appearance that the leaders of the movement desire to temper the use of their legal power with any consideration of policy or of mercy... Has any

19. Weighing machine workers, c.1927.

feudal baron ever exercised his powers in the manner in which the leaders of this great trade union [the Miners Federation] are now using theirs?

All this was exaggerated, of course, in the cause of political rhetoric, but the speech does illustrate the apprehension in some upper- and middle-class circles at the rise of Labour. It was not only the impact of Labour on national politics, of course, but the success of Labour in local government elections which was of concern to the Conservatives. As we have seen, Labour representatives in Birmingham were being elected to the City Council, and also sat on the School Board. They were even being appointed Justices of the Peace.[65]

Thus the trade union movement both nationally and in Birmingham was transformed between 1850 and 1914, and especially after 1880, from a small organisation representing the older craft unions to a much larger body including both skilled and unskilled trades, with separate representation in parliament, and the power to influence government decision-making. Their power was much stronger on the shop floor than in parliament, of course, but its strength is shown by government intervention into threatened national strikes before 1914.

Was there any justification for Balfour's alarm when the Birmingham scene before 1914 is surveyed? Not really: our elderly retired worker would not be likely to testify to the tyranny of trade unionism in Birmingham, but the decline of the old sub-contractor system and of the factor made the division of forces in industry into those of employer and worker much more clearly defined. The older, more complicated organisation of small masters, sub-contractors and charge-hands had been more complex, and had emphasised co-operation and mutuality. The newer emergence of two distinct classes in industry, employers and workers, made organisation of the workers much easier and more straightforward, especially in the newer industries with their large-scale work forces.

So by 1914 life at work had changed, both in its essentials (length and nature of working day, working environment and so on) but also in acquiring a new context, provided not only by government regulation, but also by the increasing authority of the local trade unions. The Birmingham Trades Council itself had played a part in the establishing of the Labour Representation Committee which led to the setting-up of the Labour Party in 1906. Thus, by 1914, there was an unseen presence in the Birmingham factory and workshop, the influence of the local trade union in determining wage rates and conditions of labour. Yet this must not be taken too far: in assessing the strength of trade unionism as a proportion of local populations, the Webbs in their pioneer work on the history of trade unionism, put Birmingham fifth from the bottom in a list of eighteen areas, with a density of 4.1% of population, compared with Northumberland at the head of the list with 11.2%.[66] Then again, the tradition of co-operation between trade unions and employers in Birmingham was still strong at the end of the nineteenth century. During negotiations in 1899, W.J. Davis told employers that 'we meet... to rescue our trade, and to make secure the property of employers as well as of workmen'.[67]

Lastly, an instructive comparison might be made of the views of Davis and the aggressive attitudes displayed by unionists in other parts of the kingdom, such as South Wales, where there was bitter antagonism between the mine owners and the miners. In 1911 a committee of the South Wales Mining Federation published a pamphlet, *The Miners' Next Step*, advocating one union to include all the extractive industries of Great Britain. The idea of one massive union for each major industry was popular among syndicalists, who regarded this as a first step to the revolution of the workers. Syndicalism was strong in South Wales, in Dublin and on Clydeside. In 1912 Tom Mann, a convert to syndicalism, was prosecuted for his 'Don't Shoot' appeal in *The Syndicalist* to British troops not to fire on strikers –[68]

> You are working men's sons.
> When we go on strike to better our lot, which is the lot also of your Fathers, Mothers, Brothers, and Sisters, you are called upon by your Officers TO MURDER US.
> Don't do it...

It will be recalled that Mann founded a branch of the SDF in Birmingham as early as 1886, but fought subsequent municipal elections with little success. A Scottish pamphlet of 1908, setting out syndicalist ideas of 'the pulsations of the class struggle' went on to declare that ultimately the vast new industrial unions in place of strikes, should institute the General Lock-Out of the Capitalist Class.

Syndicalism did not spread very far nationally before 1914, and its ideas certainly did not suffuse trade union thinking very widely; but views of this kind provide a sharp contrast to the conservative thinking of most Birmingham trade unionists, and emphasise yet again the co-operative attitudes which they displayed.[69] Certainly syndicalist beliefs would have been anathema to W.J. Davis, with his constant desire to avoid lengthy confrontations and to obtain the best deal for both sides. This spirit was the essence of the alliance system, and it was still in evidence during the changing circumstances of the First World War, as will become apparent in Chapter Seven.

CHAPTER FIVE

LIVING CONDITIONS

In Chapter One a brief, preliminary sketch of living conditions in Birmingham about 1850 was undertaken, the emphasis being on working-class housing. In this chapter it is proposed to discuss both middle-class and working-class housing during the second half of the nineteenth century, though the larger amount of space will necessarily be given to the latter. To start with middle-class housing: earlier in the century there were still some manufacturers who lived in the central areas of the town – Joseph Gillott is a good example, living at first in Newhall Street, close to his workshops – but increasingly middle-class employers moved out to Edgbaston, a suburb to the south of the town centre which soon developed, especially in the 1840s, into an exclusive estate of spacious and impressive houses. Many of these were on a considerable scale, with large gardens: when Gillott moved to Edgbaston, for instance, it was into a house situated at 9 Westbourne Road, with six bedrooms, a library, wine cellars, two picture galleries, stables, an aviary, greenhouse and carpenter's workshop.[1]

The Calthorpe trustees exercised a strict control over the grant of building leases. Plans were rigorously inspected, and alterations were frequently demanded. All working-class housing, together with any form of speculative building, industry and trade was prohibited. The result was the creation of a most attractive leafy suburb with spacious gardens and many trees. It is not surprising that Edgbaston was by far the healthiest place to live in Birmingham; its inhabitants were undoubtedly the best-fed, clothed and washed in the whole area. Thus, in 1838 Edgbaston had the lowest death rates due to measles, scarlet fever and typhoid, and the highest frequency of water closets. Death rates for the working classes living elsewhere in Birmingham were much higher, but there was no working-class housing at all in Edgbaston before 1850.[2] Two other areas of predominantly middle-class housing (but on a smaller scale) were to develop in districts adjacent to Edgbaston; these were Harborne on the west side, and Moseley to the south-east of the city centre.

Working-class housing in the central areas of Birmingham in the mid-nineteenth century was on an entirely different scale, of course, from anything at all recognisable as middle-class housing. Much of it had developed in these central areas as industry had expanded from the mid-eighteenth century onwards, and was therefore quite old. Additional accommodation was also provided on the outskirts of the town, for example, in the Deritend area. The most typical form of working-class housing was built in rectangular courts. Some of the older courts by 1850 were undoubtedly in a bad condition, but perhaps the most important preliminary generalisation which can be made about Birmingham working-class housing of the time is that it varied considerably in quality from one district to another. It is a popular misconception that all Victorian urban housing was slum-like in nature. Certainly some of it was very bad, giving the minimum shelter from the elements in wretched, insanitary conditions to the very poorest, or most unfortunate, or most disreputable of the working classes. But not all housing was like this, and as Professor F.M.L. Thompson has rightly remarked, although Victorian slums were nasty, and were affronts to the wealth and civilisation around them, it is important to remember that four-fifths or nine-tenths of the people did not live in slum conditions.[3]

This is certainly true of the working people of Birmingham in the second half of the nineteenth century. Better accommodation was available for the skilled workman who could afford a higher rent, while the poorest housing would be occupied by the unskilled labourer, whose earnings were often intermittent, thus permitting only the lowest rent to be paid. This simple fact may be demonstrated by reference to Chadwick's Report, published in 1842. The Birmingham section of this report, compiled by a Committee of Physicians and Surgeons (the only town report to be compiled in this way) is illustrated by plans and elevations of selected houses.[4] Thus, at one extreme, are the so-called three-quarters houses in Tennant Street, off Broad Street. They were built in twos, with a central tunnel entrance and front doors opening to left and right off this passageway. Each house had a ground floor parlour at the front, measuring 13ft by 12ft, and a kitchen of the same size to the rear. There were two bedrooms above on the first floor, and a further two bedrooms on the second floor. At the back there was a brewhouse and a privy for each house. These houses were rented at a stiff 7s a week – certainly well above average.

At the other extreme, much humbler accommodation was available in the form of court houses in Ann Street (off Livery Street) where two-room houses were available for only 2s 6d per week; while in the Pershore Road, houses with three one-room floors (ground floor 14'4" by 11'8") could also be rented for 2s 6d per week. On the whole, housing in the older, more insanitary courts appears to have been slightly cheaper than in the newer, more spacious courts. Thus, the older court houses in Bromsgrove Street had either two or three stories, with an entry into the court measuring only 2'11". The two-story houses cost 3s a week, and the three-story houses 4s 6d. The houses in Bradford Street (south of Digbeth) were in newer courts, with a wider entry of 3'3". They were mostly on three floors and had cellars, and were rented at 3s 6d a week. Their rooms were larger than those in Bromsgrove Street.

A substantial number of Birmingham working-class houses were back-to-back houses – that is, they were only one room deep, and literally back-to-back with other houses. These are a notoriously cheap and poor form of housing, but curiously enough, the 1842 Committee of Physicians and Surgeons did not think them necessarily bad, provided the rooms were large and lofty and had chimneys, and that the doors and windows were of a good size. They observed that disease was no more prevalent in them than in houses of different construction. They went further by remarking that even if the houses could be separated by a few yards, the space between would only be used for pigs, rabbits or poultry, and made the receptacles for rubbish and filth. Their report contains plans and elevations of back-to-backs in Great Russell Street. The houses here were three stories high, with two rooms on the ground floor, side by side. Above them were two bedrooms, and above these bedrooms was a third, very small bedroom directly under the roof, with a ceiling height of only 5'2". Outside was a yard, with one privy and a brewhouse for every four houses.

In 1849 a petition was presented by more than a tenth of the ratepayers asking that the terms of the very mild Public Health Act, 1848 be applied to Birmingham. The result of this was a report by Sir Robert Rawlinson to the General Board of Health on sanitary conditions in the town.[5] This report emphasised the general good state of public health , but dwelt (as had the earlier reports) on the bad state of the older courts. There were about 2,000 close courts without proper drainage and many were unpaved. The privies were described as 'a frequent source of nuisance'. The results of a survey of 285 courts in both the older and the newer parts of the town were as follows:

	Good	Bad	Imperfect	None
Drainage	134	74	77	-
Level	134	49	99	-
Repair	159	43	78	-
Water Supply	177	80	-	20

In the majority of cases, there was one privy to every four houses. The report also commented on some of the newer houses in the suburbs with rents of 5s per week. These were described as being better designed. Thus, plans of cottages in Bridge Street West contain two ground-floor rooms, two bedrooms, a cellar, a washhouse or brewhouse, a privy and a pump, and small gardens back and front. In the opinion of Rawlinson, these cottages had 'a clean, neat and cheerful appearance when new', but the cesspool near the privy 'could not fail' to drain into the well, so that the water supply was likely to become contaminated. There was also a want of proper drainage, something which applied to both working-class and middle-class housing on the outskirts. In these areas there was a lack of local authority power to drain and pave the streets, and many of even the best houses drained into the public road (a case of this happening in the otherwise salubrious Hagley Road was mentioned in Chapter One).

Since workers needed to live close to their place of work, those working in the same industry usually lived in the same neighbourhood. This certainly seems to apply in Birmingham in those areas where domestic or workshop industry had taken root. For example, in the gun trade, there was a strong concentration of workshops and gun workers' housing in the area of St Mary's, while jewellery workers were to be found on the Newhall and adjacent Vyse Estates. The button trade, however, was more dependent on the labour of women and children than other trades, with the result that the housing of these workers was more dispersed, dependent on the occupation of the householder, and was often to be found in the gun and jewellery quarters. Brass foundries were also widely dispersed, and the residential pattern of brass workers was similarly scattered, too.[6]

Although the Reports of the 1840s appear to give a reasonably full picture of the range of working-class housing in Birmingham, they are surprisingly uninformative on the subject of housing erected by working-class terminating building societies. In fact, the town was well-known for building clubs of this kind.[7] The *Morning Chronicle* in 1850-51, however, contained one or two references to them of a surprisingly critical nature; one would have thought that such houses, erected through the initiative of enterprising workmen, would have been of reasonably good quality. However, an article on social conditions in the *Chronicle* in March 1851, alleged that in Birmingham the clubs erected 'small and mean houses and cottages, built without any pretensions to beauty, and very often of the flimsiest materials'. Yet the article had to admit that their quality exceeded that of speculative building in Lancashire.[8] Twenty years or so afterwards, the Royal Commission on Friendly and Benefit Building Societies, 1870, had some interesting evidence on the extent of working men's building societies in Birmingham. As we saw in Chapter Four, by this time the societies had all become permanent building societies, and a spokesman for the societies claimed they had 13,000 houses in the town which belonged to working men. Moreover, he also alleged that there were streets more than a mile long in which every house belonged to the working classes. It must be said again that all this sounds somewhat exaggerated, but it still seems likely enough that the numerous class of comparatively well-paid workmen in Birmingham would make home ownership an important if relatively minor element in the housing of the working classes in the town by 1870.

What else needs to be said about living conditions in Birmingham in the mid-years of the nineteenth century? Of course, the lack of modern sanitary arrangements and of a tapped water supply are obvious enough, but they were aspects of urban life in all towns of the time. The major point remains that the town was on the whole a healthier place to live in than many other manufacturing towns. This was due not only to the physical characteristics of the town, such as being well-drained and having good supplies of pure water, but also because it was not subject to the overcrowding which was such a feature of town life in Manchester and other places; there were no cellar habitations, for example. Mortality rates suggest the claim made in the 1844 Report that Birmingham was 'perhaps one of the most healthy of our large towns' had some substance. Details of the mortality rates in other towns seem to bear this out for the three years 1840, 1841 and 1842 –[9]

	Mortality Rates (%)
Bath	2.6
Birmingham	2.7
Bristol	3.1
Dudley	2.6
Hull	3.0
Liverpool	3.5
Manchester	3.2
Wolverhampton	2.8

As for the physical well-being or otherwise of the working people of Birmingham at the time, there are some interesting comments in the Children's Employment Commission, 1842, Report. Two witnesses, Mr T.F. Cox, a surgeon, and a Sergeant Buchan, gave their opinions on the physical state of the recruits for the marines enlisted in Birmingham. Mr. Cox considered that they were much inferior in strength to men employed in agriculture; the Birmingham

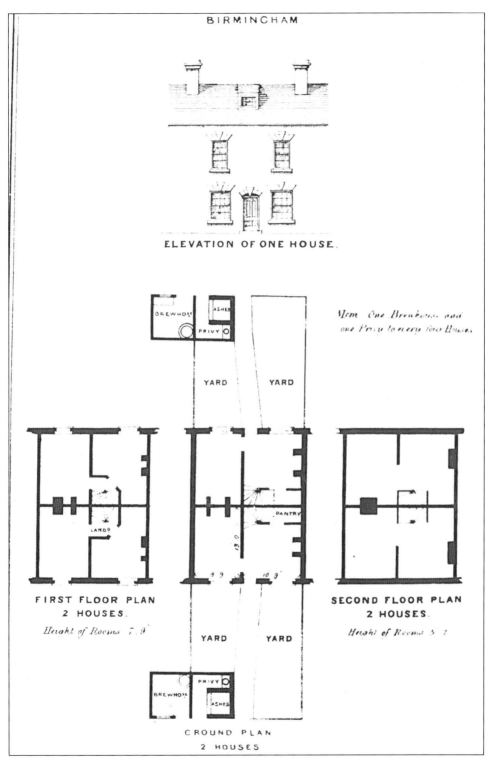

20. *Chadwick's Report, 1842 - back-to-back houses, Great Russell Street.*

recruits were shorter and more puny. Many were rejected because they were below the required standard of height, which in the marines was 5'6". Sergeant Buchan agreed that many men were not tall enough for the marines. The general height of Birmingham men, he said, was from 5'4" to 5'5" – they were shorter than in any town he had known. Many were rejected for narrow chest and want of stamina.[10] Of course, we do not know whether volunteers for the marines constituted a fair sample of the male working population as a whole, or indeed how far service in the marines was likely to be attractive in a town full of thriving industries paying good wages for skilled labour.

Other opinions as to working-class diets expressed in Chadwick's Report are that when trade was good, the work people would buy the best joints and the most delicate meats. As we saw in Chapter One, many working men had their main meal, the midday dinner, in a cook shop where a plate of meat cost 3d, and potatoes or bread another penny. The meat was usually roasted, though inferior joints would be mixed with vegetables in a stew. Cook shops also sold soup at a penny a pint, and older, less well-paid men might make do at midday with soup and bread. There were ninety-five cook shops in Birmingham, and many public houses also provided cooked meat for dinner. At home, the wife and children dined on bacon and potatoes, though some housewives might provide a meat stew with potatoes and onions. If the bread-winner came home to dinner, he would expect meat in the form of steak or chops, and on Sunday a good joint of meat was usual. All these comments obviously relate to an ideal situation when the principal wage-earner is a skilled man, earning a good and steady wage. It could be very different where he was only a labourer, or was out of work. Nevertheless, the average workingman's diet in mid-nineteenth century Birmingham was likely to be somewhat better than that of his rural counterpart, simply because rural diets were notoriously poor for most of the first half of the century. In the countryside, meat was somewhat of a luxury item, not to be eaten every day.[11] To sum up: working-class living conditions in Birmingham in the mid-nineteenth century depended very much on the occupation of the head of the family: if he was a skilled worker and in regular employment, he would generally live in better accom-modation than the unskilled worker whose employment was more intermittent. It was the labourer who had only his brute strength to offer the employer, and who was the first to be dismissed when trade was depressed; the skilled man was not so easily replaced, and might be retained, at least for the time being, until trade improved.[12]

This simple economic fact was a major reason for class division within the working classes, and helps to explain variations in the standard of living of working-class families. So the better-paid worker lived in housing for which he paid a higher rent than the unskilled labourer. There was nothing unusual in this. In London, for example, the worst housing was occupied by the worst-paid and most irregularly employed; living space increased roughly with the amount of wages and the regularity of employment.[13] In Birmingham the better housing was in the newer courts, and some of the new housing away from the city centre might have small gardens. In some cases, as we have seen, occupants might even own their own houses through building societies (though the number of these relatively affluent householders was likely to have been very small, in spite of the evidence given before the Royal Commission in 1870). Water supplies were reasonably good, pumps being generally available, but Rawlinson noted in his report that in addition to private and public wells and pumps, many private water carts traversed the town, charging a ha'penny a canful (3.5 gallons).[14]

The worst housing undoubtedly was to be found in the old courts in the middle of the town. The reason for this is probably that many were erected in the great building boom of the second half of the eighteenth century, when Birmingham's population appears to have increased by more than three times. Hutton was greatly impressed by the extent of building which took place, and observed that 'Perhaps more are erected here, in a given time, than in any place in the whole island, London excepted'.[15] Hutton was also critical of the lack of control over the builders' methods as they rushed up the new housing. The result was, in his words, 'evils without a cure; such as narrowness, which scarcely admits light, cleanliness, pleasure, health, or use'.[16] These buildings were erected speedily to meet a need. The quality of materials used was unlikely to have been very high,so that by the mid-nineteenth century they were showing their age. Housing of this kind was to remain a serious problem right up to 1914, and beyond.

Nevertheless, the greatest sanitary problem affecting both old and new housing (and even some middle-class housing) was the use of earth closets. They were the usual and traditional form of privy in the countryside, of course, where at a distance from the cottages they did not necessarily constitute a major health hazard; but it was very different in the close-packed courts of the new industrialised towns. In theory, the privies were emptied regularly by nightsoil men, but in practice they were often neglected, and made the subject of frequent complaint and condemnation by visiting health commissioners in the 1840s. Some of the entrances of the older courts were too narrow to permit the entry of carts, so that the nightsoil had to be removed in baskets or other containers, the contents of which were deposited in the street in great noisome midden heaps. The threat to health through flies, contamination of water supplies and so on, is obvious enough.

Little can be added to what has already be said about diet. It is clear that a hard-working population needed to eat heartily to provide enough energy to see them through a long working day. In times of prosperity, such as the 1850s, '60s and early '70s the skilled man ate well (the head of the family always had the greatest share, since it was essential to keep up his strength, the welfare of the whole family depending on him). In leaner times, it could be short commons all round, and sometimes even near-starvation. Here, membership of a friendly society by the better-paid worker could be a great help; the ultimate degradation would be to go to the poor law guardians, of course. In the longest perspective, the general health of the working classes of Birmingham depended on a number of factors – family income, diet, health (or ill health) and housing. There were no especially dangerous trades in the town: accidents at work were confined to sprains and contusions, wounds, fractures, burns and scalds, with an occasional serious accident, due to unguarded straps, bands and wheels.[17] To judge from mortality figures, living conditions in Birmingham in the mid-century years were probably superior to conditions in many other industrial towns.

The housing accommodation described so far in this chapter constituted the basic housing stock for the rest of the century, with additions mostly in suburban areas as the population

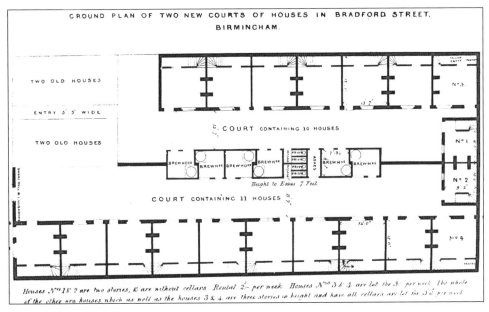

21. *Chadwick's Report, 1842 - two new courts, Bradford Street.*

continued to increase. By the 1870s the population had grown by about 50% since 1851 (from 230,000 in round figures in 1851 to 344,000 in 1871). During this time, little or nothing was done about the state of the old courts which contained the worst housing, and as was noted in Chapter Three, during the mayoralty of Joseph Chamberlain, an investigation was undertaken into the central slum areas. Even though all three of the major public health enquiries of the 1840s had commented adversely on these slums, nothing had been done about them. In 1875, the Medical Officer of Health, Dr Hill, reported on the state of the slum area in St Mary's and Market Hall wards as follows:[18]

> Narrow streets; houses without back doors or windows, situated both in and out of courts; confined yards; courts open at one end only, and this opening small and narrow; the impossibility, in many instances, of providing sufficient privy accommodation; houses and shopping as dilapidated as to be in imminent danger of falling, and incapable of proper repair.

Dr Hill went on to describe the evils following from this state of affairs as 'want of ventilation, want of light, want of decent and proper accommodation, resulting in dirty habits, low health, and debased morals on the part of the tenants'. He pointed out that the death rate in St Mary's ward was twice as great as in Edgbaston – 26.82 per thousand compared with 13.11 in Edgbaston over the previous two years. The general low condition of health led to indulgence in stimulants and to other vicious habits.[19] These allegations were confirmed by Councillor White, whose description of the area has already been given in Chapter Three. He commented further that —[20]

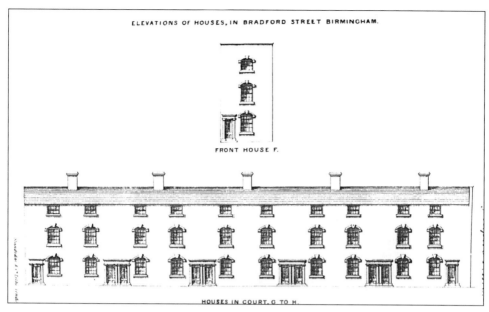

22. Chadwick's Report, 1842 - houses, Bradford Street.

The only prosperous people in that neighbourhood are publicans. There is light and warmth in their dwellings, if not sweetness. They are the only escape of the people from the darkness of their lives. The more misery, the fewer bakers and the more publicans; that is, I believe, the experience of every town.

So at last, as was seen in Chapter Three, Chamberlain's Improvement Scheme resulted in the demolition of an area of slum properties which hitherto had been a disgrace to a forward-looking local authority. Chamberlain's Improvement Plan followed on his municipal take-over of the local gas and water supplies, and was undoubtedly a great step forward – the first major slum clearance of the century.

The downside, of course, was the failure of the Council to provide adequately for the tenants who had been dispossessed, or indeed to do anything beyond building a limited number of council houses in Ryder Street and Lawrence Street, together with the two-bedroom flats in Milk Street (see Chapter Three). Though the reluctance of the City Council to compete with private builders is understandable enough, it has already been pointed out that other local authorities, notably in Liverpool and London, showed much more initiative in municipal building. Admittedly efforts were made to refurbish properties, and in some cases, courts were opened up later by demolishing one side of the court; but the fundamental problems of slum clearance were left almost untouched before 1914. This meant that by that date there were still large areas of slum properties especially in the central wards of the city, much of it quite unchanged from the 1850s. The special committee of enquiry appointed by the Council and chaired by Joseph Chamberlain's son Neville, made this quite clear when it issued its report in 1913. It was hardly to the credit of the City Council that there were still

42,000 properties with no separate water supplies, sinks or drains, and more than 58,000 householders with no separate lavatories.

The one advance for the occupiers of so much slum property was the beginnings in the 1870s of a campaign for the removal of earth privies and of midden heaps. A specially appointed Sewage Enquiry Committee reported in 1871 that there were only 3,884 premises, accommodating 20,000 persons, with 7,065 water closets (which drained into the sewers); whereas there were 70,000 houses with about 320,000 occupants, connected with 19,351 privies and ashpits or middens. Nearly 14,000 of these ashpits also drained into the sewers. The contents of the sewers were conveyed to Saltley, where the solid matter was held in tanks, the remainder passing into the River Tame.[21] The major results of the Committee's report were twofold: first the extension and improvement of the sewage farm at Saltley (though initially there was much opposition to this by Sir Charles Adderley, the local landowner); and secondly, the institution of the pan system of collecting night soil.[22] To quote directly from Bunce –

> Beneath each closet seat is placed a metal pan, capable of affording closet accommodation for a week. In the yard is placed a wooden or iron tub for the reception of dry ashes and vegetable and other refuse from the houses. Once a week these receptacles are cleared of their contents. The closet pans are carried away in closed vans, each containing about eighteen of the pans, and holding also about one ton of ashes from the ash tubs. The pans in process of removal are fitted with close-fitting metal lids, fresh pans being left in their places. The pans are then taken to the Corporation wharf in Montague Street, are emptied, thoroughly cleansed and disinfected, and are then again ready for use.

Bunce adds that this system met with considerable opposition at first, both on the grounds of expense and of alleged uncleanliness and offensiveness, but had been improved since its inception. Since the beginnings of the system in 1874, when the number of pans in use was 3,845, by 1884 the removal of pans had reached 1,922,752, and 129,000 loads of ashes and other refuse (altogether over 100,000 tons weight) were removed. By this date the number of water closets in the borough had risen to about 10,000.[23]

A beginning was thus made on the task of removing one of the greatest threats to the health of the working classes at the time – the system of earth closets and midden heaps. It was not the only source of working-class ill health, of course; the decayed condition of the cheapest housing in the older courts, malnutrition and attendant ill health, the cost of medical attention and so on, all played their part. Something was done in 1898 and 1899 to improve paving and scavenging in the courts, and in 1899, for example, cleansing of 2,519 courts was carried out. Nevertheless, the basic problem remained of how to provide sanitary housing for those living in the worst accommodation. Opinion on the City Council was deeply divided on this issue, since the Housing Acts of 1875 and 1890 were permissive and not mandatory, and as already emphasised, many thought it wrong in principle for the municipality to erect working-class housing in competition with private enterprise. This division of opinion could only result in weak compromise policies of patching-up existing properties. For example, in 1899 and under the 1875 Act, only eighteen

23. Lichfield Street, 1883, houses demonlished in Improvement Scheme.

houses were demolished, and 119 houses closed; while in the same year, under the 1890 Act, twelve houses were closed, forty-five made habitable, but not a single house demolished.[25]

Another way of assessing living conditions is by reference to mortality figures. In the years up to 1880, average death rates fell, but in spite of the city's sanitary advantages, from then on, death rates showed little change. In 1880-84, they averaged 20.8; in 1885-89, 19.8; in 1890-94, 20.7; and in 1895-99, 20.3. C.A.Vince, writing about this period in 1905, considered these figures to be disappointing, but suggested that one cause was the migration to the suburbs of the better-paid, wage-earning class, carrying with them their capacity for improving the statistics of health and mortality, 'while the idle, careless, and uncleanly, who live in wilful and ignorant resistance to sanitary regulations and the laws of health, remain in the City and help to raise the death rate.'[26] This is to recall Charles Booth's somewhat harsh and condemnatory comments on the two lowest classes in his survey of the London poor in the 1890s —[27]

> Their life is the life of savages, with vicissitudes of extreme hardship and occasional excess. Their food is of the coarsest description, and their only luxury is drink... they render no useful service, they create no wealth; more often they destroy it. They degrade whatever they touch, and as individuals are perhaps incapable of improvement.

No doubt, in the opinion of critics such as Vince, some of the poorest in the slums of Birmingham fell into this category. However, Vince does pinpoint the fact that the death rate was much higher in some wards of the city than in others. For example, in 1899 it was 27.1% in St Bartholomew's, 25.6% in St Stephen's, and 29.7% in St Mary's, while in the salubrious districts of Edgbaston and Harborne, it was only 13.0%. Moreover, the death rates in the three wards just noted can be linked significantly with back-to-back low-rented accommodation. In 1897 a survey in these wards estimated that 42,000 houses out of a total of 105,000 were without through ventilation, that is, were back-to-backs –[28]

No. of streets	Death rate	Houses without through ventilation (%)	Houses rented at 3s 6d a week and under (%)
6	Under 20	38	13
25	20-25	50	20
25	25-30	55	34
21	30-35	62	39
14	Over 35	65	54

On this evidence, it would seem that the belief expressed in Chadwick's Report, 1842, that back-to-back houses were not necessarily a worse health hazard than other types of housing had become open to question; though of course by this time, back-to-back housing was among the oldest and most decayed type of housing, and among the cheapest. In fact, mortality figures tell a similar story of the greatest incidence occuring in the most impoverished wards. Thus, in 1891, the city average death rate was 171 to every thousand born. In the central district of Market Hall it was 240; in Edgbaston and Harborne, it was 119.

So it seems quite clear that although by 1914 the city benefitted from a better water supply (which facilitated the installation of water closets), cheap gas, the pan system since 1874, and better paving in the old courts, there was still a great deal of bad, slum-like housing in central areas. Housing further out (provided by private builders, of course), was by no means ideal, consisting very often of terraced rows of tunnel-back housing, but certainly superior to the central slums. These slums were concentrated in the seven central wards of St Martin's and Deritend, Market Hall, Ladywood, St Paul's, St Mary's, Duddleston and Nechells, and St Bartholomew's. These wards were grossly overcrowded. In 1938 they were still twice as densely populated (sixty-two persons per acre) as the ten Middle Ring wards (thirty-two persons per acre), which wards in turn had a density twice that of the seventeen Outer Ring wards (fifteen persons per acre).[29] On the other hand, although the Central Wards were strongly working-class in character (the working classes there constituted about 90% of the population in the wards), in 1921 they amounted to only 27.6% of the working population of the city as a whole, a figure which had shrunk to 18.8% by 1938 (by this last date 28% of the working population lived in the Middle Ring of roads, and over 50% lived in the Outer Ring). Thus, immediately after the Great War, only just over a quarter of the working classes lived in the worst slum housing. The rest lived in the Middle and Outer Ring of wards. Even in the Middle Ring, housing was distinctly better than in the Central Wards. Although Middle Ring houses seldom had a bathroom, they did have sinks and running water, and proper water closets. The same can be said of the Outer Ring housing in which up to half of Birmingham's working population lived by 1938.[30] It is therefore necessary to take all these facts into consideration if we are to reach a fair assessment of the variations in quality of working-class housing in Birmingham in 1914.

24. First houses for senior Cadbury workers at Bournville, 1879.

We may now return to a point made earlier in this chapter: not all the working classes lived in slums in Victorian and Edwardian times. Certainly they did not in Birmingham. The worst slums were in the Central Wards, but as we have seen, only a minority of workers lived there by 1914. However, conditions were undoubtedly bad in the Central Wards: buildings were dilapidated, many lacked separate water supply or separate lavatory, and death rates and infant mortality rates were high. To give one last example: in Park Street centrally in 1904, where most of the housing was back-to-back, and the occupants were unskilled labourers earning 17s to 21s per week, the death rate was 63%; in Edgbaston it was 12.1%.[31] Of course, all this is only to be expected: the meanest housing was usually old, insanitary, and was the cheapest to rent. The tenants were usually poor, ill fed and sickly. Hence the high infant mortality, and the high death rates.

How far can the City Council be criticised for the slum conditions in the Central Wards? How far did the Civic Gospel prove a failure in this respect, at least, especially when it is recalled that in the mid-century, Birmingham was considered a rather healthier place than many other industrial towns? It must be reiterated that much of the city slum property was very old, dating back to the eighteenth century, an unenviable legacy of early industrialisation. Even after Chamberlain's Improvement Scheme, many areas of slum housing remained. The problem was to decide the best way of solving the problem. In spite of the idealistic ambitions of some believers in the Civic Gospel, it seemed highly unlikely that in a city where entrepreneurial zeal was so strong that municipal building would be seen as the answer. On the contrary: most re-housing was left to private enterprise, and very little undertaken by the Council. It was not until the inter-war period that a vigorous programme of council house building was at last undertaken.

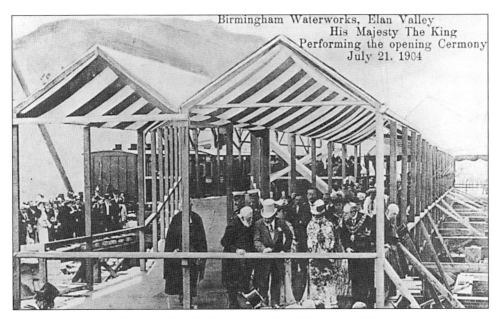

25. King Edward VII opening the Elan Valley Works, 1904.

However, it would be only fair to say that only a very few local authorities embarked on such building before 1914, pre-eminent among them the new and progressive London County Council. Further, the policy of what has been called 'slum patching' was pursued doggedly by the Council. Landlords were compelled either to demolish unfit houses or to refurbish them, and (as mentioned earlier), some courts were opened up by demolishing altogether one side of the court. By 1913 landlords had reconditioned 3,311 houses, 2,774 houses had been knocked down and 165 council dwellings had been built. This is a modest record when compared with Manchester's achievements – more than 11,000 houses improved, 5,500 houses demolished and 2,322 council properties built; but some progress at least had been made in Birmingham, and the cost to ratepayers was only 15s a head.[32] Council house building was undoubtedly costly (in Liverpool, the cost was £56 per head of ratepayers) and it took time to recoup capital costs through the rents collected. When a massive programme of municipal building was embarked on at last between the wars, it was with the help of government subsidies.

To return to the subject of middle-class housing with which this chapter began. One famous development for mixed social occupancy was the Bournville estate established by George Cadbury. It was intended not only for his employees, but for other classes of occupants as well. Houses were built in pairs, threes or fours, with ample gardens, wide tree-lined roads and open spaces. At first the houses were sold on long leases; by 1900, 313 houses had been erected, and the estate covered 330 acres. By 1914 the number of houses had risen to 894, and the estate had grown to 587 acres. The houses were of good quality, and some (for bigger families, obviously) had four bedrooms, though baths were originally concealed in the kitchens. Later on, houses were made available to rent, the rents ranging from 4s 6d to 9s a week. Among the amenities provided were an infant school, a church hall and retail shops (but no off-licences or public houses).[33]

Another interesting building development took place in Harborne, where a new company, Harborne Tenants Ltd, laid out the Moor Pool Estate. The company built 494 houses on an area of fifty-four acres, starting in 1908. It also provided shops, a club house, tennis courts, a bowling green and public halls. Rents were between 4s 6d and 9s per week. A third building scheme was proposed by the Ideal Benefit Society in 1908 for a 'workmen's garden colony' at Bordesley Green. This ideal village was to contain 225 houses and a number of shops. The City Council was interested in the project, but in the event it went ahead as a private venture. The Ideal Village turned out to be less attractive than either Bournville or Harborne. Long blocks of terraced houses were erected; but there were still a number of trees planted, and a public park was also laid out.[34]

Although municipal building as such was so limited before 1914, the idea of town planning and of encouraging the growth of garden suburbs was not unpopular on the City Council. J.S. Nettlefold, chairman of the Housing Committee from 1901 to 1911, was in fact an enthusiast for the garden suburb idea, and supported proposals that the city should buy land and then supervise private building on it. Support for such ideas grew after a visit by a deputation of the Housing Committee to Berlin in 1905, and was strengthened after the passing of the Housing and Town Planning Act, 1909. As a result of that act, a planning scheme was submitted to the government, covering Quinton, Harborne and Edgbaston; it was the first of its kind to be accepted by the central government. There were to be no more than twelve houses per acre, and no industry, with two areas set aside for parks and open spaces. In 1913 another proposal, the East Birmingham Scheme, was also approved; it covered 1,673 acres in Saltley, Washwood Heath, Little Bromwich and Small Heath. The district was to be laid out for both factories and domestic housing (between twelve and eighteen housee an acre), while 51 acres were reserved for allotments. Other schemes under consideration by 1914 were for North Yardley (3,164 acres) and for South Birmingham (8,400 acres). Active planning of controlled development in selected areas was therefore very noticeable before 1914, and indeed, Professor Cherry has suggested that Birmingham was foremost among local authorities for advancing the cause of town planning.[35]

Little remains to be said about living conditions in Birmingham in the period from 1850 to 1914. The city was by no means among the worst-housed among the great industrial cities of the time, even though it had become the largest of them all as a result of the Greater Birmingham Plan of 1911. It could now take the proud title of the Second City of the Empire. By 1914 housing conditions and the living conditions of the bulk of the population had certainly improved to a marked extent, given the better working-class housing in the Middle and Outer Rings of the City wards. After the completion of the Elan Valley water project in 1904, the more plentiful supply of water speeded up the replacement of the pan system by water closets. In this way one of the greatest evils of the old sanitary system, the earth privies, was at last eradicated (though there were many houses still without separate water closets in 1914). Municipal amenities had proliferated since the 1870s as a result of the Civic Gospel – the city was at last properly paved and lit, a new and handsome shopping street had been constructed, local transport had greatly improved, and more parks and open spaces had been provided. In all these ways the city environment had changed for the better, and even in the poorest working-class residential areas, overcrowding was not nearly as bad as in London and in the north east.[36] However, by 1914 a serious housing shortage had developed in Birmingham, the number of empty working-class housing falling to only 1.34%. Only 1,396 houses were built in 1914 when it was estimated that 2,000 new houses were required to house the increasing population. The years 1909 to 1914 saw a slump in the local building industry.[37] Thus in spite of a general overall improvement in the previous fifty years or so in working-class housing, problems remained.

These problems were twofold: the most immediate was the shortage of new housing to accommodate the increasing numbers working in the city (there was indeed a national shortage of housing at the time due to a variety of reasons, such as the increasing cost of building resulting from more stringent building regulations). The second was the continuing problem of the slums in the Central Wards of the city, the legacy of the industrial expansion of the late eighteenth century and early nineteenth century. There were some slum-like properties in the Middle Ring, too. All these slums remained unaffected by the mass of new building which took place in the Middle and Outer Rings, and still constituted a massive problem. What could be done to remove this blot on the achievements of the so-called best-governed city in the world?[38] The outbreak of the Great War on 4 August 1914 was to postpone any further efforts to find a solution to the problem of the Central Ward slums until peace returned, and the national government was forced to take action to alleviate a national housing shortage.

CHAPTER SIX

THE SOCIAL SCENE

Efforts have been made so far in this book to deal with the most prominent aspects of life in Birmingham in the second half of the nineteenth century and up to 1914, with particular reference to economic change, working and living conditions, and the Civic Gospel; but what of other aspects of daily life such as religious observance, schooling and leisure pursuits? These important facets of day-to-day life in the city will now be considered in this chapter. Taken together, they constitute an important part of the culture of a maturing industrial community, and for convenience will be discussed under the headings of the middle classes and then the working classes. This is not to suggest that class divisions necessarily became more marked by 1914 – the chapter dealing with working conditions has argued that relations between employers and workmen continue to be on the whole amicable enough before the Great War – but all the same it is clear that by 1914 a more distinct and greater working-class identity had been established. To this point we shall return at the end of the chapter.

THE MIDDLE CLASSES

It was pointed out in Chapter One that Birmingham was not high up on the list of church and chapel attendances compiled by Horace Mann from the Religious Census of 1851. In fact, although by 1851 the number of churches in the town and in Edgbaston had more than trebled, the provision of seats had failed to keep up with the growth of population; there were seats for only 13.3% of the town's inhabitants. This was far short of the 58% that Mann considered necessary to accommodate all those available to worship at any one time (deductions had to be made for those too old or too young, or sick, or at work, or otherwise not free to attend). Over the country as a whole, roughly half of those judged free to worship actually attended church or chapel on Census Sunday. In Birmingham, the figure was 36.1%, a not surprising figure for a large industrial town, but below Wolverhampton (53.1%), Dudley (55.3%), and Worcester, an ancient cathedral city (66%). Birmingham's figure was considerably higher than in Leeds or Manchester. Although Dissent had always been strong in Birmingham, the Church of England percentage of total attendance for the town was 47%, as compared with the figure for the Dissenters of 45.9%.[1]

Although we have no statistical means of proving the point, there is little doubt that the majority of attenders in Birmingham were middle-class. For them, attendance (up to three times on Sunday if all the morning, afternoon and evening services were attended) was in any case a social obligation; not to attend might well attract comment and criticism. Again, we have no means of measuring the depth or sincerity of the religious belief of those who attended, but it is clear that for many it was a very real thing. Their education would have been dominated by Christian beliefs, with emphasis on the literal truth of the Bible. Evangelicalism was still so strong nationally that Bibles were provided on reading-stands in main-line railway stations to help travellers pass the time to the benefit of their souls as they waited for their trains. Parliamentary business was always prefaced by daily prayers and clergymen were present at most public ceremonies.[2] Family prayers at which the domestics were required to be present were very common. However, although Dissent was strong in Birmingham, the Church of England attendance as a proportion of total attendance, as we have just seen, was higher than in the chapels. Where Dissent had great influence in the life of the town was in the great dissenting preachers who were mentioned in Chapter Three – in particular, George Dawson, H.W. Crosskey and Robert William Dale.

The influence of these ministers was great, and was not confined to their Sunday sermons. Indeed, the extent of their activities in running a variety of religious societies associated with their churches and chapels is extraordinary. Thus, the societies organised at the famous congregational Carr's Lane Chapel at the end of 1859 were described as follows –[3]

> We are not one whit better than some others... we have now an organisation for the London Missionary Society which raises as its regular contribution nearly £500 per annum... for the Colonial Missionary Society we raise annually £70. For our Sunday and day schools, which comprehend nearly two thousand children, we raise £200. We support two town missionaries at a cost of £200. Our ladies conduct a working society for orphan mission schools in the West Indies...

The same source goes on to say that the ladies of the congregation also ran a Dorcas Society for the poor of the town and a Maternal Society for visiting the sick poor. The chapel had a religious tract society, employing ninety distributors, which spent nearly £50 a year in the purchase of tracts. In addition, there were the Our Village Preachers' Society, employing twelve or fourteen lay agents, and a Young Men's Brotherly Society for general and religious improvement; the latter had a library of 2,000 volumes. Then there were night schools for young men and women, and Bible Classes. Lastly, the chapel had many and liberal subscribers to its public societies, such as the Bible Society, the Society for the Conversion of Jews, and other objects of Christian zeal and benevolence. Thus Carr's Lane Chapel provided for very much more than simple weekly services designed to uplift the spirit. It was clearly a positive force for spreading the gospel and for succouring the poor. For many of its numerous supporters (especially female members, one suspects) its activities must have filled much of their spare time, not excluding opportunities for meeting the opposite sex.

There is thus a good deal of evidence to show that regular attendance at church or chapel was more than merely a matter of social conformity on a Sunday. Moreover, Chapter Three on the Civic Gospel has made it clear that Unitarian beliefs as preached by George Dawson and H.W. Crosskey (minister of the Unitarian Church of the Messiah, attended by the Chamberlains, William Kendrick and R.F. Martineau) had a direct influence on implementing the Civic Gospel. It should also be remembered that many of the leading advocates of civic reform lived in the leafy suburb of Edgbaston, frequently dined together, and were in and out of each other's drawing rooms. As Professor Cannadine has put it, for the civic élite, 'Edgbaston was but the

Council House at home'. So it is not surprisng that Unitarianism, although very much a minority religious belief, exercised a potent influence in local politics. Quakerism, too, had a marked influence on civic affairs; between 1872 and 1900, Quakers and Unitarians provided more mayors than any other two bodies.[4]

By the 1890s religious attitudes were changing and secularism was growing. This seems to have been due to a variety of causes, among them increasing doubts as to the literal truth of the Bible. Lyall had published his *Principles of Geology* in 1830-33, while Charles Darwin's *Origins of Species* dates from 1859, and his *Descent of Man* from 1871. These works did not deny directly the essential truth of Christianity but questioned the Biblical version of the creation of the Earth and of Man. The belief in the Darwinian theory of evolution found a strong and aggressive supporter in Thomas Huxley. Meanwhile the growth of secularism was shown in the decline of family prayers, the relaxing of the strict sabbatarianism of the earlier years, the opening of London museums and art galleries to the public on Sunday afternoons, and the running of cheap railway excursions on Sundays by the National Sunday League. Inevitably, all this led to a falling-away of attendance at church and chapel, as was shown by a series of surveys in 1881 of church attendances in a number of major cities, and later in London in 1902-03.

Against this background we may examine developments in religious belief in Birmingham in the 1890s, for in 1892 a local religious census of church and chapel attendance was carried out.[5] As might be expected, this showed an overall fall in attendance to 32.4% of the population (in 1851, the figure was 36%, although boundary changes and the rise in the population make direct comparisons unsafe). The Church of England's share of adult attendance was 38.6%, little different from the figure for protestant dissent of 39.1%. Sunday school attendance remained high, particularly in the dissenting churches and chapels – over half of all children of school age went to Sunday school.

These figures show a falling-off of attendance since 1851, but perhaps on a rather smaller scale than might have been expected, given the fact that in some of the 1881 surveys elsewhere, attendance was much lower – for example, in Liverpool it was 19.9%, in Sheffield 23% and in Nottingham 24.2%. It is interesting to see that although Anglican church attendances in Birmingham were little different from those in the dissenting denominations, attendances were below the overall Birmingham average in the strongly middle-class areas of Edgbaston and Harborne. Edgbaston had a population of less than 25,000, and was served by four churches and ten clergy, yet it had an attendance figure of only 20.8%. In Harborne, the figure was 24.4%. From this it appears that even in these overwhelmingly middle-class residential areas, church attendance showed a marked decline.

No further figures are available for church or chapel attendance in Birmingham between 1892 and 1914, but in those twenty-two years it is reasonable to suppose that they either declined further on trend, or at best simply remained static. It certainly seems very likely that in Birmingham they were affected by the national mood of secularism which manifested itself in a greater indulgence in leisure activities and indeed in what the historian R.C.K. Ensor, looking back in the mid-1930s to his own Edwardian youth, simply called 'hedonism'. It was a period in which the upper classes in particular indulged themselves in ostentatious and extravagent display, in expensive dinner parties, balls and weekend parties in their spacious stately homes, waited on by large retinues of servants. While at Sandringham, the leader himself of London society, the Prince of Wales, attended church only briefly and required sermons to be limited to ten minutes. It is no wonder that the active participation of the middle classes in Birmingham in church and chapel activities in the mid-century years was noticeably reduced in scale by 1914. It was not simply a loss of faith, but also a widening of leisure opportunities which seemed to make church and chapel attendance less important in the years before the Great War.

It would be wrong, perhaps, to leave the subject of religious observance among the middle classes in Birmingham without a last reference to the significance of dissenting beliefs, and especially to Unitarianism. Although it has been emphasised that this creed was confined to only a minority of worshippers – in 1892, Unitarians constituted only 1.8% of all adult attenders – yet Unitarian beliefs were a powerful force behind support for the Civic Gospel. The Unitarian Church of the Messiah thus had a political influence out of all proportion to the size of its congregations. The Wesleyans, on the other hand, contributed the greatest number of dissenting attenders in 1892 – 13.8% of all adult attenders – yet they played only a limited part in secular affairs. The comparison brings out very well the influence which can be exerted in local affairs by a minority religious group, especially perhaps, if their adherents include forceful business men with strong personalities such as Joseph Chamberlain.[6]

Chamberlain, of course, was not born locally, and was educated at University College School, London, but many of his supporters were educated in Birmingham, and in particular at the King Edward VI Grammar School. This school is largely synonymous with middle-class education in Birmingham in the nineteenth century, and although the wealthier business men might send their sons to public boarding schools outside the area, or if dissenters, to Edgbaston Proprietory School, established 1837, and afterwards merged with the King Edward Foundation,[7] the majority of middle-class boys went to the King Edward School in New Street. This school dates from the sixteenth century, of course, and was an Anglican foundation. Its curriculum was heavily classical as might be expected, but by 1850 some reform had taken place. In 1837 a new commercial or English department had been set up. Of the 465 pupils at the time, 250 were in the classical school and 215 in the English school. In the former school, the sons of professional men numbered about a quarter, but they were not to be found at all in the latter; many of these boys were destined for university, where the curriculum was still based on classical learning. In the English school, nearly all (six out of every seven, in fact) were sons of manufacturers, clerks, and tradesmen, and left school to enter industry, commerce, or the service trades.[8]

By the 1860s the King Edward school was increasingly unpopular with Liberal supporters for its exclusiveness. Admission to the school was still by individual nomination, and the governing body was still unrepresentative of local interests. The Report of the Endowed Schools Commission, 1868 (the Taunton Commission), put this last point forcibly enough –[9]

> No Dissenter within the memory of man has been a governor; no mayor of the town has until the present year been a governor; no member of the borough, except one, a Conservative; not one town councillor.

26. Edmund Street, 1912.
27. New Street, late nineteenth century.

The exclusively Anglican nature of the school became an increasing cause of complaint among dissenters by 1870. Reform came at last with the introduction of reform schemes in 1875, 1878 and 1883. These modified the old structure of the foundation, so that the eight small branch schools were converted into grammar schools, nomination of pupils was replaced by competitive examinations, and a third of pupils were awarded free foundation scholarships. In 1885 a new constitution for the governing body was issued. Henceforth there were to be eight governors from the town council, one each from the universities of Oxford, Cambridge and London, eight appointed by co-operation, and one elected by the teaching staff. In 1900 an Act of Parliament promoted by the governors abolished any remaining control by the Charity Commissioners, and an additional representative from the new University of Birmingham was added to the Board of Governors.[10]

In the period 1850-1914 King Edward VI High School (as it was called from 1883 onwards) therefore underwent a certain degree of reform, but its classical tradition remained strong, and the school prided itself on the teaching of the classics. It was even suggested by its headmaster to the Schools Enquiry Commission, 1864-68, that it deserved to rank in eminence with the leading public schools investigated by the Clarendon Commission, 1861-64 – a suggestion that was not favourably received, as the school's clientele was considered to be far too local.[11] What happened in practice was that it was far cheaper as a day school for most middle-class parents to send their sons there than to a boarding school at a distance. As just noted, professional fathers kept their sons on the classical side with their eye on Oxbridge entrance; others, less ambitious perhaps, were content for their sons to stay on the English or Commercial side. So King Edward's remained a major element in middle-class education before the outbreak of war in 1914.

But what about the education of middle-class girls in Birmingham? It did not make much progress at the secondary level until 1883 when a branch of the King Edward Foundation for girls was established in New Street. Fifteen years previously the Taunton Commission had pointed out that more money available in educational trusts throughout the country ought to be used for the education of girls. At last the King Edward Foundation acted on this suggestion, with the founding on a small scale of the present High School for Girls. Before 1883 it is difficult to discover any schools for girls with high academic standards in the Birmingham area, the emphasis more often being on genteel accomplishments than on academic achievement. This is certainly true of the many private schools thought suitable enough for girls. According to Victor Skipp, about 170 of the 250 schools listed in Kelly's Directory for 1874 were girls' schools run by spinsters or married women. Two more pretentious establishments were the Misses Grimley's ladies boarding school at Stratford House, Camp Hill, and the Howells' ladies' school at Metchley Abbey. The latter was run by three sisters thought to be 'highly educated', and their pupils were Wesleyans, whose parents paid high fees. Many private schools for girls were very small, and occupied domestic houses with only a limited number of rooms, as for example in Victoria Road, Aston Park, where there were six establishments in 1874.[12] The traditional belief that women's place was in the home and that her educational needs were really minimal was beginning to change towards the end of the century, but the rate of change in the provision of academic education for girls was still relatively slow in Birmingham before 1914.

To turn now to middle-class leisure activities: for the more thoughtful and caring, church and chapel continued to provide outlets for charitable work, as we have seen, and middle-class women seem to have become more and more active in this field. No doubt towards the end of the century the decrease in the size of their families gave them additional time for this. One interesting example of this is the extension of the scope of social work to include a campaign against prostitution in Birmingham. In 1878 Mary Showell Rogers founded a reform home for young prostitutes, and a girls' Night Shelter was opened in 1888. Both Mrs Rogers and Mrs Elizabeth Cadbury were active members of the Birmingham Ladies Association for the Care of Friendless Girls.[13] Voluntary social work of this kind was of increasing importance among middle-class women, helping them to acquire a new sense of independence and giving them experience in organising and directing activities outside the home. Women profited, too, from the new sport of lawn tennis, very popular on the spacious lawns of Edgbaston, while the cycling craze of the 1890s appealed to the younger, more adventurous women. Women could be both voters and candidates on school boards, and on parish councils in and after 1894. In the political sphere, by 1900 there were over a million female voters for county, borough and poor law elections.[14] By 1914 there were two women councillors on Birmingham City Council. Meanwhile, in 1903, the Women's Social and Political Union was formed to campaign for the parliamentary vote, and the suffragette movement had begun. Both nationally and in Birmingham, women – and especially middle-class women – were emerging from the restrictions imposed by large families and a traditional subordinate role in the home.

Social and charitable work for middle-class men and women covered a wide spectrum of activities in Birmingham before 1914. For some, it was limited to what might be loosely called civic duties, such as serving on the City Council, on the Board of Guardians, on the School Board, or on the Bench as JPs. For others, it could include membership of one or the other of the vast number of committees in the town, such as the organising bodies of the great Triennial Music Festivals (which had begun in the eighteenth century), the Hospital Saturday Fund (inaugurated in 1869), and the Botanical Gardens at Harborne. The middle classes also played a part in the establishment and organisation of the city's great football clubs such as Aston Villa (founded 1874) and Birmingham City in 1875 (an off-shoot of the Holy Trinity Cricket Club in Bordesley). The Moseley rugby club, which offered active participation to middle-class males, was founded in 1873, and again owed its origin to a cricket club, the Havelock Cricket Club. Warwickshire County Cricket Club dates from 1882, the first match being played on ground at Edgbaston donated by Lord Calthorpe; the first test match to be played there was against Australia in 1902. Other sports appealing to the middle classes were golf and lawn tennis, already mentioned as a sport easily adopted in the large gardens of Edgbaston.

Two other forms of mainly middle-class entertainment continued to flourish up to 1914. The first was the theatre. The Theatre Royal dated back to 1774. The Alexandra, a newer creation, first opened in 1901 as the Palace of Delights. The Hippodrome was the town's leading music hall, and much patronised therefore by the working classes, while another theatre, the Prince of Wales, also a music hall, first opened in 1856. Certainly the most famous theatre of the present day, the Birmingham Repertory Theatre, opened in 1913 with a performance of *Twelfth Night*

28. The Old Farriers Arms, Lichfield Street, c.1880.

produced by Barry Jackson, who made the theatre famous between the wars and subsequently as a nursery for some of the country's leading actors and actresses.[15] As for music, the Triennial Music Festivals, begun in 1768 as a way of financing the founding of the General Hospital, had acquired a national reputation by the 1840s. According to one visitor in 1847 –[16]

> No town of its size in the Empire spends more time and money in concerts and music festivals than Birmingham: no small proportion of its people are amateur performers; almost all are musical critics; and the organ in its great Hall, the property of the town, is with the exception of that at York, the largest in the Empire, and the finest, it is said, without any exception.

This is lavish praise indeed. The reference to the great Hall, of course, is to the Town Hall, which came in to use in 1834. Previously concerts had been held in St Philip's, usually of sacred music, especially oratorios, but the town hall was much larger, and possibly the largest in England, with seats for 3,600, or 9,000 standing when the seats were removed.[17] The Musical Festivals came to an end in 1912, but between the wars regular concerts were provided by the City of Birmingham Orchestra and supported financially by the Council. The visual arts were catered for by the Academy of Arts, founded 1814, which was replaced by the Society of Arts in 1821, holding its first exhibition in 1828. After 1850 Birmingham was to produce its own distinguished artists among the Pre-Raphaelites, among the best-known being Sir Edward Burne-Jones. The present-day Municipal Art Galleries, of course, have a splendid collection of pre-Raphaelite art.

Middle-class influence over a wide spectrum of social life in Birmingham was therefore very strong, a consequence perhaps of the determination of the town's business élite to do things according to their own notions, and free from the influence of the local landowning classes (there is an interesting contrast to be made here with some parts of the Black Country; for example, in West Bromwich, friendly relations were maintained with the Earl of Dartmouth, and similarly in Dudley with the Earl of Dudley).[18] Peers of the realm do not figure very often or very largely in the nineteenth century history of Birmingham. So civic life, cultural life and leisure activities all owed much to middle-class participation. Indeed, the same names re-occur constantly throughout the second half of the nineteenth century – the Chamberlains, Kendricks, Martineaus and the Cadburys. The history of the city would be immeasureably different without their active leadership.

THE WORKING CLASSES

If church and chapel attendance was limited in 1851 among the Birmingham middle classes, then it would not be expected that the working classes were any more zealous in attendance. We have no figure for estimates of working-class attendance other than the very speculative figures given in Chapter One. There can be little doubt that relatively few working-class men and women attended services in the mid-century years. A variety of reasons have been advanced for this. One of the simplest is that in Birmingham, as in many fast-growing industrial towns, chuch and chapel building failed miserably to keep pace with the rapid growth of urban population; and this is certaily shown by the limited number of seats available in Birmingham (enough for 13.3% of the population) in 1851. However, even if more seats had been on offer, it is doubtful if they would have all been filled. To refer again to arguments already put forward in Chapter One: many of the immigrants from the countryside coming to Birmingham simply found better things to do than go to church or chapel on Sundays, having escaped from the vigilant eye of squire and parson in their native village. Even those inclined to attend might be put off by the pew rents which were peculiarly plentiful in Birmingham in both church and chapel, and were an essential source of income for some congregations (even in 1892, according to the *Church Times*, only seven of the fifty seven churches were entirely free).[19] Even then, even those among the working classes prepared to go to church or chapel might be embarrassed by the placing of free seats at the back, or by their own lack of suitable Sunday dress.

Above all, perhaps, was the simple fact that the Church of England was regarded by most of the working classes as essentially part of middle-class society (and the large and prosperous chapels were not much better), attended by the respectable classes whose attempts to lure into church or chapel their working-class brethren were regarded with suspicion and some dislike. It is noteworthy that the Primitive Methodists, who usually had substantial working-class support in the Black Country, had only three chapels in Birmingham in 1851, with a total attendance of 1,053 (that is, allowing for multiple attendances, about 702 actual worshippers). Probably it was the better-paid, artisan class who provided the majority of working-class support in the churches and chapels, being strongest among the Roman Catholics (though they had only a small number of churches), the Wesleyans and then the Primitive Methodists. There was a sprinkling of self-employed craftsmen among the Unitarians, Quakers and Baptists, but again their numbers must have been small.[20]

The situation is unlikely to have been any better and indeed was likely to have been considerably worse in 1892. It is still surprising that the Birmingham census of attendance in that year, as we have seen earlier on, seems to show that overall attendance had held up relatively well since 1851 (32.4%, as compared with 36.1% in 1851). The strongest dissenting group was that of the Wesleyans (13.8% of adult attendances, as compared with the Church of England's 38.6%), but of course they played little part in secular affairs.

Does all this mean that by the end of the nineteenth century the working classes in Birmingham were sinking into a state of utter indifference to religion? Not really: figures for church and chapel attendance are not the only guide to religious belief, and they take no account of occasional attendance at Easter, Whitsun or Christmas. Then again, according to Roy Peacock, half of all school children in Birmingham went to Sunday school in 1892.[21] In addition, the majority of school children attending elementary school in the city attended church schools where religious instruction was a key element in the curriculum. Even in the secular board schools, children were accustomed to hearing Biblical texts. For these reasons, the younger generations in Birmingham were still gaining some idea of the fundamentals of the Christian religion. It is simply that fewer members of the adult working classes thought it necessary to attend church or chapel regularly, though no doubt retaining vague beliefs in a Christian God. They certainly still believed in getting married in church, having their children baptised there, and being buried with the rites of the church.

Some were attracted into political activity as believers in socialism – witness the setting-up of branches of the Labour Church – though some leading trade unionists held devout dissenting beliefs all their lives; others were simply drawn into the leisure activities which became so much more extensive at the end of the century. It would seem to be apathy and indifference rather than a widespread and positive loss of faith which characterised working-class attitudes to religion in Birmingham by 1914. This is so in spite of valiant efforts such as that of the Pleasant Sunday Afternoon Movement to attract those with a lingering interest in religion by quasi-religious programmes of music and readings. The Salvation Army, founded in 1878 by William Booth, was another attempt to evangelise the ungodly, especially among the poorest. The clergy themselves were very conscious of the growth of indifference, both in Birmingham and the Black Country. In 1914 the vigorous vicar of Quarry Bank near Stourbridge delivered an address with the arresting title, 'Is Religion played out?'

As for working-class education, the situation in 1850 has already been outlined in Chapter One. To recapitulate briefly: literacy rates were still low (29% of Birmingham bridegrooms could not sign their names, nor could 47% of brides), schooling was not compulsory, and there were more privately-run dame schools and common day schools than church schools, either Anglican or nonconformist. Attendance at school usually lasted only a short time and many children were sent out to work as soon as they were capable of earning a few pence. In more specific terms, according to a survey carried out in 1868-69 by the Birmingham Education Society, of a sample of 37,122 children aged five to fifteen, only 14,464 (that is, 39%) were attending day school and the average attendance for boys was only one year, nine months and for girls, two years, three months. Of attenders, 64% fell into the age range three to nine; only 11% into the range eleven to thirteen. Over the whole sample, 50% were unable to write and 36% unable to read.[22]

After 1850, however, the demand grew nationally for more schooling for the working classes, and one of the recommendations of the Newcastle Commission of 1861 was that the cost of local schooling should be met out of the rates (a suggestion strongly opposed by many nonconformists, who suspected Anglican influence would predominate). Finally, Forster's Education Act, 1870, brought in additional elementary schools (board schools) financed out of a school rate, and elementary education became first compulsory (1880), then free (1891). Then in 1902 Balfour's Education Act transferred the board schools to appropiate local authorities, and made limited provision for county secondary schools. Between 1870 and 1914, therefore, a national system of education for the working classes came into existence. What part was played by Birmingham in these important educational changes?

In fact, Birmingham played an important part in the events leading up to the passing of the Education Act, 1870. In 1869 the leading radical reformers in the town founded the National Education League which aimed at a national system of free, secular and compulsory education. Its chairman was George Dixon, the acting chair was Joseph Chamberlain, and its secretary Jesse Collings. Its branch committees were organised by Thomas Martineau, the Treasurer was John

Jaffray, while on the Executive Committee were such well-known names as Timmins, Dale, Vince and Dawson – an impressive array of Birmingham's progressives (or in the modern term, Great and Good).[23] In fact, Forster's Act was a great disappointment to them. They strongly objected to the continued existence of the church schools (Forster had no intention of abolishing them, and sought to supplement the church school system, not to supplant it), and schooling was not compulsory under the Act, neither was it free. Fees of up to nine pence a week could be charged in all the schools. A further reverse for the reformers first lay in the fact that the Conservative and Anglican party won the first election to the School Board in Birmingham in 1870 by the adroit use of their votes (voters were allowed up to three votes each, the so-called 'cumulative' vote, and they distributed their votes wisely). Moreover, the new School Board actually decided to use the proceeds of the school rate to pay fees in all schools, both church schools and board schools; and in spite of legal action taken by the reformers, the Board's decision was upheld by the High Court. However, the ruling was never enforced by the Board in view its extreme unpopularity and of the fact that many school ratepayers would have refused to pay anyway. By the second school board election in 1873, the Liberals had learned their lesson. The Liberal caucus of strictly controlled voting patterns had been set up (today it would probably be called tactical voting), closely supervised by local committees, and they secured a majority which they were to hold for many years to come.[24]

What of the other key elements in the national campaign of the National Education League? In 1871 the Birmingham School Board decided to make education compulsory between the ages of five and thirteen, with Standard IV necessary for full exemption, and Standard III for half-time exemption. The first Attendance Officer was appointed in 1872. Lord Sandon's Act,1876, laid it down that it was the moral duty of parents to send their children to school, but it took another four years before Gladstone's 1880 Act made schooling legally compulsory for all children between five and ten. Children were supposed to stay on beyond that age unless they could obtain exemption, and the age of compulsion was extended to eleven in 1893 and to twelve in 1899.

As for fees in the new board schools, they were fixed originally at 3d per week for children over seven, and 2d per week for those under seven; later the fees were reduced to a penny a week. In 1891, Lord Salisbury's Act in effect abolished fees altogether by recompensing all schools who chose to do this. Curiously enough, some church schools continued to collect fees from parents who were prepared to pay up in order to preserve the social status of their schools by keeping out children from the poorest homes. As for the form of religious instruction in the new board schools, this was a subject on which the National Education League held strong views, of course. It was a matter which had caused much controversy when Forster's bill had first been introduced. Finally an amendment was accepted by which religious instruction should not be distinctive of any religious catechism or religious formulary (the Temple-Cowper clause); in other words, it should be undenominational. In the Birmingham board schools, this at first took the form of voluntary instruction after school hours. A Religious Instruction Society was set up, with a panel of voluntary teachers, but difficulty was experienced in recruiting a sufficient number of teachers. In and after 1879 the scheme was replaced by simple Bible reading.

29. Colmore Row, late nineteenth century.

In the twenty years or so following Forster's Act, the new board schools became a familiar part of the educational scene in Birmingham. They had no easy task. It is true that they were newly-built and better-constructed than many of the old church schools (though a few were former church schools, handed over because the church society did not wish to continue running them). The main problem facing the board schools was that they were expected to teach the very poorest children whose parents had not been able to afford school fees or had simply not bothered to send their children to school. These were the children of the *residuum*, living in areas where the church societies had not thought it worthwhile to build schools. *The Schoolmaster* put this bluntly enough in 1872, referring to 'the younger years of school board life, while the unbroken youth of our country are being raked in from the gutter, the dunghill, and the hedgerow'.[25] The school boards themselves seemed to recognise that some of their schools contained very rough children, and indeed the London School Board charged fees varying with the class of children, so that better-off parents could send their children to better schools than could the poorest parents. It appears that the Birmingham School Board followed a similar policy of social differentiation.[26] Nevertheless, the new board system bedded down in time and by 1880, twenty-eight new schools had been built, providing 28,787 additional places. Attendance was good, averaging 89% in 1879.[27] The curriculum was simple, being limited to the three Rs, together with grammar, history and geography for the older pupils, and needlework for the girls. Special educational treatment was introduced for backward children in 1894. Meanwhile, higher grade schools were established in Bridge Street and in Waverley Road. Scholarships were also available from the elementary schools to the High School.

The period between 1870 and 1902 therefore saw a remarkable expansion of elementary education in Birmingham. It had at last become compulsory, on the whole free and (as far as the board schools were concerned) unsectarian. However, the Education Act, 1902, was to bring an end to the Birmingham School Board. This Act was passed as a result of a number of factors, not least being the urgent need of the church societies for more financial support. Another cause was the creation towards the end of the century of new local authorities such as county councils, county borough councils and local councils with smaller powers such as urban district councils and rural district councils. Lastly, there was mounting criticism that schools boards were more and more using ratepayers' money not only for elementary education (their primary function) but for higher-grade schools with more ambitious curricula, evening classes and other educational purposes. The result of the 1902 Act was not only a sweeping away of the school boards, and the transfer of the board schools to new local educational authorities, but also the giving of financial support to the church schools from the rates in return for appointing up to one-third of the managers by the local educational authority.

This 'putting of the church on the rates' (as it was called at the time) drew great protests from dissenters, and especially from Joseph Chamberlain, who tried unsuccessfully to get the government (of which he was a member) to make this part of the act optional. So authority over the former board schools in Birmingham was transferred to the local county council – that is, to Birmingham City Corporation – and they became the responsibility of the new Education Committee. Its chairman was George Kenrick, who had been a member of the old school board for more than twenty years. Board schools became known as council schools. By 1902 there were more than sixty of these schools, and they catered for 70,000 children (an additional forty-three council schools were acquired in and after 1911 as a result of the Greater Birmingham Plan). Another provision of the 1902 Act was that county councils and county borough councils were to survey the need for more secondary schools in their area, and to provide new county secondary schools where necessary. However, Birmingham already had its High School for Boys (and a High School for Girls since 1883), together with eight grammar schools all dependent on the King Edward Foundation, so no new grammar schools were founded directly as a result of the 1902 Act.

However, the two higher grade schools (Waverley Road and Oozells Street) officially became secondary schools, as did the municipal day school in Suffolk Street. In 1906 the George Dixon School in Oozells Street reopened on a new site in City Road, Rotten Park, its old site becoming a pupil teacher centre. In addition, in 1911 the Yardley Secondary School was taken over, and the new secondary school at King's Norton (both provided by Worcestershire County Council). So by 1914 Birmingham Educational Authority was responsible for five secondary schools in all.[28]

Substantial progress was made in elementary education in Birmingham in the second half of the nineteenth century, and the Birmingham School Board acquired a national reputation for its efficiency. This reputation was enhanced as a result of the additional school services provided after the Liberal governments of 1906-14 had introduced school meals for poor children in 1906, and school medical inspections in 1907. Birmingham Educational Authority became responsible for both these services, and the statistics are impressive. In the year ending March 1914, the total number of meals served in the form of breakfasts was 274,069, an average of 751 a day. Dental and medical care was also provided: in the following year (to March 1915), 11,792

30. Corporation Street, early twentieth century.

children had dental treatment, 468 children had tonsil and adenoid operations and 220 children were X-rayed as treatment for ringworm. In the year ending December 1914, spectacles at cheap rates were prescribed for 2,533 children and 4,471 were treated for minor ailments. Also in 1914 there were 152,769 examinations for verminous children (38% had nits, 8.2% other vermin and 53.4% were declared clean).[29] The extent of Birmingham's school medical services were to receive high praise during the Great War.

Space forbids further reference to elementary education in Birmingham in the period 1850-1914, and to the Education Committee's three technical schools, special schools, industrial school and evening classes, but it would be wrong to leave the subject of working-class education without some reference to the extent of voluntary work in the mid-nineteenth century years directed to education. Much of this was due to middle-class efforts in founding new schools. The majority of these were church schools: about 52 National schools (i.e. Church of England schools) were founded in the borough in the period 1839-70, but there was also a number of other schools, such as the Ragged Schools,which were free to very poor parents, and date from the 1840s. There were nine of these in all, the first being William Chance's School in Windmill Street, 1845, with 200 children. Another, the St Philip's Ragged School, Litchfield Street, 1846, moved to Gem Street, and became the Birmingham Free Industrial School which taught trades and industrial occupations as well as the three Rs. In addition, there were some factory schools, and others such as Josiah Mason's Orphan School (1868) and a new workhouse school for boys at Winson Green (1869). Altogether at least 130 new schools of all kinds were founded in the period 1839-70.[30]

It must not be forgotten,either, that there was another side of the coin: many working-class adults were anxious to improve themselves, and in particular to learn to read and write. Adult

31. The Old Leather Bottle, Digbeth, c.1885.

Sunday schools existed before 1850, but the movement really seems to have taken off with the opening of Joseph Sturge's First Day School in 1845. By 1860, 654 men and 300 women were attending, being taught by up to fifty members of the Bull Street Meeting House congregation. Subsequently Early Morning Schools were organised, and by 1880 were attended by 2,397 men and 684 women. Evening classes were also held; there were twenty-four evening schools in 1838, but they were quite expensive, costing from 4d to 1s a week.[31] One can only admire the determination to acquire skills and knowledge which drove men to attend classes either before or after a twelve-hour working day. This drive is also to be seen in a different context, the establishment of the Midlands Institute in 1854. It was the idea of Arthur Ryland to bring together a number of smaller bodies to form a single institution which would serve both as a general scientific and literary association (appealing to the middle classes) and an industrial institute (providing adult education for the working classes). Charles Dickens strongly supported the idea and raised £300 as a contribution. The Institute was incorporated by Act of Parliament in 1854, and moved into a new building in 1857. By 1862, the Industrial Department had 717 students, of whom 8% were manufacturers or their sons, 31% manual workers, 16% women, and the remainder mainly clerks and shopmen.[32] The Institute has continued to the present day as a valuable centre for part-time adult education.

To sum up: the story of working-class education in Birmingham between 1850 and 1914 is of a change from a fragmented organisation of church schools and private schools to a compulsory and free system of local authority education into which the church schools had been incorporated, but on a voluntary basis. In some ways this might seem to be the logical outcome of the Civic Gospel but, as we have seen, the roots of change were in the Education Acts of 1870 and 1902. One valuable aspect of this change was the beginnings of the schools meals service and of the schools medical service. The emphasis throughout was on what was beginning to be called elementary education for the working classes, but this does not mean that working-class and middle-class education were entirely and mutually exclusive. Indeed, the opinion has been advanced that many artisans sent their children to the lesser private schools, while many of the middle classes sent sent children to the better National, and British Church schools.[33] This is as may be; there was still a world of difference, of course, between an education at a church school and one at the High School. Here and there, able working-class boys might transfer from an elementary school by means of a scholarship to a secondary school of the King Edward Foundation or even to one of the five secondary schools administered by the Corporation in 1914; but overwhelmingly the education on offer to the working-class child was of an elementary nature, ending at twelve if the requisite standard of proficiency could be reached. Real secondary education was something different, and was not to be extended to working-class children for some years to come.

Nevertheless, the educational changes of the time had a profound effect in many ways on the working-class family. The new routines of regular attendance at school brought an unaccustomed regularity into many family lives (reinforced in some cases by the visits of the Attendance Officer), and also by 1914 by the free school meals for the neediest, and the school medical inspections, which might lead to attendance at the School Clinic and interviews with a schools Medical Officer. Family life was no longer what it had been in 1850, when the male head of the family could batter both his wife and the children if he thought fit. By 1914 his children were part of a school community, and violence in the home increasingly resulted in a visit by the 'cruelty man' (the National Society for the Prevention of Cruelty to Children inspector; the Society was founded in 1889). Family life was becoming more civilised, and free, compulsory education played no small part in this.

If family life changed by 1914, so had working-class leisure activities. As we saw earlier in this work, St Monday gradually died out from the 1860s onwards, to be replaced by the Saturday half-day, while from the 1870s and after there was a shortening of the working day. Then again, in spite of the hardships experienced in some parts of industry in the worst years of the Great Depression, there was a fall in the cost of living and a rise in real wages. As a consequence of these changes, there was more leisure time available in 1914 than in 1850, and an increase for many in spending power. The public house and the clubs of the Union of Workingmen's Clubs and Institutes (founded 1862) remained the principal venues for working-class leisure and entertainment, still offering warmth, companionship, cards, dominoes and so on in a congenial atmosphere. Nationally, the consumption of alcohol was still on a massive scale.[34] The pubs themselves changed very little in the period, though gas lighting became universal. Some of the larger establishments had become rather more ornate, with elaborate brass work and fancy glass – the so-called gin palaces. For the more serious-minded, the growth of the public library system offered greater opportunities for reading, and of course literacy had spread very widely among the working classes by 1914 – generally speaking, only among the elderly was illiteracy still to be found. There were still plenty of ways in which those of an enquiring mind could extend their knowledge in evening classes in the city, or at the Midlands Institute, while the politically-minded had a choice of small political clubs, mostly of a left-wing and socialist outlook (see Chapter Four). The friendly society movement still flourished, of course, with its monthly meetings in public houses for the payment of dues and the consumption of liquor.

However, during the second half of the nineteenth century, some of the earlier and brutal forms of entertainment died out such as bear-baiting, dog fights and cockfighting (of these, cockfighting is said to have continued a shadowy and illegal existence). Wakes also died out – they were local holidays lasting three or four days, and often crude and violent affairs. Wakes were disliked by the middle classes because of their rumbustious nature, and also by the borough police, established by Act of Parliament in 1842. Fairs on the other hand were rather more peaceful than wakes, and the two annual fairs, one in spring, the other in autumn, continued right up to 1914, long after the wakes had died out.[35] Their popularity was such that excursion trains were organised for those wishing to attend from outside Birmingham. Railway excursions were also available from the 1840s to beauty spots in Warwickshire, Shropshire and Wales, and later on to sea-side resorts such as Blackpool, Morecombe, Skegness and Scarborough. In the mid-years of the nineteenth century, local expeditions, termed gipsy parties, in the form of works outings to places like the Clent Hills became very common.

Four new forms of leisure activity also became very popular in Birmingham during the last decades of the nineteenth century. The first is cycling, which dates from the invention in the 1880s of the modern bicycle frame with two wheels of equal size. In 1888 Dunlop patented his pneumatic tyre, and this led to a national cycling craze in the 1890s, with an estimated more than 1.5 million cyclists, mostly among the working classes and lower-middle classes. Cycling became not merely a convenient way of getting to work, but also an excellent means of getting into the countryside for recreation. In Birmingham there developed a number of 'Clarion' cycling clubs, formed by readers of the 'Clarion', Robert Blatchford's socialist periodical, so that the pleasures of exercise in the open air (for example, on trips to Sutton Park and further afield) could be pursued in the company of fellow socialists.[36] The second form of outdoor activity is that of organised sports such as football and cricket, and especially the development of professional football and cricket. Local leagues were formed, while the Football Association was established in 1863, in 1871 the first FA competition being held; in 1872 the first international football match was played between England and Scotland. All this was made possible by the fact that Saturday afternoon had become available for sporting activities, and for attendance at Aston Villa, Birmingham City and Bromwich Albion matches. This is the beginning of mass spectatorship of sport, especially of professional football, which is a remarkable example of what was mainly a middle-class sport, dominated by middle-class officials and amateur teams, being taken over by the working classes as their favourite sport. Professional cricket has a longer previous history as a spectator (and betting) sport than football, and was played at mid-week, as well as at weekends, which necessarily limited working-class attendance. It remained very much a middle-class game, dominated by the amateur spirit, but there were still plenty of working-class supporters on Saturdays at the county cricket ground at Edgbaston from the 1880s onwards.

32. Birmingham & Midland Motor Bus, 1913.

The third new and popular working-class entertainment was the music hall, which developed from the earlier saloon theatres, this being the reason why the programme of individual turns would be presided over by a chairman, while patrons could drink as they watched the performances on the stage. By 1868 there were thirty-nine music halls in London and nine in Birmingham. The leading performers acquired national fame; their repertoire of songs appealed to working-class taste, and were often of a racy and suggestive nature. For this reason there were plenty of middle-class critics of the music hall, who deplored the deleterious effect of the music hall on the nation's youth. Certainly there were Birmingham critics of the music hall. Thus the Rev. Henry Pelham, Domestic Chaplain to the Bishop of Birmingham, spoke out strongly against their malign influence on the younger generation –[37]

> The influence of the crowd, the suggestiveness of the performance, and the spectacular appeal to his excitement or emotionalism are rotten to the very core. An occasional visit may do no great harm, but the boys usually become habitués, and it is in this that the evil lies.

Whether the Birmingham music halls had a peculiarly corrupting effect on the city's youth is not known, but it seems very unlikely.

The last great new form of indoor entertainment was the cinema. The earliest shows seem to date from 1896, and they soon became immensely popular. By 1914 Charlie Chaplin's two-reelers were great favourites, and by this date Birmingham had forty-seven picture dromes of various sizes, with seats for 33,000 in all. Three afternoon performances were provided, and two in the evening. Admission charges were very low – children could get in for a few pence. Most boys in Birmingham went to the cinema about twice a week. As the films were silent, of course, the grander cinemas would have a pianist to provide music appropiate to the action taking place on the screen. Most programmes consisted of half a dozen or so short films of a very varied nature. Arnold Freeman, writing about Birmingham youth in 1914, thought that the cinema had unquestionably become the greatest formative influence of the time on the life of the average boy. In his book Freeman supplied specimen programmes of films available in Birmingham in 1914. A typical example is as follows:[38]

THE STOLEN SYMPHONY

Bunny all at Sea   Tootles buys a Gun

MUSIC HATH CHARMS

DUPIN IN SEARCH OF QUIETNESS

HAWKEYE HAS TO HURRY!

BLUDSOE'S DILEMMA

Freeman was critical of the cinema, though he did not go so far as Pelham in his criticism of the music hall. All the same, Freeman obviously still thought that the leisure activities of the working classes should be educational and uplifting; 'rational recreation' was what was most suitable for them (as opposed, for example, to drunken brawls after closing hours). However, he was prepared to admit that there was not much that was vicious that was shown, and as simple entertainment, there was little to be said against the cinema; but he still thought that 'the higher powers of the mind are rather lulled to sleep than spurred to activity in a show which leads nothing to the reason or the imagination'.[39] Whether Freeman assessed the cinema of his day unfairly or not (to judge from the titles he gives he does not seem unduly critical), the cinema was to become enormously popular in Birmingham between the wars, and the greatest form of entertainment outside the home for the working classes.

Little else needs to be said about the great changes in the leisure interests of the working classes in Birmingham between 1850 and 1914. It is evident enough that at the root of the changes just surveyed were the increased amount of leisure time available, and the improvement in the standard of living. These changes made possible the mass attendance at Saturday afternoons at sporting events, the popularity of the music halls and cinemas, and the continued thriving trade of the public houses and beer shops. Nor must the decline in sabbatarianism be forgotten – the Sunday stroll in the local park in summer where a band might be playing (though cinemas still shut on Sundays before 1914) and the cycling excursions with the Clarion and other clubs, such as the Cycling Touring Club. Newspaper reading increased, of course, as literacy increased. In the mid-nineteenth century, the only newspapers catering directly for the working classes were the more lurid Sunday papers such as *Lloyds*, *Reynolds* and the *Illustrated Police News*. By 1914 a number of new papers had emerged, aimed directly at the skilled working man – *Tit Bits* (1881), *Answers* (1896), *The Daily Mail* (1896), the *Daily Express* (1900) and the *Daily Mirror* (1905), all aimed at the newly literate.[40] The new literacy helped, of course, the development of the trade union movement, and the participation of working-class men and women in both local and national politics. By 1914 then, much had changed in working-class leisure habits, at least for the better-paid and those in steady employment; but it was otherwise for the 'submerged tenth', and perhaps as many as a third in all below the poverty line who still lived wretched and degraded lives in the less salubrious parts of the city.

At this point we may return to the subject touched on briefly at the beginning of this chapter: the extent of class divisions in Birmingham by 1914. It goes without saying that class antagonism is difficult to assess, and to some extent is in the eye of the beholder. Certainly for the Marxist historian it must always be present in nineteenth century society – for those of this persuasion it is an article of faith, even if the working classes themselves fail to recognise the class struggle, and how far they are unjustly exploited by the ruling class. Nevertheless, it is suggested in this work that co-operation rather than class struggle was a distinctive feature of Birmingham society and of labour relations in the period 1850 to 1914. The evidence is strong for this, and it was pointed out in an earlier chapter that syndicalism was weak in Birmingham, and its pronouncements of a kind entirely unacceptable to labour leaders such as A.J. Davis. However, this is not to say that class-consciousness was not sharpened in Birmingham by 1914 as compared with 1850. In all probability the thinking man and woman were much more conscious by 1914 of being in a distinctly different class from their employers, even though some of the largest employers were noted for their philanthropy and were much respected. Changes of attitude became inevitable with the spread of socialism, the rise of the Labour Party and the emergence of collectivist ideas. However, an increase of class-consciousness does not necessarily mean an increase in class hostility. For the many Birmingham working men and women with no particular interest in politics, the major point of interest may well have been whether their employer paid a fair wage and provided good working hours and conditions. On this basis it seems fair to suggest that class awareness had very likely increased by 1914, but that labour relations remained amicable on the whole. The course of events described in the next chapter provides further evidence of class co-operation rather than class antagonism during the war years.

In conclusion, it is perhaps worth recalling a few typical glimpses of the Edwardian city before the shadows of the Great War closed in. It is a world of tarmacked streets, with gutters and proper drains, lit by gas, with elegant shop fronts in New Street and in the tree-lined Corporation Street, the latter having become the most fashionable shopping area in the city. The roads are busy with traffic, mostly horse-drawn, but there are occasional motor cars to be seen, together with tram cars and omnibuses. Policemen on their beat are a common sight, sometimes pedalling by on their bicycles. Newspaper boys with their posters carrying the latest headlines are also to be seen in all the mainstreets, and advertising billboards everywhere assault the eye in garnish profusion. Crowds throng the streets in shopping hours, especially on Saturday after-noons, the working men easily distinguishable by their cloth caps and rougher dress, the gentlemen by their top hats or hombergs, the women in bonnets or shawls. All this is familiar enough to us at the present day, thanks to the street photographs which were so popular at the time. The point to emphasise here is that it all represents a vast change from the Birmingham of 1850 with its oil street-lamps, imperfectly drained and roughly-paved or even cobbled streets, and noisome midden heaps and cesspools off the main throughfares. Only in the slum areas of the central city in 1914 could one catch glimpses of the old world of the nineteenth century. Much progress had been made since 1850 in the making of the modern second city; but much more remained to be done between the wars.

Chapter Seven
The Great War, 1914-1918

In common with all industrial cities during the First World War, life in Birmingham suffered from the strains imposed by the demands for manpower in the armed forces and by the equally strong demands for maximum war production. The government struggled throughout the war to maintain a balance between these two demands, but as early as March 1916 it was forced to introduce conscription, which by 1918 was extended to men up to the age of fifty-one. Conscription, of course, was unprecented, and it raised issues of exemption from service, either on grounds of conscience or because of essential work on war supplies. Even before this, the trade unions had entered into stronger relationships with the government because their co-operation was vital for maximum output of munitions. After conscription, their support was even more important in deciding who served in the forces and who stayed in industry; and from the beginning they had agreed to forgo strikes and to accept dilution by unskilled labour and particularly female labour. Naturally then, in addition to the enormous demands for service in the forces, all industrial towns found their industries geared to the needs of war production, and all experienced considerable advances in the authority and influence of the trade unions. How then did Birmingham respond to the challenges presented by the four years of war?

To take military service first: the earliest Birmingham men to serve in France were the Reservists and Territorials who were called up at the outbreak of war, followed by volunteers who flocked to the Colours, including three City Battalions raised by the Lord Mayor, Sir William Bowater. By early 1915, recruitment had tailed off to less than a hundred a week after the first initial rush to join up, but the numbers recovered to a weekly total of more than six hundred, following the Lord Mayor's appeal for recruits in May 1915. By the end of the war, Birmingham had contributed at least 148,000 men to the armed forces, this figure representing about 54% of men of military age in the city. More than 11,000 Birmingham men were killed serving their country, and their names are recorded on the city's Roll of Honour in the Hall of Memory, erected in 1925, which stands in front of Baskerville House. The roll of men killed is one of the longest in the country, and eleven men in all were awarded the Victoria Cross.[1] Birmingham may well take a just pride in its contribution in this respect to winning the war. We will return to Birmingham's military record at the end of this chapter.

To turn now to industrial production: according to Professor G.C. Allen, the major effect of the war on Birmingham industry was to speed up changes which had already been taking place more slowly before 1914. The principal change took the form of an increase in size of the average work unit, especially where the plant was easily adapted to war production: Austins at Longbridge, for example, were well placed in this respect and they expanded enormously, employing about 20,000 workers by the end of 1918. Some minor trades also benefitted from the demands for war production, such as saddlery, harness, sword and bedstead manufacture. A few trades suffered as a result of the war, such as the jewellery trade, while the sporting gun trade was seriously affected, its rudimentary mechanical equipment not being suitable for mass production; glass manufacture, on the other hand, benefitted from the removal of foreign competition, particularly from Germany.[2]

At first, before the extent of the demand for munitions was fully grasped, there was actually a period of trade depression, with short-time working in some factories, for example, at the Metropolitan Waggon Works. At the time, there was also some discussion of the opportunities suddenly made available to seize German markets, but by the beginning of 1915 it had become obvious that Birmingham would have to concentrate on production for war purposes – shells, fuses, small arms ammunition and so on – and also to employ more unskilled labour, especially women. A local co-ordinating Munitions Committee was set up in 1915 which established the National Shell Factory at Washwood Heath, and the second half of that year saw a great drive to increase production of fuses, shells, Lewis guns and Mills bombs (which were invented in the city). The production figures achieved were quite remarkable: between May 1915 and the end of the war, 15 million finished shells were produced in the district.[3] The production figures for individual firms are equally impressive. Kynock's, for example, were contracted to supply each week 24 million rifle cartridges, 300,000 revolver cartridges, 110,000 18-pounder brass cases, and 300 tons of cordite. In 1918, their output of rifle cartridges rose to nearly 30 million a week. At the BSA works, the pre-1914 average weekly output of 135 rifles was raised to 10,000 rifles, and the weekly output of Lewis guns went up from 50 to 2,000 a week by 1918. In all, 145,397 complete Lewis guns were produced. The Vickers subsidiary, Wolseley Motors, manufactured over 4,000 cars for war purposes, 4,500 aero engines and 700 complete aeroplanes. Austin's labour force was about 2,800 in 1914; as already mentioned, it went up to 20,000 by 1918. A special railway station was constructed on site and was used by 10,000 every morning, and 20,000 meals were served in the canteens every twenty-four hours.[4] As Sir John French was reported as saying in 1915, 'The issue is a struggle between Krupps and Birmingham'[5] – a striking testimony to the city's importance as a centre for the manufacture of munitions.

All this could not have been achieved without the active co-operation of the trade unions in Birmingham. At first, just before war was declared, the unions were actually alarmed at the appoach of war, and two well-attended meetings were held in protest in the Bull Ring, but the invasion of Belgium by Germany – a clear breech, it was thought, of international law and an attack on a country whose neutrality Britain was pledged to maintain – soon changed attitudes. Only the Independent Labour Party in Birmingham continued to oppose the war.[6] From then on, majority opinion among Birmingham trade unionists was strongly pro-war, at least until the last year of hostilities. The willingness of trade unionists nationally to support the war effort was demonstrated by the Shells and Fuses Agreement of March, 1915, and the Treasury Agreement reached shortly after at a conference held at the Treasury, whereby trade unions engaged on war work agreed to give up the right to strike for the duration, disputes were to go to arbitration, trade union restrictions on output were suspended, and no worker was to leave a job in munitions without a certificate of consent from his employer. All this was put into statutory form by the Munitions of War Act, 1915.[7]

In Birmingham, the pro-war faction among trade unionists found a strong leader in Edward Hallas, secretary of the Municipal Employees Association in 1914. From 1915 onwards, Hallas was joint secretary of the Amalgamated Society of Gas, Municipal and General Labourers. He and John

Beard, of the Workers' Union (another general, non-craft union) actively supported recruiting, which was still opposed in Birmingham by the small but active Independent Labour Party. In fact, both wings, right and left, of the trade union movement in Birmingham disliked conscription in principle because it was feared that it might lead to industrial conscription; and when the bill was introduced into parliament in January 1916, the Trades Council was split over the issue, and a motion condemning conscription, moved by Councillor Kneeshaw (a member of the ILP), was carried in the Trades Council. However, once the bill became law as the first Military Service Act in March 1916, there was no turning back; and the Amalgamated Society of Engineers and the smaller skilled unions were mollified by the introduction of the Trades Card Scheme in November 1916. By this scheme, skilled men could be given exemption cards, issued through their unions, which protected them from military call-up. It constituted a significant acknowledgement of the importance of the craft unions, but was an inefficient and indeed doubtful mode of control of the labour market. In the spring of 1917, under further pressure to provide more troops, the scheme was abolished by the government, who replaced it by a Schedule of Protected Occupations which tightened up the criteria for claiming exemption.[8]

The first three or so years of war therefore saw the Birmingham trade union movement growing stronger, especially in the membership of new general unions such as the Workers Union. Nor was its influence in Birmingham confined to its role in improving war production. Increasingly the trade unions were seen as speaking on behalf of the whole working community, and not merely members of trade organisations. This is shown in the setting-up of the Birmingham Citizens Committee on which the unions had representatives (including the veteran W.J. Davis). The committee was supported by forty district committees, all of which also had TU representation. After the introduction of the Rents Restriction Act in December 1915, freezing house rents, the Trades Council publicised and explained the act, advising tenants of their rights and supporting them in court. By the end of the war, there were fifteen tenant associations, with about 20,000 members. By 1916 the Trades Council was investigating food prices, and in October of that year estimated that they had risen by 71%.[9]

Meanwhile, on the national scene, the labour movement was achieving increased importance. In 1915, Arthur Henderson, the secretary of the Labour Party, joined the coalition government as President of the Board of Education and unoffical adviser on labour matters, while William Bruce, a miner, became an under-secretary, and G.H. Roberts, a printer, became a government whip. When Lloyd George became Prime Minister in December 1916, Henderson was promoted to be a member of the small inner war cabinet, John Hodge of the steel workers became Minister of Labour, and George Barnes of the engineers became Minister of Pensions. This represented extraordinary progress for a small party which had formed its parliamentary party only ten years previously.[10] Thus, the trade union movement was acquiring an enhanced status not only in Birmingham but also nationally in the affairs of the nation.

However, it must not be thought that relations between the leading unions in Birmingham were always cordial in nature.[11] The principal union in terms of age and prestige was the Amalgamated Society of Engineers (ASE), and although Lloyd George readily acknowledged it was an 'engineer's war' (and there is no doubt that engineering was Birmingham's biggest industry by 1914), nevertheless the ASE did not have things all its own way. Admittedly, as a well-established craft union, the ASE had to be treated with respect, and it has already been mentioned that the Trade Cards conferring immunity from conscription were issued for a time through the ASE – a considerable acknowledgement of the union's importance. The problem was that the fast-growing general union, the Workers Union, was the most powerful of all the general unions, and had twice the membership of the ASE by 1918. Further, it had as members many unskilled and semi-skilled workers in engineering, including a good number of women. Engineering as a trade was changing even before the war, as noted in a previous chapter, because the increased use of machine tools permitted the employment of more semi-skilled workers and feminine labour. Thus, there were some grounds for friction, especially over the ASE's near-monopoly of the issue of trade cards. Moreover, the Workers Union regarded the ASE's jealously guarded rights as a craft union to be selfish, unpatriotic and contrary to the workers' real interests. In March 1917 the general unions threatened strike action if the use of the trade cards was not extended or abolished altogether (they were done away with in April 1917). In general terms, the Workers Union and other general unions believed in democratic and evolutionary methods, and co-operation with employers to achieve high wages and improved conditions. Ultimately they believed that war collectivism was a development to be welcomed, a sort of quasi-socialism, and that increased control of industry by the workers would come through state nationalisation.[12]

By 1917 political opinions in the labour movement nationally began to change. The stalement on the Western Front, continuing heavy casualties, the two Russian revolutions in 1917, long hours of work and (very important on the Home Front) the high cost of food all contributed to this. A number of Commissions of Enquiry into Industrial Unrest in June 1917 placed considerable emphasis on this. Thus, the report on conditions in the north-east stated that –[13]

> The high prices of staple commodities have undoubtedly laid a severe strain on the majority
> of the working classes, and in some instances have resulted in hardship and actual starvation.

This report went on to concede that improved wages could compensate for increased food prices, but there were some workers whose wages had risen only slightly, or had even diminished.

There seems little evidence to show that the high cost of food was a major cause of dissatisfaction in Birmingham (wages figures will be given later in this chapter), but undoubtedly there was increasing anxiety about the apparent lack of military progress at the time. This is shown most clearly by the growth of left-wing attitudes in the Trades Council. In January 1917 the pro-war president, George Stanway, was defeated in a Trades Council election by an anti-war opponent, F.W. Rutland, by sixty-three votes to fifty-four.[14] The Trades Council became increasingly anti-war in attitude until Hallas accused it of being 'captured and exploited by the pacifist ILP section'. A number of pro-war representatives thereupon resigned from the Council in April 1917. By July 1918 feelings were high enough for Hallas, Beard, Davis and others to set up a new Trades Union Industrial Council for Birmingham, designed to work on non-political lines. Hallas and Davis even supported a national effort to set up a Trade Union Labour Party, the intention being to replace the existing Labour Party which it was thought had become too political with its new constitution and its Statement of War Aims. Both proposals – for a substitute Trades Council and a new Labour Party – died the death.[15]

In surveying the role played by the unions in Birmingham during the Great War, a number of interesting points emerge. The first is that as the government was forced to co-operate more and more with the national labour movement in the interests of war production, so in Birmingham it seems that the needs of the community helped to change local TU representatives from speaking for a minority of organised workers to being spokesmen for the whole working-class community on issues such as rents, pensions, war allowances and the like. This constituted an important extension of power and influence. Secondly, although the ASE remained a formidable union, it was already weakened by 1914 and subsequently by changes in the engineering industry which brought in many semi-skilled workers who could be recruits for the Workers Union as much as for the ASE. Thirdly, the support of the Workers Union (and of other general unions) for war production and their opposition to the engineers' attempts to preserve their traditional rights and privileges, helped to maintain the good relations with employers which were so prominent a feature of the industrial scene before the war. Asa Briggs has commented that there was little loss of production due to strikes or lock-outs in Birmingham during the war. This is largely true, though not entirely so: there were strikes at Longbridge in January 1918 (12,000 men out over alleged victimisation), in the following May (4,000 out over cuts in bonus pay), and two strikes in July 1918 (again over bonus pay and proposed limitation of numbers of skilled men employed). These strikes were no doubt part of the war weariness which characterised the last year of the war, and perhaps some indication of the growing radicalism of the rank and file. This had manifested itself to a minor degree in the unofficial shop steward movement, but this movement did not develop to any degree in the Birmingham area, and died away after the war. The tradition of good labour relationships remained largely intact when Armistice Day came at last on 11 November 1918, though it is clear that the trade unions were emerging as a new force on the political scene. In the 1918 General Election the Labour Party won fifty-seven seats and gained 2 million votes as compared with less than half a million in the last General Election in December 1910.

What of women workers in Birmingham during the Great War? It is common knowledge that women were called upon to fill the many vacancies resulting from the demand for male recruits. In Birmingham, of course, women were already employed in industry before the war, even in the engineering industry as the use of automatic or semi-automatic machinery increased; they worked on capstan, press, milling, drilling, grinding, polishing, screwing and gear-cutting machines. Opportunites for such work before the war had increased with the development of the new industries of cycle and motor car manufacture, the electrical and rubber industries. In addition, women were employed extensively in outwork of various kinds, in clothing, domestic service and retailing. Most working-class girls went into factory work when they left school, and even after marriage, 19% of married women worked, 70% of them in factories on light press work.[16] Following the outbreak of war, demand grew for a vast increase in the already considerable numbers of women engaged in

Birmingham industry. Some indication of the additional numbers of women employed nationally, especially in the metal and chemical industries and in government establishments, may be gained from the following table:[17]

Industry	July 1914	November 1918
Metal industries	170,000	596,000
Chemical industries	40,000	103,000
Textiles	863,000	818,000
Clothing	612,000	557,000
Paper	148,000	141,000
Government establishments	2,200	246,000
Total industries	*1,835,200*	*2,461,000*
Transport	18,000	115,000
Total	*1,853,000*	*2,576,000*

In Birmingham, the greatly increased demand for labour attracted women from afar, and it is estimated that about 15,000 women came into the city, some from as far away as Orkney and Jersey.[18] This increased the housing problems in the city, and a special clearing house for munitions workers was opened up, St Mary's Hostel. Much of the work in munitions was of a kind previously performed by women before the war, but they were also employed as welders, core-makers, shapers, solderers, metallurgists, wood-workers and works chemists. In transport, women worked as ticket collectors, conductors, van drivers, carriage cleaners and repair-shop labourers. In public utilities they worked as scavengers and road sweepers, postwomen and sorters, and as general labourers in gas and electrical works. Transport was the first to use female labour, though they were not given the responsibility of driving trams.[19] Work on the trams and railways was popular since it was paid at the same rate as men. This was exceptional, in that women's rates before the war were usually half or less than half the rates for men. By 1917 it was estimated that girls were earning three times what they would have earned in 1913,[20] though the cost of living about doubled by the end of the war. In munitions, women were first paid £1 per week, but by 1918 were earning not less than 6d an hour, with a minimum of 24s a week (some were earning much more than this). Many awards were made by a special arbitration tribunal. By way of comparison, the National Award for skilled men on munitions was 46s per week, plus 16s 6d, plus 12.5% or 7.5%, by the end of 1918. Even the unskilled labourer, who pre-war was on 23s per week, was paid 36s plus 26s 6d, plus 12.5% at the end of the war.[21]

The attitude of the unions to the employment of women is interesting, and varied from union to union. Generally speaking, the craft unions maintained their hostility to female labour, and would not admit female members. The Workers Union and the Amalgamated Society of Gas, Municipal and General Workers were rather more liberal in attitude, and the WU in particular had a famous women's organiser in Julia Varley, who set up the first Domestic Servants Union in Birmingham.[22] Varley had left the National Federation of Women Workers (a small organisation in numbers) because she thought women should organise with men, not separately.

What were the results in Birmingham of all this massive influx of women workers into industry, transport and office work? It is often assumed that women's war work made possible a great step forward in the story of female emancipation. It is certainly true that towards the end of the war there was a growing awareness of the important contribution made by women to the war effort, not only in industry, but in nursing, office work, and in voluntary work. In Birmingham, for example, much voluntary work had been undertaken by women in the Women's Voluntary Reserve (established in 1915), in ambulance work, in serving in canteens and in providing comforts for the troops; the Lady Mayoress' Depot had organised clothing for the troops and other comforts on a considerable scale. The need was felt to acknowledge this by some public gesture. The most obvious way of doing this was to give women the vote as demanded by the pre-war suffragette movement, and this was done by the Representation of the People Act, 1918 which gave votes to all women of thirty or over provided they or their husbands possessed the minor local government property qualification necessary to vote in local government elections. Moreover, the Sex Disqualification (Removal) Act, 1919, provided that women might now serve on juries or become magistrates, and become members of most professions save that of minister of the Church of England or member of the Stock Exchange. In 1919 Lady Astor took her seat in the Commons as the first woman MP. The vote would have been given at the age of twenty-one (the male age for the franchise) but for the fact that women voters would then have out-numbered the male voters, and this was thought inappropiate.[23]

However, these advances must be seen in perspective. Votes for women came in the wake of the pre-war suffragette movement, and might have been granted before 1914 but for the hostility roused by the violent tactics of some suffragettes. Further, the 1918 Act owed as much to the need to extend the male franchise as to the need to give votes to women. This was because before the war only two-thirds of the male adult population had the vote, and during the war, residence qualifications were lost due to service abroad. The voting registers were hopelessly out-of-date due to this (and to the deaths of so many men in action) so that it was urgent to modernise the male franchise by basing it on a simple residence qualification. As for the provision of the Sex Disqualification (Removal) Act, this was important for middle-class women, but had very little relevance for working-class women, of whom the vast majority had to give up their jobs as the munitions factories closed down, and the men returned from the trenches to resume civilian employment.[24]

So what were the major results of the war for the women workers of Birmingham? Those of thirty or over had gained the vote (extended in 1928 to women aged twenty-one and over), but for many except the small minority interested in politics it was not a matter of great significance, especially if they had been widowed during the war, and had to face the responsibility of bringing up a family without a father. Many had earned good money during the war (though admittedly working long hours and seldom for equal pay). Rather more jobs became available in offices, and the general employment of women secretaries, typists and clerks in banks, the civil service, insurance and local government became common, although lower middle-class women were often preferred for these jobs. For those who had had responsible posts in industry during the war it could be that they had gained more self-confidence and had become more independent in outlook. This was commented on during the war, and it was observed that women smoked more in public, visited public houses more openly and went out alone more often (the illegitimacy rate went up by 30% by the end of the war). Nevertheless, the end of hostilities must have brought hard times for younger girls who had earned good money on munitions and were now out of a job. According to the *Daily Sketch* on 30 December 1918 –[25]

> Everyone agrees that the splendid army of munition girls, their contribution to winning the war completed, have a very strong claim... In Birmingham there are at least 7,000 who have signed the Unemployment books at the Labour Exchange. What is to become of these girls? The large number of girls thrown onto the labour market is not likely to solve the domestic servant problem. Wages are too low, but the chief factor which sets the girls against domestic service is what they regard as their loss of freedom.

The *Daily Sketch* was probably right in emphasising the loss of freedom felt by some at the prospect of domestic service; and the numbers of domestic servants certainly showed a significant decline after the war. Nevertheless, traditional attitudes remained strong after 1918, and among them was the belief that a woman's place was in the home as a wife and mother. Married women were expected to give up work when starting their families, and thereafter to remain in the home. The economic and social advances enjoyed by them during the Great War were therefore more limited in nature than might at first appear.

What part was played by Birmingham Corporation during the war? In general terms, the Corporation provided whole-hearted support for the war effort throughout. It has already been mentioned that successive Lord Mayors encouraged voluntary enlistment, and Sir William Bowater not only raised money for war purposes, but also founded the three city battalions. Nearly 7,000 municipal employees joined the services, of whom just under 800 were killed. More and more men in uniform were to be seen about the city, while New Street Station saw the arrival of wounded soldiers en route for hospitalisation at the University of Birmingham campus at Edgbaston.[26] There the Great Hall and other parts of the Aston Webb building were taken over by the military authorities for use as the First Southern Hospital, which became the centre for forty-seven other military hospitals. By November 1918 the hospital at the university provided 3,293 beds in all and had over-flowed into marquees in the grounds. Altogether the hospital handled about 64,000 casualties.[27] On the walls of the Entrance Hall to the Great Hall there are inscribed the names of members of the university who fell in both World Wars,[28] while over the doors to the Great Hall itself is a sombre inscription which reads –

> From August 1914 to April 1919 these buildings were used by the military authorities as the 1st Southern Hospital. Within these walls men died for their country. Let those who come after live in the same service.

However, one great difference between the two World Wars as experienced in Birmingham was the absence of air raid casualities in the first war. There were only three Zeppelin attacks, the first coming in January 1916, when lighting restrictions were in place; no damage was done, and the airships went on to raid the Black Country. The second raid was in 1917 when there

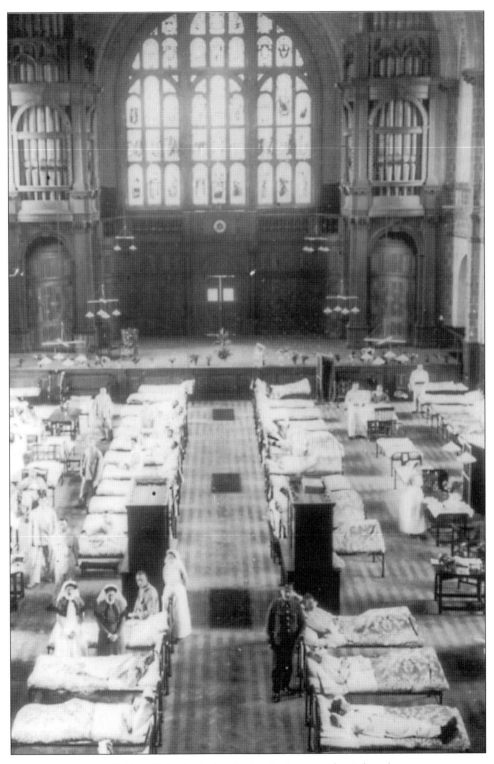

33. Great Hall, Birmingham University, in use as a hospital ward.

was another attack by a Zeppelin. Again, no damage was done in the city itself, though bombs were dropped on Longbridge, where rather remarkably the works were brightly lit. A third attack was made by five Zeppelins in April 1918, which apparently was designed as an attempt to bomb a number of targets in the Midlands. The airships were strongly attacked by anti-aircraft fire, and they dropped their bombs harmlessly in open countryside. Birmingham was still out of range for the German Gotha bombers which had attacked London and southern towns earlier on.[29]

Air-raid precautions were therefore not a major part of the Corporation's responsibilities in the First World War, though the high price of foodstuffs by 1917 gave it increasing concern. The Corporation therefore set up a Food Committee in May 1917, and introduced food cards to be used on a voluntary basis and as an encouragement to food economy. In August 1917, the Food Committee became the official Food Control Committee which issued ration cards at first for sugar, and then in December for tea, butter and margarine. In July 1918 the government introduced uniform, national ration books, and Birmingham issued 870,885 of these books. The government's scheme was closely modelled on Birmingham's experimental scheme of December 1917, so that Birmingham may be said to have led the way in food rationing.[30]

The Corporation was also concerned at the shortages in the supply of coal. In 1916 the Lord Mayor, Neville Chamberlain, set up a Corporation Coal Purchase Committee, setting aside emergency supplies of coal, and in the cold spring of April 1917, 600 tons of this reserve stock were distributed to coal yards. In 1918 the City Council established a further Fuel Committee which drew up registers of all coal dealers and coal consumers; drawing up these lists was a lengthy task, and necessitated the employment of 200 officials. During the hard winter of 1918, the Committee had to issue special permits for emergency supplies of coal.[31] Coal was therefore in very short supply, but the system of food rationing was relatively light as compared with the strict system introduced during the Second World War as early as the spring of 1940.

One other area of Corporation civic responsibility must be explored, and this is education. As the result of the Education Act, 1902, Birmingham became responsible as the second largest local education authority for a widespread network of elementary schools. It is often too readily assumed that there was a marked increase in early leaving from elementary schools during the war because of the shortage of labour. Indeed, the President of the Board of Education, H.A.L. Fisher, stated categorically in the House of Commons in August 1917 that 600,000 children had been withdrawn prematurely from school and were engaged in industry;[32] but what he failed to make clear is whether any of these early leavers had left illegally before the minimum leaving age of twelve, or subsequently between twelve and fourteen, when it was possible to leave early quite legitimately, for a variety of reasons. In fact, before the war, about half of the age range appears to have left school before fourteen. In Birmingham, early leaving never seems to have been a serious problem. It is true that prosecutions of parents for non-attendance rose from 2,818 in 1915 to 4,706 in 1917, but in 1918 they fell to 4,202. Prosecutions of employers for the illegal employment of children numbered 325 in 1915, then 196 in 1916, ninety-three in 1917, and only four in 1918. Presumably employers had learned their lesson by 1918 (or the authorities had become progressively more lenient). Whatever the truth of the matter here, attendance figures in the war years in Birmingham elementary schools remained over 87%, and the number of twelve and thirteen year olds in them actually increased slightly between 1914 and 1918. There is little to show that early leaving was much of a problem, though the temptation to do so obviously existed in a great industrial city where there was a heavy demand for labour. The Birmigham Education Committee stood firm on the issue. When a Memorial from Employers and Parents was presented to them in 1916, urging that the school leaving age be reduced for the duration, it was rejected, it being pointed out that a child between twelve and fourteen could work full-time only if he passed the Labour Examination in Standard VII and obtained a Labour Certificate. If his employment was under the Factory and Workshop Acts, he had to be thirteen before being employed full-time. If employment was to be in farming, the farmer had to be able to show that he could not obtain other labour owing to the war, whereupon the Committee might permit full-time work between thirteen and fourteen provided they were satisfied as to conditions of work.[33]

However, there were some shortages of teaching staff. The number of Birmingham teachers serving in the forces on 31 December 1916 was 426, together with 103 local government officers in the Education Department, and fifty-six caretakers.[34] By the end of the war, the total number of Education Department employees who served in the war was 757; at a guess, about 500 of these were teachers.[35] The majority of these would have been elementary school teachers. Given the fact that there were 189 elementary schools in Birmingham in 1918, the average number of vacancies to be filled during the war would have been between two and three per school. These vacancies would have caused inconvenience, of course, dependent on the size of the school; larger schools with bigger staffs had greater flexibility in timetabling. The shortages were of young male teachers, though women who had retired on marriage could be brought back into the schools, as were retired male teachers and even occasionally disabled ex-servicemen. Towards the end of 1915, it was decided to ask headmasters with an average atten-dance of not more than 350 pupils to take a class while the war lasted. The peripatetic science staff was also re-arranged.[36] All in all, there were clearly some problems arising from the shortage of young male teachers, but they hardly appear insurmountable.

Other problems arising from war conditions were the cessation of all new school building and the cuts in the school medical and dental services. Certainly some schools were overcrowded, and addi-tional buildings were required. In Birmingham there was a shortage of elementary school accom-modation before the war, so that permission had to be given for classes to be taught in the school hall in a number of schools.[37] Although reductions in the school medical services were made necessary nationally due to the high demand for doctors and dentists in the military hospitals, these cuts were not very large, and the Board of Education went so far as to observe that the work of medical treatment was well maintained in some places, and even developed. In 1917-18 about 70% of normal numbers nationally were inspected.[38] Birmingham was one of the LEAs where medical services were maintained at a good level and actually improved. Dental treatment for 6-8 year olds had started in early 1913 and tonsil operations in October of the same year, these operations being performed three times a week. Unlike other authorities, Birmingham kept the children overnight after the operation and brought them back three weeks later for breathing exercises.[39] Spectacles were prescribed, and X-ray treatment given for ringworm. Inspections for vermin continued, though on a reduced scale;

34. Birmingham University Guild of Undergraduates Committee, 1919-20.

nevertheless prosecutions rose from 309 in 1915 to 628 in 1917.[40] Such was the Birmingham record that it was commended in the Annual Report of the Chief Medical Officer of the Board of Education in 1917. Moreover, after the war in 1924, the Education Committee thought that it was probably true that there had been greater progress in the school medical service during the previous ten years than in any other branch of the Committee's activities.[41]

Another concern of the Education Committee was the play centre scheme, which was based on the centres in London organised by the well-known novelist Mrs Humphrey Ward. The aim of these centres was to keep the children off the streets and to reduce the level of juvenile crime which had risen during the war. The causes of this increase in crime were ascribed to the absence of fathers on military service and also of mothers engaged on war work. In January 1917 the Board of Education issued Circular 980 which authorised grants of up to half the cost of maintaining the centres.[42] In Birmingham the idea was taken seriously, and it was planned to open five centres in schools on 1 October 1917, while the Birmingham Street Children's Union proposed to open no less than forty-five Junior Clubs on the lines of play centres, mostly on their own premises. Rooms were made available to this body by the Education Committee in an additional nine schools.[43] It is not clear when these centres closed down, though one source claims that they went on till 16 April 1919, after a most successful session, with average attendance of 230 in each of the mixed centres, and 120 in the others (there were ten centres in all, opening two evenings a week, by the time the centres were disbanded).[44]

Towards the end of the war, in an effort to improve existing educational services, the government drew up an education bill which in its original form was opposed by the local authorities, but in a revised form became the Education Act, 1918 (commonly known as the Fisher Act). The Bill is generally regarded as disappointing in that its provisions were seriously damaged by the economy cuts of the early 1920s. Birmingham was initially affected by two reforms introduced by the act. The first is that the system of part-time attendance between the ages of twelve and fourteeen, common enough in Lancashire and Yorkshire, was henceforth abolished. The school leaving age was to be fourteen without exception, with a further raising of the age to fifteen when it was considered appropiate to do so. In fact, in Birmingham the part-time system did not operate at all, and any other form of early leaving by the Labour Certificate was very limited. Indeed, it was thought that the abolition of all leaving before the age of fourteen would not increase school rolls to any noticeable extent, so that it would not be necessary to appoint any additional staff.[45]

The second major and potentially far-reaching reform in the Fisher Act was the requirement that day continuation schools should be set up for part-time schooling between the ages of fourteen and sixteen. This proposal clearly required considerable planning and expense on the part of local authority educational authorities, and indeed the Birmingham Education Committee did begin preparations for implementing this part of the act, but the idea was abandoned once the cuts in government expenditure were made in 1922 (the Geddes Axe, named after the chairman of the committee recommending the cuts). However, one further section of the Act should be noted: all local educational authorities were to survey the educational needs of their areas, and prepare a scheme to meet those needs. Birmingham's 1920 Plan thus provides a useful survey of existing educational facilities, and was the springboard for a limited extension of the number of secondary schools between the wars.

What other municipal services were provided by Birmingham Corporation during the war? Strong support was given to voluntary recruitment, as already noted, but from 1916 onwards conscription necessitated the setting-up of tribunals which heard appeals against call-up. 90,721 cases were heard, 34,760 appeals failed, and 7,749 were given exemption certificates. In the last year of the war, there was a further combing-out of men under twenty-three in protected occupations, the result being that nationwide, the munitions industry lost 104,000 men in six months.[46] Because of the food shortage, the Corporation encouraged the growing of more food. By 1918, about 1200 acres had been made available in the City for this purpose. Even though Birmingham was a heavily industrialised city, it had two recruitment committees for the Women's Land Army. By 1918 the Warwickshire total of land girls was 173, though the numbers in Greater Birmingham were only nineteen.[47] In September 1916 a Municipal Bank (the first of its kind in the country) was established, the idea being to encouraged working-class savings, and to give loans to the government. In July 1919 the bank was put on a permanent footing by an Act of Parliament.[48] Lastly, the Gas Department of the Corporation pioneered a number of useful technical advances. Toluol was produced for high explosives, chrome steel was developed as a substitute for rare tungsten, and a new tube furnace constructed for hardening metals. The Technical College was also used for training munitions operatives.[49]

When the war ended in November 1918, central parts of the city remained much as they were when the war began in August 1914. There had been no damage due to air raids. The major immediate differences which might strike the observant visitor would probably be the number of men to be seen in uniform (or possibly in hospital blue) and the number of women doing men's jobs on the buses, trams and elsewhere. Otherwise things looked more or less the same as in 1914. In the industrial areas, the main impression might well have been of the sheer size of some of the works, the numbers of workers employed (including women), and the pace of work in the long working day. In sum, dramatic changes in the busy life and appearance of the city were not really apparent, unlike the battered look of the city after the air raids of the Second World War; but real and indeed striking changes had taken place in the lives of many of Birmingham's citizens.

At this point we may return to the subject dealt with at the beginning of this chapter, namely, Birmingham's military contribution to fighting the war. The figure of 11,000 killed in battle many not seem a large proportion of the total national deaths of 750,000, but it must be remembered that many of the Birmingham dead were married and had children. Nationally, 300,000 children lost their fathers during the war, and 160,000 wives lost their husbands,[50] so that grief over the death of loved ones was not confined to parents of young men, but extended also to wives and children. Moreover, many widows were faced with the task of bringing up children on meagre widows' pensions (and on unequal pay when they could find work). We should therefore not underestimate the grief of those who lost relatives , or the often grim experiences of those who served and survived. It is worth emphasising that the Great War was a traumatic experience for the nation as a whole, and also among Birmingham people – a war which was not over by Christmas, and dragged on for four years with ever-mounting (and quite unprecedented) casualities. Hitherto Britain had a very large navy and a small army; never before had the whole nation's manhood been called up to serve in the army. The consequences were shocking. Children growing up between the wars could not fail to be aware that even though Germany had been defeated, the war had been some kind of a national catastrophe – every year they were reminded of the war by the Two Minutes Silence on 11 November, the wreaths of poppies and the war memorials in parks, public places and schools. Some of the children's teachers bore visible scars of military service. Enoch Powell entered King Edward's High School in 1925, and there observed the effect that the war had had on some of the masters who served in the trenches. His biographer has commented that Powell, a highly sensitive and intelligent man, felt a shadow being cast over him and his generation, with the memory of the war saturating everyday life.[51] Powell was not alone in sensing the psychological damage resulting from the war; it had been a dreadful business, its after-effects going far beyond the physical suffering of those who fought in it. Some in Birmingham had actually profited from the war, of course, especially manufacturers of munitions, but rarely those who had served at the Front in what C.E. Montague was afterwards to call the life of 'mud, stench, and underground gloom'.[52]

CHAPTER EIGHT

BETWEEN THE WARS, 1918-1939

In the memory of many of those who grew up in Britain between the two World Wars, two characteristics of life at the time loom large – unemployment and the approach to war at the end of
the period. Unemployment in itself was nothing new; it had been serious enough (as we have
seen) in the 1870s and 1880s for the term 'The Great Depression' to have been coined. It led to
the word 'unemployment' coming into common usage for the first time; but between the wars,
unemployment became so widespread that the term 'Great Depression' was again used to
describe economic conditions, especially in the early 1930s. After a brief post-war boom in 1919
and 1920, trade declined markedly, unemployment climbing to over a million in 1921. Thereafter
there was some recovery in the later 1920s, but following the Wall Street crash in 1929, the
number out of work climbed to new heights in the early 1930s, reaching over 3 million. It was
still over a million in 1939. The worst affected industries were the so-called staple industries
(textiles, coal, iron and steel, and shipbuilding). The social consequences of unemployment on
such a scale could be devastating. J.B. Priestley described the unemployed men and women
whom he met in Stockton on Tees in 1933, victims of the depression in ship-building –[1]

> ...middle-aged men who looked like old men, sucking their empty pipes and staring at
> nothing, and grey-faced women remembering new clothes and good meals and holidays and
> fun as if they had once lived in another and better world.

Birmingham between the wars remained a great industrial city, of course, but it could hardly
escape entirely the effects of the great national depression in trade which was particularly severe
in the 1930s. However, it had the good fortune not to have the basic staple industries at the basis
of its economy. Moreover, it had a number of newer industries which have been described in
Chapter Two, and these were all expanding in the inter-war period. As a result, Birmingham
suffered far less from the slump between the wars than other industrial towns. In the pages which
follow it is proposed to describe and discuss first the development of industry, then working and
living conditions, and then finally the major changes in leisure activities.

At the outset it should be noted that the boundaries of the city remained largely unchanged
between the wars, though by the Birmingham Extension Act, 1927, the central part of the Urban
District of Perry Barr was brought within the city, while in 1931 certain parts of Castle Bromwich
and Sheldon were acquired.[2] Thus, the pre-war Greater Birmingham was not further enlarged to
any great extent, and the main areas of industry were still the same in the inter-war years. The most
striking change in the location of industry was the industrialisation of the valley of the Tame from
Perry Barr in the west to Bromford and Castle Bromwich in the east. Otherwise industry
continued to grow in the well-established central areas, and at Hay Mills, Kings Norton and at

Longbridge.[3] One indication of the relative prosperity of Birmingham's industry is the increase in the city's population between the wars – a net growth rate of about 38%, which was greater than in any other provincial city in the years since 1911. By 1938 the population was estimated at 1,048,000, of whom the working-class population constituted about 86%, or 901,303.[4] There was some movement from the city in the early 1920s and again in the early 1930s (times of relatively short-lived trade depression) but these were more than counter-balanced by a strong inward movement after 1935 and by the natural growth of population.[5]

As for the fundamental nature of industry itself, it continued to be based very largely on the processing of metal. In 1931 it was estimated that 31.7% of all those in industry, trade and commerce worked in the metal trades.[6] Some of the older industries declined between the wars, notably the gun trade, which dropped from 2% of the occupied population to less than 0.5%; jewellery also declined, from 5% to 1.5%. Metal work and engineering, on the other hand, increased its share of the workforce from 35% in 1881 to 45% in 1951.[7] The important new industries which had grown up before 1914 continued to increase after 1918 – the motor industry, electrical engineering, rubber goods (especially tyres), aluminium, plastics and hollowware. Some of the plants which had expanded during the war grew still further when peace returned. For example, Austins at Longbridge employed 23,000 by 1937 and Cadbury's at Bournville employed 10,000 by 1927.[8] This raises the obvious question of how far Birmingham industry as a whole had gone over to large-scale production, having finally abandoned production in the traditional small workshops of the town. At first, this seems actually what did happen. Dr Barbara Smith gives the following numbers of factories and workshops in Birmingham which appear to illustrate the process –

Numbers of Factories and Workshops in Birmingham

	1895	1931	1951
Factories	3,321	5,856	7,877
Workshops	4,868	2,545	727

Dr Smith goes on to say that by 1927 there were many Birmingham concerns employing several thousand workers, and that the average size had increased in every trade except those in decline. Only a small proportion of very small plants survived by 1949, giving the 'satisfying illusion to many that Birmingham was still the home of the small firm'.[9] Further, Professor Briggs says that in the 1930s there were many Birmingham factories employing thousands of people.[10]

However, both these authorities appear to have overlooked the fact that between the wars workshops were re-defined as workplaces *without power*. Yet by the 1930s relatively few workshops were without electrical power, and most workshops were re-classified as factories. The truth of the matter is shown by the numbers employed by each plant. As late as 1957, plants with eleven to ninety-nine workers in Birmingham constituted 76% of all plants, and works with 100-499 workers another 18%. Really large-scale works with more than 2,000 workers numbered only eighteen, and were only 1% of all firms.[11] Briggs also muddies the waters by remarking in another place that in 1938 there were over 10,000 factories employing on average less than twenty persons each.[12] A reasonable conclusion would seem to be that there was an increase in the size of Birmingham works between the wars, and works employing 200 or so had become common, but that the numbers of very large firms was not great, and must not be exaggerated. Many men and women continued to work in quite small work places; even in 1957, about three-quarters of all Birmingham firms had less than 100 workers.[13]

The quality of life at work in Birmingham really depended on whether employment was in the smaller workshops still utilising more or less traditional work practices, or in the larger factories which were more likely to introduce new approaches to production methods such as new forms of flow-production and specialisation. The size of the larger work units was in some cases increased by further horizontal mergers. For example, early on in 1919 Vickers took over the Metropolitan Carriage, Waggon, and Finance Company, while ICI gained control of Elliott's Metal Company (which had previously taken over the Muntz Metal Company), Lucas absorbed two large firms in 1925 and two other firms in 1926, while the Morris Motor Company took over Wolseley Motors in 1927. Thereafter large-scale mergers were much less common. One interesting merger in 1921 was that of the two large Quaker chocolate firms, Cadbury's in Birmingham and Frys in Bristol, though production continued on the two separate factory sites,[14] and they went on marketing their products under their separate brand names.

It was only in the very largest firms, of course, that the emphasis on rationalisation and mass-production really made itself felt. Taylorism and the later and more elaborate Bedeaux system were both systems of so-called 'scientific management' which were imported from North America between the wars, aiming at greater productive efficiency. Not surprisingly, Taylorism was unpopular in trade union circles, and was attacked by the Birmingham Trades Council as 'an inhuman system'.[15] Attitudes at the higher level of the Trades Union Congress were rather less hostile, and in 1933 the TUC reported that Bedeauxism might be applied in a manner which made it less harmful than other systems, though full consultation with the trade unions was essential.[16] In Birmingham, W. & T. Avery appear to have been one of the earliest firms to introduce job analysis and time-study in 1921; it has been said there was little resistance among the rank and file, but rather more from the foremen, who insisted on controlling the scheme and retaining shop floor control.[17]

Generally speaking, neither Taylorism nor the Bedeaux system made much impact on Birmingham in industry, though occasional efforts by managements to introduce Bedeauxism could lead to strike action. Thus, in January 1932, 10,000 girls struck successfully at the Lucas Motor Accessories Works. There was another strike in the following month at Amalgamated Carburettors involving 300 women and 150 men, and similar strikes at Kynocks and Mass Gear. At Rovers there was a twelve months' experiment with Bedeaux before a return to normal piecework. The most important strike of all perhaps against the Bedeaux system was in the spring of 1933 at Hope's Steel Window Works at Smethwick, led by members of the Communist Party.[18] On the whole, therefore, it seems fair to say that scientific management did not make much progress in Birmingham industry between the wars, though it could be a disruptive influence. It could be that the upset it caused discouraged managements from persisting with it.

What were working conditions like in the factories and workshops of Birmingham between the wars? Clearly enough, it is impossible to define the length of the working day precisely over the whole twenty years – it would vary with the industry, market conditions (including seasonal fluctuations), overtime and short-time working, and the age and sex of the worker. Nationally, there was a remarkable reduction in the working day immediately after the war in 1919. Whereas before the war, the 60-hour week and 10-10.5-hour day were common, in the metal trade and engineering, the working day was reduced from 53 or 54 hours to 47 hours. In jewellery, hours fell from 50-54 hours to 47 hours; while in chocolate making, the hours were also reduced to 47.[19] All these changes were particulaly relevant to Birmingham industry; Birmingham edge tools' working hours were singled out in the *Labour Gazette* as being reduced from 54 to 47 or 48 hours weekly. In the following years, some minor increases took place, but the trend was downwards, no doubt as productivity increased. In 1936, for instance, the national reduction weekly was 804,500 hours, and in 1937, 953,000 hours. In 1935, in the Midland Division of the Factory Inspectorate, the electrical, rubber and chocolate industries were working either a 43 or 44 hour week, while the motor, motor cycle and bicycle industries were on a fifty-five hour week for six months, and forty-eight hours for the six winter months.[20] In 1937, motor engineering firms with more than ten workers (76.6% of the total) were reported to be on a forty-seven-hour week.[21] In that year, the Factory Act ended the legal maximum sixty-hour week (55.5 hours in textiles), and for women and young persons the new legal maximum was forty-eight hours, with a daily maximum of nine hours.[22] It is clear then that the major industries in Birmingham benefitted from a significant reduction in hours worked per week in the early 1920s, while in 1937 young persons (aged fourteen to eighteen) and all women workers gained a forty-eight-hour week.

The working environment in Birmingham between the wars again varied from one workplace to another, from the decrepit state of the oldest workshops to the modern buildings of newer factories such as Fort Dunlop, opened in 1915, and the newer buildings at Longbridge. The many trades in the city were not notoriously dangerous, but the power presses increasingly used in the metal trades were known to to inflict severe injuries if used improperly and without appropiate guards. There were 270 accidents involving power presses in 1920 in the Midland Division of the Factory Inspectorate, out of 604 in the whole country.[23] Throughout the years between the wars the Factory Inspectorate made great efforts to improve the safety of working conditions. Cadbury's were well-known for their paternalistic attitudes, of course, and they established an Accident Committee by 1927 (a sub-committee of the Works Committee set up in 1919).[24] Two years later the Safety in Factories Order had been applied to eighteen or twenty works in East Birmingham (by now the largest of the three industrial areas of the city), while in Birmingham south, seventeen firms had appointed Safety Supervisors.[25] At Austins at Longbridge, a determined campaign to reduce the number of accidents was begun in April 1929. By 1931, in less than three years, a reduction in the accident rate of 41% had been achieved.[26] As for the overall pattern of accidents, the annual total recorded by the Factory Inspectorate in Birmingham rose to nearly 10,000 in 1924, and remained at just under this figure for most of the period, with a drop in the early 1930s, and a rise to a peak in 1937 of 12,967. Most of these accidents occurred in Birmingham East (as might be expected), and the largest number of fatal accidents was notified in this division. The number of fatalities per year for Birmingham appears to have dropped by up to a third; there were twenty-nine in 1937 and twenty in 1938.[27]

All the official evidence goes to show that there was some improvement in safety at work between the wars, but much depended on the type of machinery employed, the attitude of the management and the strength of trade union representation in the firm. The largest firms would have more resources than the small firms, and could afford to provide ambulance or first aid rooms, or even a nurse. Cadbury's not only employed a full-time doctor with three nurses, but also three dentists, a dental mechanic and five dental nurses; they also supplied free toothbrushes and dental powder to employees under sixteen (very appropiate for a firm making chocolate and sweets). Safety supervisors were supposed to be appointed in all firms but no doubt this legal requirement was ignored in some cases, and it is possible that not all the smaller firms could even find the first aid box in an emergency. Differences between the larger and smaller firms could also be seen in the provision of canteens, mess rooms and rest rooms. In the 1920s, such amenities were confined to the larger workplaces, and were often supported by voluntary effort. The Lady Inspector, Miss Schofield, provided a description of one Birmingham messroom in 1920 which she said was very popular 'as having the atmosphere of cheer in it'. She continued –[28]

A gas cooker and a tea urn are available, and crockery and cutlery are provided. A woman caretaker prepares the room and clears away after the girls have left. A piano is apparently a great attraction, and there is a fire in winter. Each worker pays a small sum per week for use of the accommodation.

Basic amenities such as the provision of water closets were already compulsory by 1919, but the law was tightened up by the Factory Act,1937 with reference to washing facilities, accommodation for clothing, adequate seating and drinking water.[29] 'Music While You Work' was introduced as early as 1930, and by 1937 gramophone records or radio programmes were broadcast over the Tannoy system in many factories. It was generally believed that musical entertainment of this kind increased production in Birmingham factories.[30]

As for the length of the working week, there was a general move to the five-day week. In 1920, the great majority of works nationally closed at twelve or one o'clock on a Saturday, though employment continued in a few to the legal limit of two, three or even four o'clock.[31] By the 1930s, the five-day week had become increasingly common. Originally it seems to have been adopted in times of slackness of trade, but in the course of time employers favoured it because it reduced overheads, provided time for maintenance work and even (it was said) improved timekeeping and reduced absenteeism. The advantages for the worker were obvious – a longer weekend off work, more time for recreation and sport, and where he or she lived at a distance from work, a possible saving in fares.[32] Austins appear to have been on a five-day week in 1932, but this might have been a temporary measure due to short-time working.[33]

Longer holidays between the wars were limited in number, of course, when compared with the present day situation. In the early 1920s the minimum number of days off nationally as required by the Bank Holiday Acts was six days annually, but nationally it was the common practice to extend the Bank Holiday weekend by an additional day or so, and a week's holiday (usually without pay) was common in the summer.[34] Holidays with pay were largely confined to clerical workers and were exceptional among manual workers; only about 3 million workers enjoyed them before 1929. However, the Holidays with Pay Act, 1938 brought in about 11 million workers by June 1939, covering about half the manual workers in the country at that time.[35]

So far the picture presented of Birmingham industry and of life at work has not mentioned unemployment or life on the dole. How bad then was unemployment in Birmingham between the wars? The key factor here has already been touched upon: textiles and coal formed no part of the local economy – there were no cotton or woollen mills, or coal mines, or major iron works in the locality. Instead, there were new and thriving motor, electrical, rubber, aluminium and plastic industries. Hence unemployment in the 1920s was not much above the pre-war figure of around 20,000, except during the post-war slump, when the numbers given out-door relief by the poor law authorities rose in July 1922 to 73,681. This figure included other than the unemployed, of course, and it dropped a year later to 44,093, and by July 1924 was 31,596. Thereafter, apart from 1926 (the year of the General Strike) when it was 20,488, it fell to below 20,000, and in 1929 was 13,000.[36] The number of unemployed in the years 1927-30 fluctuated between 25,000 and 60,000, then reached a peak of 76,000 in August 1931.[37] The average unemployment for this year in Birmingham was 17.7% of the workforce, as compared with the national figure for England of 20.7% (Wales 33.5, Scotland 27.4%).[38] Thereafter the figures declined – overtime was being worked again in the motor industry by September 1932. By November 1934 Birmingham's unemployment figure was 6.8% (the national average was 16.6%). By 1936 the number of unemployed was 15,742 – the lowest ever recorded up to then – and a national newspaper, the *News Chronicle* (owned by the Cadburys) referred to the shortage of labour (not of jobs) in the area. In September 1937 the unemployed percentage was 3%, a figure which Beveridge later considered to represent full employment. Though the numbers out of work rose in 1938 to 28,560 (nationally it was a year of recession), any unemployment in 1939 was absorbed by the armaments industry when war broke out.[39]

This sketch of the incidence of unemployment in Birmingham between the wars demonstrates that its extent was very different from what was experienced at the time in the textile towns and mining villages. There were less prosperous years, of course, especially in the post-war slump, and again in 1931, a year of unparalleled depression in trade; but Birmingham recovered quickly, and the immigration into the area is a sufficient testimony to this recovery. There is also a marked contrast to be drawn between what happened in Birmingham and the experience of the adjacent Black Country. There, both the iron industry and the coal industry had been in long-term decline even before 1914. Between the wars the decline continued. This is shown clearly enough by reference to the unemployment figures in the Black Country towns. In 1931, when the Birmingham figure was 17.7%, Dudley's figure was more than double this, a striking 38.8%. Again, of the fifteen Black Country towns, only Smethwick was below 20% (18.9%) in this year of deep depression.[40]

To sum up: for the working people of Birmingham, life at work was necessarily at the centre of their existence. At times there were dark periods due to unemployment, but on the whole the inter-war years were years of mild prosperity, thanks for the most part to the existence of the new industries and the absence of the staple industries. Hours of work were shorter than they had been in 1918, and working conditions were on the whole rather safer. Moreover, the paternalism of the nineteenth century had by no means entirely disappeared. It was still strongly in evidence at Cadbury's, of course, where consultation with the workers was undertaken through the two Works Committees (set up in 1918 following the Whitley Committee Report, 1917, on joint consultative committees). Later these committees were supplemented by Shop Committees and Group Committees – a somewhat elaborate system. The firm was famous not only for its welfare provisions but also for its sports facilities. Friendly relations were maintained with the trade unions.[41] Herbert Austin was rather less friendly towards trade unionism at Longbridge, but he still took a practical interest in work on the shop floor, and went on tours of inspection. The sports club at Austins was very popular, offering a wide range of activities, and new employees were expected to participate.[42] Even smaller firms might provide some sporting facilities: the *Ariel* motorcycle, a leading make, was manufactured in Selly Oak, and the firm had its own tennis club near the county club cricket ground in Edgbaston with six courts.[43] All this was hardly typical of the vast majority of Birmingham firms, of course, but it at least goes to show that concern for the welfare of the workers and good labour relations did not die out completely between the wars.

Since a good deal of attention was paid in the last chapter to the increased power and influence of the trade unions in Birmingham during the war, it might be expected that further advances took place after the war. In fact, the trade unions made only modest progress between the wars; and their major contribution to the welfare of the working classes took the form of the traditional co-operation with employers in the process of collective bargaining. An example of this was the setting up of joint councils with trade unionists in the trading departments of the City Corporation (gas, electricity, water and tramways), and a joint consultative committee for non-manual staff in 1929.[44] The General Strike in 1926 was well-supported by the unions and passed off without major incident, except that on the last day of the strike the Birmingham TU General Emergency Committee was arrested, and charged with spreading alarm in their own publication, the *Strike Bulletin*; ten of the twenty members of the committee were each fined £10. Subsequently as a result of the Trades Disputes and Trade Union Act, 1927, seven branches of the Post Office Workers and three of the Post Office Engineers had to leave the Trades Council since the Act *inter alia* forbade civil servant workers from being members of bodies affiliated to the TUC.[45] The collapse of the second Labour Government in 1931 was naturally a blow to the Birmingham trade unions. In 1924 the Labour Party had won one of the twelve Birmingham parliamentary seats, and four in all in the 1929 general election, but lost all of them in the 1931 election, and failed to regain any of them in the next general election in 1935. As for local elections, only limited progress was made: Labour had ten seats in 1921, but still only thirteen seats in 1932. By 1938 the situation had improved so that there were twenty labour councillors and seven aldermen; but they were still heavily outnumbered by the eighty-three Conservative councillors and twenty aldermen (there were also three liberals and three independents). However, rank and file membership of the unions increased in the flourishing conditions of the last three years of peace. This is illustrated by the increased membership figures of the AEU in Birmingham –[47]

1935	*1936*	*1937*	*1938*	*1939*
5,760	6,240	8,096	10,083	12,245

To turn to life away from work: the vital statistics show an overall distinct fall from the pre-war averages to the mid-1920s, followed by a minor fall thereafter:[48]

Crude Death Rates for Birmingham 1901-1939

	Average
1901-05	16.5
1906-10	15.0
1911-15	14.6
1916-20	13.4
1921-25	11.5
1926-30	11.6
1931-35	11.2
1936-39	11.4

Infant mortality rates dropped quite dramatically. From 1901-05 they averaged 157. By 1919 the figure was down to 89. The average for 1920-29 was 77.4; for 1930-39, it was 64.l, the last three years of the period giving figures of 60, 61 and 60. Lastly, birth rates in Birmingham fell over the inter-war period as a whole, and especially in the 1930s. For example, in 1930 the rate was 17.4; in 1935, 15.7; and in 1939, 16.6. This correlates positively with the reduction in the size of the family unit both nationally and in Birmingham.[49]

Size of the Family Unit

Percentage of families of –

	3 or less	*4 or less*	*More than 6*
England and Wales			
1911 census	40.8	58.9	16.3
1921 census	44.5	63.1	13.6
1931 census	52.7	72.1	8.2
Birmingham			
1931 census	49.3	70.0	8.9
1938 survey	55.0	76.3	5.3

Thus, it can be seen that in Birmingham there was a marked increase in the number of smaller families (three or less) between 1931 and 1939, and in fact, 76.3% of all families in 1938 consisted of only four persons (adults and children) or less.[50] This is a remarkable contrast with the size of the family in the mid-nineteenth century, when the typical family contained about six children.[51]

However, the death rates given do conceal a good deal of variation in rates from one ward of the city to another. In 1936, when the death rate for the city as a whole was 11.5, in the seven Central wards the average was much higher: the three highest figures were St Mary's 15.7, St Paul's 13.8 and St Martin's 13.8. In the ten Middle Ring wards, the figures range from Balsall Heath 14.6 to Lozells 12.7, to Washwood Heath 8.7; while in the seventeen Outer Ring wards,

35. Broad Street, c.1930 (showing Church of the Messiah).

the highest figures were in Soho (12.9) and Handsworth (12.7), and the lowest Hall Green (6.7) and Perry Barr (6.1).[52] Nevertheless, although the death rates were clearly highest in the thickly populated central area, it was in these wards that the death rates fell fastest in the inter-war years.[53]

Birmingham Death Rates by Wards

	1916-20	*1931-35*	*Percentage Decrease*
Central Wards	17.9	13.4	25
Middle Ring Wards	12.7	11.8	7
Outer Ring Wards	10.3	9.6	7

Obviously enough, between the wars Birmingham became a healthier place than it had been before 1914.[54] The most striking improvement was in the infant mortality rates. The worst area for ill health and early death was in the oldest, most over-crowded central districts, though these were improving noticeably as slum clearance went on; and a remarkable migration took place out of these wards and into the Outer and Middle Rings. The fall in the birth rate is linked directly, of course, to the decline in the size of the family. By 1939, more than three-quarters of Birmingham families had two or less children. Only one in twenty families had as many as four or more children. Thus, the proportion of the family income devoted to feeding, clothing and the care of the children diminished in Birmingham between the wars. This is a crucial point with reference to nutritional standards to which we will return later in the chapter.

When we turn to housing between the wars, it is to be remembered that the state of pre-war housing in the Central Wards was very poor. Acccording to the City Enquiry of 1913, centrally there were about 200,000 people housed in 43,366 back-to-backs; 42,020 houses had no separate water supply, sinks or drains; 58,028 houses had no separate water closets; and there was much overcrowding.[55] The situation was made worse by the virtual cessation of house-building during the war. Indeed, by 1918 the national pre-war housing shortage had grown to such an extent that the government was forced to take action, especially in the light of Lloyd George's promise made in November l918 of 'homes fit for heroes'. It was clear that the government would have to subsidise both private and municipal building, and this was done through a succession of housing acts – Addison's Act, 1918, Chamberlain's Act, 1923, and Wheatley's Act, 1924.

The results for Birmingham were striking indeed. The pre-war hostility to municipal building was dropped abruptly, and ambitious plans were adopted. Birmingham built more council houses between the wars than any other local authority, more of them before 1931 than after, when private housing erected more houses than before as house prices became cheaper and building society rates for mortgages fell. The total numbers of council houses built was 51,681, housing about 200,000 people, at a cost of £23.59 million. Private builders built 59,744, making a grand total of 111,425.[56] New municipal estates developed in the Outer Ring – there were thirty-one of these estates by 1935 – and in June,1939 the 50,000th council house was opened. An outstanding example of the new council estates was the Kingstanding Estate (1928) at Perry Barr (Kingstanding, Kettlehouse, Witton Lodge Farm and Oscott College) which covered nearly 1,000 acres, and provided up to 9,000 houses, with a population at the time as large as that of Shrewsbury; it was the largest municipal estate in England outside the London area. On another large estate, the Lea Hall estate to the east of the city, a further 3,500 houses were erected by 1939.[57]

Meanwhile, slum clearance had begun in the Central Wards, and about 8,000 houses were demolished in the 1930s. In spite of this, in 1935 there were still 51,794 houses without a separate WC, a decrease of only 11% on the 1913 figure. Some progress had been made, however, in providing a separate water supply, the number still without this facility showing a decrease of 68%.[58] In St Mary's Ward, for instance, of 509 houses, 131 were demolished, fourteen bought in order to open up the courts by pulling down one side of the court, and the remainder re-conditioned. In December 1938 the Council drew up a new scheme, recommending the building of a further 25,000 houses within five years, of which 4,000 each year were to be allocated to slum clearance and overcrowding. 10,000 of the 25,000 dwellings were to be houses, and the rest were to be in equal numbers of flats and maisonettes which were to be erected on cleared sites in the central areas.[59] The decision to build flats and maisonettes is interesting, in that for many years previously the Corporation had been strongly against building flats, but had gradually changed their minds on the matter, erecting four three-story blocks of flats in Garrison Lane in 1927, with other flats built on the Ashcroft estate and also in Emily St in Highgate, 1934. Maisonettes were also erected in 1933 in Great Brook Street, Duddeston, and Kingston Road, Bordesley, in 1937.[60]

If the housing situation as a whole is surveyed between the wars (and no doubt the reader has had enough of the statistics for the time being) it is clear that much remained to be done in the Central Wards, where the Medical Officer of Health estimated in 1938 that there were still 17,500 houses unfit for human habitation. However, determined efforts were being made to improve the situation, and by 1938 only 18.8% of workers lived in the area. In the Middle Ring there was plenty of bad housing, too, though many of the houses here were of the 'tunnel back' variety, with extensions to the rear to include a scullery, WC and coalhouse at ground floor level, with a third bedroom above. The 'tunnel back' was usually much more spacious than the back-to-back, with three bedrooms in all (in the Central Wards, just under half the houses (49.6%) had only three rooms *in all*; the equivalent figure in the Middle Ring was only 15.1%).[61] Housing was much better in the Middle Ring than centrally, even if it was mostly terraced and dark, built in conformity to bye-law regulations. Many of the tenants were artisans and blackcoated workers, who paid higher rents than labourers in the central back-to-backs; but less than a third (28.6%) of the working classes lived in this area. The largest sector of the working classes lived in the Outer Ring, many in new or nearly new houses built on the 'universal plan', that is, the standard three up, two down semi-detached or short-terraced house of a kind found on both private and council estates. By 1939, a good proportion of the working classes in Birmingham lived in relatively new housing; it has been estimated that in that year about a third of the total population of around a million lived in houses built since 1918.[62]

What did the tenants on the new council estates think of their new houses? For many, for the first time in their lives they had roomier accommodation, internal supplies of water, proper sinks and drains, and an internal WC for their exclusive use. The quality of building was generally good, and there were gardens front and rear. Most estates had trees and grass verges, and were entirely residential, without factories or business premises. On the Kingstanding estate, most households were small: 33% (1,700 households) had no children under fourteen; 46% had either one or two children (2,450 households); only 21% (1,150 households) had three or more children.[63] Fewer mouths to feed meant more income available for food, clothing and other household expenses.

On the other hand, there were drawbacks: one frequent cause of complaint was that rents were higher on the council estates than in the Central Wards (though there were rent subsidies later on). There were also increased travelling costs; for example, 34.4% of tenants on council estates worked in the Central Wards.[64] However, only 3% travelled more than six miles to work, and only 3.3% spent over 5s a week in travelling to work (most of these were in the north-west of the borough).[65] Others working locally would either walk, cycle or take the bus or tram to work. Other complaints were that the larger premises required more furniture, that prices in estate shops were higher than in the central shopping area, and that children's appetites were keener on the estates and that they cost more to feed... Another complaint (with more substance, perhaps) was that the new estates were windy, lonely places, and that there was little communal life because public amenities such as churches, clinics, libraries, swimming baths and club premises were often insufficient in the early days. It was pointed out that in 1932 the town of Shrewsbury, with a slightly smaller population than the Kingstanding estate, had thirty churches, fifteen church halls and parish rooms, and two public libraries. Kingstanding at that time had only one church and one hall.[66] (It was scarcely a fair comparison, since Shrewsbury was a long-established county town, and Kingstanding later on did acquire public houses, schools, cinemas, a public swimming bath and several communal playgrounds).

On the whole, most tenants seem to have welcomed life on the new estates when all the domestic amenities available were taken into account. Some certainly missed the friendly neighbourhood feel of their former life in the central back-to-backs, but recognised that their new homes were far more civilised than their previous abodes. Unfortunately, the poorest in the central slums were not the first to be offered the chance to move. This is because the City Council wanted the first occupants to be respectable and reliable tenants, and rents were kept quite high. It was not until after 1935 that the policy was changed and rent subsidies were made available for tenants out of work. By the 1926 rent scale, a tenant of a three-bedroom non-parlour house with wife and children was required to earn a minimum of £3 10s a week; for a three-bedroom parlour house, the minimum was £4. Yet only 16.5% of Birmingham's population earned £4 or more a week in 1934. Even when rent subsidies were introduced, they could cause ill-feeling among tenants because they resulted in different rents being paid for similar kinds of houses on the same estate. Discontent among tenants at the level of rents led to a rent strike in 1939.[68]

The amount of rent payable raises the whole question of the level of rents, prices, and the standard of living in Birmingham between the wars. Over the city as a whole, rents were relatively cheap, and for slum property in the Central Wards, especially low, the majority ranging from 8s to 10s or so per week, and for the largest, four-bedroom parlour house on a municipal estate, up to 20s a week. There was not much difference between the rent of a council house and that of a privately-owned house of the same size in the same area. In the city as a whole, more than 20% paid less than 8s rent per week, and about 44% less than 10s.[69] As for food prices, they fell from 1920 to 1933-34, when they rose slightly. Wages nationally were stable for the most part during the inter-war years, and in 1938 they were 5% to 6% higher than they were in 1930, and about double what they had been in 1913. When these facts are taken together, real wages are seen to have improved by about 30% on the 1913 figures. When the national reduction of hours and improved holidays are taken into account, it has even been claimed that the total real gain by wage earners between the wars was of the order of 50%.[70] Whether this figure could be justified for Birmingham workers is another matter, but certainly of the two main items in the family budget, food and rent, food prices remained low and rents were relatively cheap.

However, the 1930s saw increasing discussion of the standard of living of the working classes, especially among social investigators and social workers, who were concerned at the extent of unemployment and its effect on the health of the unemployed. Surveys of the extent of poverty were carried out in York (1936), Bristol (1937), London (1938) and Merseyside (1928-32). An investigation by Sir John Boyd Orr into nutritional needs in 1936 actually claimed that half or more of the entire population were undernourished (afterwards reduced from a half to a third). In spite of the evidence for a rising standard of living just reviewed, how much hidden poverty was there in Birmingham between the wars? How much malnutrition? The Reports of the Birmingham Schools Medical Officer provide interesting information on this last subject. As early as 1932 it was pointed out that the death rates of the five to fifteen age range were steadily improving:[71]

Death Rates among 5-15 year olds and Infant Mortality Rates

	Death Rates 5-15 age range	*Infant Mortality Rates*
1912	2.8	126
1921	2.1	83
1931	1.6	76

A separate report on malnutrition, requested by the Board of Education, was made in 1935, based on the examination of 41,300 children. In 1938, a new classification of children was adopted, based on the Board's recommendations. Throughoul the 1930s, from 1932 onwards, every Annual Report had a section on malnutrition. In 1936 it was declared that '... in Birmingham there is no high incidence of malnutrition in the child population', but it was conceded that 'the nutrition of many children might be improved'. This would depend on an increased knowledge of food values, and of a better expending of the family budget.[72] The difficulty lay in reaching firm statistical conclusions because of the different standards of assessing malnutrition by the Schools Medical Officers. For example, in 1938 the proportion of the 43,507 children examined who were classified as 'badly undernourished' was 1.4%, but if one officer's report was omitted, this figure fell to 0.5%. Further, there was the problem of determining the cause of malnutrition: an extended discussion in the 1938 Report classifies the main causes as pathological, social, dietetic and financial. Thus, among those placed in the 'badly ill-nourished' category, 21.1% were due to pathological causes and 63.2% to financial causes. The 1938 Report summed up by concluding that the most important factors were shortage of food due to lack of means, and illness, past or present. Compared with the school population at large, the amount of malnutrition among Birmingham school children seemed about the same. Children receiving free school meals appeared to be healthy and well-nourished. As might be expected, cases of malnutrition were more numerous in the Central Wards (1.29%) than on the new estates (0.27%).[73]

A study of nutrition and the family carried out on the Kingstanding Estate in 1939 helps to provide us with additional information.[74] On the estate there were about 5,300 households, and a 5% sample (269 families) was questioned. Of all these families, 33% had no children under fourteen, and 46% had either one or two children under fourteen – that is, over three-quarters (79%) had small families with either none, or one or two children under fourteen.[75] The approach adopted by the enquiry was to compare the minimum standard of spending on food necessary for each family to maintain adequate health (using the BMA minimum diet scale of 1933) with the household money available for spending on food. This last amount was determined by deductions from the housekeeping money for rent, fares, compulsory insurance, fuel, light, clothing, cleaning materials, voluntary insurance and regular hire-purchase payments (no deductions were made for furniture, medical charges, tobacco, newspapers, amusements, holidays or savings). The survey was carried out at a time when there was virtually full employment, and overtime was being worked. A table was then constructed, showing what proportion of families were unable to conform to a 'standard of sufficiency'; and this means that all families either on the borderline of the minimum standard (within 5% above) or definitely below the standard are shown as a percentage of the total number of families –[76]

Families on or below the Minimum Standard of Sufficiency (Kingstanding Estate, 1939)

Families with 1 child under 14	13%
Families with 2 children under 14	45%
Families with 3 children under 14	65%
Families with 4 children under 14	85%
Families with 5 children under 14	96%
Families with 6 or more children under 14	96%

This survey has some oddities: the sample is small, and the placing of families 5% *above* the minimum along with those definitely *below* the standard is peculiar. It appears to run the risk of exaggerating the numbers actually below the standard. It can also be argued that the method of arriving at the amount available to spend on food per family seems strange – see the list of items for which no deductions from gross income were made. Then there are other debatable matters, too, such as how appropriate the BMA scale really was as a guide to the average working-class diet. Nevertheless, it is hard to reject the principal finding of the survey, which is that children in the larger families were at risk of malnutrition. This point was made by Rowntree's survey of 1936, which considered that 32.8% of poverty in York was caused by low wages, even if the breadwinner was in regular work; the same view was taken by the Beveridge Report, 1942, and by supporters of Eleanor Rathbone's campaign for family allowances which was at last successful in 1945.

The conclusions to be drawn from this detailed survey of working-class life so far in this chapter are than a substantial majority of Birmingham's work people profited from steady employment, a

36. Infant Welfare Centre, Selly Oak, 1922 (formerly 'Village Bells' public house).

shorter working day, an improved working environment, better housing conditions, better health and, as will be seen later, a wider range of leisure activities. On the other hand, there was a minority, especially those with larger than average families, who still experienced poverty by the standards of the day. Many of them still lived in the slums of the Central Wards, unable to afford better accommodation. This is where malnutrition was most prevalent, death rates highest and unemployment likely to be heaviest among the unskilled and low-waged. Though some slum clearance had taken place, and water supplies improved, in 1935 there were still 38,773 back-to-backs, 51,794 houses without a separate WC and 13,650 houses without a separate water supply. According to Asa Briggs, the situation was far more serious than in many other cities, such as Manchester.[77] All that can be said by way of qualification of this gloomy picture is that life in the Central Wards was marginally better in 1939 than it had been in 1919 – it has been claimed that the standard of living of an unemployed man with children was higher in the 1930s than that of a labourer in work in 1913.[78] Welfare services improved, of course, during the twenty years between the wars. Lastly, the numbers in the Central Wards were reduced by 1938, the proportion of the working classes living there dropping from 27.6% of the whole in 1921 to 18.8% in 1938.[79]

According to Asa Briggs, the creation of the new council housing estates was the most important feature of Birmingham's civic history in the inter-war years.[80] Certainly they are a very important feature of working-class life at the time. Another important aspect of civic activity affecting working-class life was the extension of the municipal school service . This was made necessary, of course, by the increase in population and the vast amount of new housing being erected, both municipal and private. During the whole period, the Education Committee owed much to the guidance of the Kenrick family; Sir George Kenrick was chairman of the Education Committee from 1902 to 1921, and was followed by Byng Kenrick, chairman from 1922 to 1943. In the inter-war period, a good deal of progress was made in providing more elementary education, though set-backs were encountered when the government imposed economy cuts in 1922 (the 'Geddes Axe') and again in 1931. If some weakness can be detected in the Council's educational policies, it is in their failure to make available more secondary school places, as we shall see later.

To take elementary education first: some forty new schools were built in the period 1923 to 1935, some of them being very large; for example, Peckham Road School had four departments and 1,568 on roll, and there were a further nine schools built for more than 1,000 children each. Between 1936 and 1939, another twenty-nine schools and departments were opened, while older schools and departments were closed down – thirty-five in the same period.[81] Progress was also made in the Schools Medical Service, and the Free Schools Meals Service was extended, too. Of the city's non-provided or voluntary schools, some were in a bad structural condition, but the Board of Education's Black List of such schools, which earlier on had numbered twenty-one voluntary schools in the Birmingham area, was reduced to only five voluntary schools in 1938, none of them directly maintained by the local authority.[82]

The story is somewhat different for secondary education: it must be remembered that secondary schools in their own buildings and with their own ethos were comparatively rare in 1918. Most so-called secondary education in state schools took place in the upper forms of all-age council schools. However, the Labour Party was beginning to campaign for separate secondary schools for the working classes. A Labour Party educational pamphlet in 1922 claimed that it was quite wrong to suppose that secondary education was required only by the middle and upper classes:[83]

> The very assumption on which it is based, that all that the child of the worker needs is 'elementary education' – as though the mass of the people, like anthropoid apes, had fewer convolutions in their brains than the rich – is in itself a piece of insolence.

As was seen in previous chapters, Birmingham had its King Edward Foundation schools, but otherwise secondary school places were very limited. Following the Hadow Report (1926) which argued the case for more separate secondary schools, a further five secondary schools were built, making ten council secondary schools in all. In addition, there were two junior commercial schools and one technical school (increased to two technical schools in 1939). A limited number of places for children from elementary schools was also available in the eight King Edward Grammar schools, and at the two Roman Catholic grammar schools. Parental grants were available for these schools in the form of remission of fees, maintenance grants and book allowances.[84] Excellent though the education provided at secondary level might be, there were too few places. The Council was aware of this, and had two sites on hand for grammar school buildings in the 1930s, but were prevented from building on them by the cuts in 1931 and then the outbreak of war in 1939.[85] In 1918, Birmingham offered only 6.6 secondary places per thousand of population as compared with 11.8 in other large cities. By 1931 the 1918 figure had improved, and it was calculated that in 1931 it would be up to 9.6 as a minimum figure, but the cuts forced the Council to aim at only 9.4 per thousand in 1935. Pressure for secondary places remained heavy – there were 7,000 to 8,000 candidates in 1934 for 2,000 places.[86] Thus, the shortage of secondary places which was apparent in 1918 had still not been remedied by 1939, though some new secondary schools had been founded – a new school for 316 girls at Erdington, a school for 500 boys at Moseley and a mixed school for 500 at King's Norton, the old school there being remodelled for 500 boys.[87] It was still not enough, and the subject came up for public discussion again after the passing of the Butler Education Act, 1944.[88] By 1939 then, there had been real advances in the provision of elementary schools, but less so in the realm of secondary education. The belief persisted that secondary education should be reserved for the relatively small minority of academically minded children. Nevertheless, it still seems strange that in a city with such a history of skilled metal-working that there should be only one technical school up to 1936. Even in 1938-39, the combined entry to the two technical schools and the two commercial schools was only 527.[89] Plans to open a new Central Technical College were foiled by the outbreak of war.[90] One explanation for the relative lack of secondary education has been that it was believed that the system of apprenticeship in Birmingham was a sufficient education for boys, so that the city did not need as many secondary places as other towns with less skilled employment;[91] but in view of the patchy nature of apprenticeship, and its unsupervised nature, this does not seem a very powerful argument.

Another aspect of civic improvement which was very important to the welfare of the working classes in Birmingham was the extension of the city's transport system. This was made increasingly urgent with the building of the vast new council estates on the periphery of the city. Its characteristics were firstly the introduction of the double-decker, roofed trolly bus, then the gradual replacement of the old fleet of trams by a large fleet of motor omnibuses – ultimately the largest fleet of municipal omnibuses in the world. In the year ending March,1927, the trams covered 77 miles and carried 238 million passengers, while the busses covered 63 miles, carrying 43 million passengers. By March 1938 the busses had drawn ahead: omnibus routes covered 153 miles and carried 225 million passengers, while the trams clanked their noisy way over only 65 miles carrying 174 million passengers. The busses were clearly a much more flexible means of transport since they could pick their own routes, and were not confined to the middle of the roads.[92] They were also more comfortable and less noisy than the trams. The great increase in city traffic led to the installing of the first traffic lights in 1929; a one-way traffic scheme for the city centre, 1933; the first pedestrian crossings, 1934-35; and the beginnings of the construction of Elmdon Airport following the passing of the Birmingham Corporation Act, 1935.[93]

Another civic service which improved working-class lives was the municipal supply of electricity. In 1923 a new generating station was opened in Nechells and completed in 1929. From 1923 onwards, electricity replaced gas on the new council estates. With the setting up of the Central Electricity Board in 1926 and the construction of the National Grid, a large new power station at Hams Hall was opened in 1929, was extended and completed in 1939, while another power station (Station B) was also begun at Hams Hall. Between 1928 and 1938, the number of consumers went up from 57,161 to 251,864. By 1935, Birmingham's electricity supply was the largest in Britain. Curiously, the municipal gas supply did not suffer from this competition, a third of the gas produced being consumed by industry, while gas was still used for street-lighting. New supplies were also offered to about 21,000 court and terrace homes, and repayment meters were fixed free of charge.[94]

37. 'The Times' Furnishing Company, 1938.

Lastly, hospital services were improved in the inter-war period. There were twelve Birmingham hospitals in all in 1914, by far the largest being Birmingham Infirmary, a poor law infirmary administered by the Birmingham Board of Guardians. As a result of the Local Government Act, 1929, which abolished the Boards of Guardians up and down the country, the powers of the Birmingham Board were transferred to the City Council. Henceforth the Infirmary, with its nearly 2,000 beds, together with two other poor law hospitals were run by the Public Assistance Committee of the Corporation. Meanwhile, a new hospital centre was decided on, situated on a site donated by the Cadburys and adjacent to the campus of the University of Birmingham. The medical school there was opened in 1938, and the Queen Elizabeth Hospital was opened officially in 1939. There were also thirty-one welfare clinics in the city, together with a midwifery service, two maternity homes and a convalescent home for mothers who had just had their babies.[95]

It remains to say something about leisure activities; it is convenient to consider them first in the home, and then outside the home. In the home, some traditional pre-war forms of recreation continued as before – reading (of both books and newspapers),[96] gardening (where plots were available), card playing, sometimes the playing of musical instruments and, here and there, songs round the piano. On the Kingstanding estate, a few families were said to be buying pianoes in 1938 at four shillings a week over four years,[97] though the possession of a piano in the average working-class home was not the status symbol which it had been. One enormously important addition to the various forms of domestic entertainment between the wars was the wireless, at first a cumbersome apparatus requiring batteries, accumulators and either headphones or a separate loudspeaker. By the 1930 the wireless was becoming known as the radio, with simplified controls and a built-in speaker. By this time almost every home, rich or poor, had a radio, often rented or obtained on hire purchase; even the poorest seemed to regard it as something of a necessity.[98] Not all households obeyed the legal requirement to purchase a licence, but even then the number of licences issued in Birmingham trebled in the 1930s, increasing from 99,221 in 1930 to 285,995 in 1938.[99] Programmes varied in quality and ranged from plays, features, sports commentaries, Children's Hour, variety and comedy shows, to regular news bulletins (at first in the evenings only, to avoid competition with the newspapers) and late-night dance music, relayed from the London hotels (very popular with the young, who also bought dance music on gramophone records, when they could afford it). The 1930s and the war years of the 1940s were the golden years of BBC radio both nationally, and of course in Birmingham. The only other radio programmes available came from the commercial stations abroad broadcasting in English, Radio Luxembourg, Radio Fécamp and Radio Normandie.

Outside the home, pre-war interest in outdoor sport continued. For the middle classes, this centred on rugby, cricket, lawn tennis and golf. All of these sports were supported by local clubs which also had a strong social side. For the working classes, the main centre of interest continued to be association football. The Birmingham City and Aston Villa football clubs remained prominent, and Aston Villa in particular attracted immense support. Their average home attendance in 1922-23 was 28,237; in 1937-38, it had risen to 41,956. In 1938, when they played Manchester City in an FA Cup match, they achieved a new record gate of 75,000, with a further 15,000 fans locked outside.[100] Amateur football also continued very popular among young industrial workers. The Birmingham and District Works League membership included 96 works and 124 teams in the 1918-19 season. In 1938-39 there were 205 works members and 278 teams. The aims of the league as stated in its 1955 souvenir booklet are an interesting reminder that Birmingham paternalism in labour relations was still alive and kicking between the wars. These aims were 'to assist in the social unity between employer and employed', and to help by recreation to fit men better for their daily task, and to make them more contented workmen, because of their employers' interest in their well-being, and to form character and make of them better and healthier citizens.[101] These were admirable if somewhat muddled sentiments, indeed, though no doubt by the 1950s they sounded a little old-fashioned and patronising.

Other spectator sports in addition to professional football were speedway racing and greyhound racing. Birmingham's first greyhound track was opened in 1927, and by 1938 there were tracks at Perry Barr, Kings Heath and Hall Green.[102] As there were no horse racing courses in Birmingham, the greyhound tracks were the only places where legal betting could take place in public (there was, of course, much illegal off-course betting on horses, and bookies' runners and look-outs were a familiar sight in working-class districts). Another kind of legal gambling developed in the 1930s in the form of football pools. In 1937 there was a special mail train from Liverpool to Birmingham each week carrying 235,000 football coupons for the Birmingham area.[103] Cycling continued its pre-war popularity, and the Birmingham and District Association of the Cyclist Touring Club flourished, organising fifty to sixty cycle runs weekly, and by 1938, mass rallies of 1,500 members.[104] There was a great emphasis nationally on healthy, outdoor activity, such as hiking, and Birmingham Corporation provided plenty of sports facilities: by 1938 there were 186 football pitches, 117 cricket pitches, eighty hard tennis courts, nineteen putting greens, thrity-eight bowling greens and twelve boating pools.[105] For those less keen on physical exercise, the Birmingham public house remained the traditional venue for working-class leisure. A number of

38. Poolton's shop, Lichfield Road, c.1935.

new and large public houses were erected between the wars.[106] The number of licences issued was reduced between the wars, however, possibly due to the reduction in drinking hours which had been imposed during the war and continued post-war. Another cause in all probability was the growth of rival social amenities and activities.[107] Dance halls continued to be popular, especially among the young, who enjoyed dancing cheek-to-cheek in the waltz, quickstep and slow foxtrot, with the more adventurous attempting the tango and rhumba. However, one form of pre-war entertainment became immensely popular from 1927 onwards, far outstripping all other forms of public entertainment. This was the cinema, and the cause of such a sensational leap forward was the advent of the talking picture. The first talkie to be shown in Birmingham was the famous 'The Jazz Singer' , with Al Jolson as the star. The *Town Crier*, under the heading 'Amazing Scenes at the Futurist', reported the event as follows –[108]

> For four weeks the house has borne the appearance of a besieged citadel, great crowds
> controlled by a special force of police encircling the building from morn to night, and
> in spite of the fact that five performances have been given each day, the public demand
> to see and hear this wonderful film has still not been satisfied.

The film ran at the Futurist cinema from 18 March to 11 May 1929, and it is estimated that about 100,000 people saw it. Subsequently many Birmingham cinemas invested in sound equipment, and in 1933 Sunday opening of cinemas began. In 1934, seventy out of eighty cinemas were open on Sundays, and by 1938 the total number of cinemas in Birmingham rose to ninety-eight. Going to the cinema on a weekly basis became a national habit. By the end of the inter-war period, 20 million nationally were visiting the cinema every week, a quarter of these going at least twice a week. Going

39. Selly Oak cinema, 1946 (built 1929).

to the pictures became an accepted feature of both working-class and middle-class life.[109] Understandably, theatre-going decreased at this time, though in 1938 Birmingham still had four theatres, three music halls, thirty-seven billiard halls, and 191 other places licenced for public enter-tainment, together with 299 public houses licenced for music, singing and dancing.[110]

What is there left to say about the Birmingham of the inter-war years? In his *English Journey*, published in 1934, J.B. Priestley recorded some interesting comments on the city as it was when he visited it in 1933. At first, approaching the city on a bus from Coventry, he caught sight of a notice board saying, 'This is the City of Birmingham', but (he says) 'there was nothing in view but hedgerows, glittering fields and the mist of the autumn morning'. Evidently he had crossed the boundary of the new Greater Birmingham. Later he encountered houses and shops and factories, and was unimpressed. The entrance to the Second City 'looked a dirty muddle'. Once at his hotel in Colmore Row, however, things improved. In his words –[111]

> There was a sudden access of civic dignity in the place. Here in Colmore Row you could imagine yourself in the second city of England. There is a really fine view at the end, where the huge Council House turns into Victoria Square. You see Hill Street mistily falling away beneath the bridge that the Post Office has thrown high across the road. If there is any better view in Birmingham than this, I never saw it.

Subsequently he much enjoyed a visit to the Corporation Art Gallery and Museum, where he was told that attendance averaged about 800 a day on weekdays, with a sudden leap into thousands on Sundays, because on that day the galleries were a favourite spot for young people to meet each other. Priestley further noted that Colmore Row, New Street and Corporation Street gave

Birmingham quite a metropolitan air, and these streets 'had quite metropolitan crowds in them, too, looking at the windows of the big shops and hurrying in and out of cafés and picture theatres'.[112]

Unfortunately, he then decided to take an unplanned tram ride to the outskirts, which turned out to be very depressing; it was, he thought, a parade of mean dinginess, so many miles of ugliness, of poor quality shops and mean suburban housing. It is a pity that Priestley does not tell us which tram route he took. It hardly sounds like the Bristol Road, and he did not visit parks such as Cannon Hill Park, or any of the new housing estates. What he saw was part of the development of the Middle and Outer Rings, and as he himself fairly points out, what he was seeing was not so much Birmingham, but 'our urban and industrial civilisation'. Today in the early twenty-first century, there remain parts of the inner London suburbs with their dirty yellow London brickwork, garish shopfronts, nasty billboards and abundant litter which are just as displeasing to the eye as Priestley's Birmingham suburbia in the 1930s. Priestley afterwards visited Bournville, and comments thoughtfully on the good working conditions, the welfare provisions for staff, and the paternalistic ethos of the establishment.

In the final analysis we should perhaps return to the condition of the people of Birmingham between the wars. It was a strange and indeed perplexing period of history. A.J.P. Taylor pointed out long ago that 'the nineteen-thirties have been called the black years, the devil's decade. Its popular image can be expressed in two phrases: mass unemployment and appeasement'. He goes on to remark that the political leaders of the decade have been judged very harshly (none more so, one might add, than Birmingham's Neville Chamberlain); yet, Taylor goes on, 'most English people at the time were enjoying a richer life than any previously known in the history of the world: longer holidays, shorter hours, higher real wages. They had motor cars, cinemas, radio sets, electrical appliances'.[113] Most of this is true when applied to the Birmingham working classes, though they did not as yet possess motor cars; Taylor could have added to his list, with reference to Birmingham, steady employment for the most part, better housing conditions on the whole, and a wider range of leisure activities. The one major qualification to be made here, of course, is the extent of poverty in the Central Wards. To recapitulate: there the worst accommodation was as bad and as insanitary as any in the country. This is where malnutrition was still most evident, death rates highest and unemployment likely to be heaviest among the unskilled and low-waged, especially when the family was above average in size. When the school children were evacuated from Birmingham in 1939, one local business man, Mr C.H. Foyle, was so shocked by the appearance of some of them (he thought the luggage of the contingent of 150 children he saw could have been put into a decent-sized packing case) that he set up a fund to provide adequate clothing for evacuated children for £1 or so a head (this included boots for the boys and shoes for the girls, who obviously lacked proper footware).[114] All that can be said in mitigation here is that only a minority of the working classes lived centrally, and their numbers had fallen between the wars to less than a fifth of the total for the whole city. For the substantial majority, however, the story was different. It can be argued that they glimpsed briefly the future affluence of the 1960s and early 1970s when the standard of living again went up, consumer goods flooded the market, holidays abroad became the norm, and working-class life experienced an unparalleled degree of comfort.

ENVOI

What in fact led to the making of the Second City? How was it that a pioneering Midland industrial town, which in the first half of the nineteenth century had been overtaken in size by both Liverpool and Manchester, should nevertheless leap forward again by the end of the century to become the country's Second City? One simple and perhaps simplistic answer to these questions would be the passing of the Greater Birmingham Act in 1911. After the Act, Birmingham became twice the size of Manchester and also twice the size of Liverpool (and three times greater than Glasgow). The deeper question then arises, of course, of just why the 1911 Act was passed. The answers, as we have seen, are many, but the most fundamental cause must surely be economic. Birmingham industry had spread far beyond its original location in the Central Wards to areas on the periphery by 1900 closely linked by developing lines of communication in the form of railways and tramways. A large area, 13 miles across, had developed into a conurbation, based on an identity of economic interests; and it made good sense that it should come under unified local government control. Moreover, by 1900 Birmingham already was a county borough, an assize town, and was a city. Thus, after 1911 the City Corporation was no longer ringed by a variety of local boards, urban councils and rural councils; it had absorbed virtually all the more important local authorities on its former boundaries, areas already bound to Birmingham by strong economic ties. The 1911 Act was by no means crudely imperialistic in nature. Admittedly it brought in additional rate revenue, but it also brought new responsibilities to the Council. The Act made financial sense (of supreme importance in a city run by business men), and it brought a strength which saw the city through the testing times of the First World War and of the inter-war years.[1]

An especially important factor in the creation of Greater Birmingham was the contemporary interest in town planning following the passing of the Housing and Town Planning Act, 1909. In particular, as noted in Chapter Five, the influence of John Sutton Nettlefold was strong. He was chairman of the Housing Committee from its establishment in 1901, and also chairman of the Committee for the Extension of City Boundaries, 1908-11. Nettlefold (another Unitarian, who married the daughter of Arthur Chamberlain) was an enthusiast for town planning and for the creation of garden suburbs. By December 1911 there was a staff of seventeen engaged in town planning work. The ground was in effect being laid for the vast municipal estates building of the inter-war period.[2] Combined therefore with the basic economic justification for the extension of the city's boundaries in 1911 were strong beliefs among leaders in the Council on the need for town and regional planning.

The whole life of the city was based on its industrial development, and on it depended the fortunes of its inhabitants. How far did these fortunes prosper between 1850 and 1939? When it is considered that these eighty-nine years constitute a period not much longer than the average person's lifetime in the early twenty-first century, it is remarkable how much change took place affecting the lives of men, women and children of all classes. For the middle classes, the Great

War had proved a grim interlude, with repercussions and memories still painful in 1939; but everyday life in Edgbaston, Harborne and Moseley had not changed greatly. In Edgbaston, main drainage had improved, houses were lit by electricity, roads were better surfaced and lit, stables were converted into garages and gardens were leafier than ever. The constitution of the City Council was still strongly middle-class,[3] and the Chamberlain influence remained evident in the preponderance of Conservative seats, both in the Council and in the city's parliamentary representation. The great names of the second half of the nineteenth century still resonated in the inter-war years – Chamberlain, Kenrick, Cadbury and the rest. Middle-class women had not become noticeably more prominent between the wars in political circles, though some like Mrs Geraldine Cadbury continued to play a leading role in philanthropic circles.

As for the working population, the whole period 1850-1939 was one of the considerable change, and for the majority, one of material improvement. For most of the Birmingham working classes, their standard of living went up, longevity increased, infant mortality fell, and their general state of health improved. The working week no longer began with St Monday and half-day work on Saturday became the norm. By the 1930s the five-day week was beginning to spread.[4] Child labour was illegal, and all children went to school until they were fourteen. So there were more schools and more school clinics; and for adults, there were old age pensions, and a limited state health insurance scheme and unemployment benefit assistance, both the latter being the result of the National Insurance Act, 1911. The entertainment industry flourished, especially between the wars, with the advent of the radio and of the talkies. Unemployment had been a problem from time to time, but on nothing like the scale or duration of the unemployment experienced in the Distressed Areas between the wars. There was no march of the unemployed from Birmingham comparable with the Hunger March from Jarrow, and Priestley did not think it worthwhile to discuss unemployment when describing his visit to Birmingham in 1933.

The downside to all this, of course, was the continued existence of the slums in the Central Wards by 1939. How far had life changed for the better there since 1850? It will be recalled that according to the Medical Officer of Health, there were still 17,500 houses in the central areas in 1938 which were unfit for human habitation. In spite of some demolition of unfit housing, and the further provision of separate water supplies, there were still many houses without their own WCs. Rents were the lowest in Birmingham there, which is hardly surprising, for nobody would wish to live there who could afford better accommodation. So here were housed the most impoverished of Birmingham's working classes, the true *lumpen proletariat*. There is the further matter of the size of families. Even on the relatively affluent Kingstanding estate, the larger the family, the less likely that the family income would be sufficient to feed the family properly. Some labourers' wages were so low that they were better off on the dole, which provided allowances for children.[5] There is no doubt that real wages rose between the wars, especially in the 1930s, but this could be cancelled out if the family was large. Fortunately the size of the family shrank markedly over the whole period 1850 to 1939.

Another aspect of working life is that of the relationship between work people and their employers. Here the desire to maintain co-operative relations was very evident before 1914, witness in particular the famous system of Birmingham alliances, unique in modern labour history. Given the growing strength nationally of socialist organisations in the last two decades before the Great War, it is remarkable that they had such limited success in Birmingham, other than the support given by the Trades Council to the moderate Labour Representation Committee.[6] Between the wars, co-operative attitudes continued. Jim Simmons was active in Labour politics in Birmingham at the time, and he wrote later with some feelings on the subject: 'It is very difficult to wage the "class war" in British political life; so many people on the "other side" are so decent in their personal relations in spite of their public attitudes'.[7] As we have seen earlier, trade union activity between the wars was relatively limited, and both the trade unions and the Labour Party were hostile to infiltration by the Communist Party, which had a strongly-held belief in class war and the class struggle. Only in the last few years before the outbreak of the Second World War in 1939 was the membership of the AEU noticeably strengthened with the increasing demand locally for armament manufacture. Cloth-capped Chamberlainism still had influence between the wars in promoting conciliatory attitudes among the Birmingham working classes rather than class hostility.

Lastly, by way of a final comment, what can be said of the City Corporation and its achievements? Although some criticism was voiced of the Civic Gospel of the 1870s earlier on in this book, it remained a powerful force in improving the city's services to the community before 1911; and subsequently the Corporation took on greater civic responsibilities than those shouldered by any other local authority in the country save the London County Council. The import of the phrase 'Second City' is not always appreciated, especially by Londoners and even by the inhabitants of the city of Birmingham itself. The earlier increasing industrialisation of Birmingham in the first half of the nineteenth century was accompanied not by increasing class division, but by class co-operation and joint class enterprise typified by the Birmingham Political Union, the Equitable Labour Exchange, and the Complete Suffrage Union, all led by middle-class radicals.[8] In the second half of the century, class leadership was maintained by middle-class leaders still with a vision of reform summed up in the simple civic motto, 'Forward'. Between the wars, the new, greatly enlarged authority certainly went forward with its vast municipal schemes, and its expanded hospital system, including the creation of the new medical centre, the Queen Elizabeth Hospital, next door to what was perhaps Chamberlain's greatest triumph in Birmingham, the University of Birmingham. The noisy, smoky industrial town which William Hutton knew in his old age in the early years of the nineteenth century had developed into 'no mean city'; and its inhabitants might well be proud of its accomplishments over the whole period 1850 to 1939. Local government had indeed made great strides since the days of the Old Woodman Council.

NOTES

THE MID-CENTURY ECONOMY AND SOCIETY

1. The causes and course of the Industrial Revolution have been discussed at great length by historians for many years. For summaries of recent views see the introductory surveys in Mokyr, J. (ed.), *The British Industrial Revolution: An Economic Perspective* (1993), and in Hoppit, J. & Wrigley, E.A. (eds), *The Industrial Revolution in Britain, I* (1994). See also Mathias, P., *The First Industrial Nation* (2nd edn, 1983).

2. For example, see Crafts, N.F.R., 'British Economic Growth 1700-1831: A Review of the Evidence', *Economic History Review*, XXXVI, No. 2, May 1983, and also Crafts, N.F.R., *British Economic Growth during the Industrial Revolution* (1985).

3. Chambers, J.D., *The Workshop of the World* (1961), 21-2.

4. Young, A., *Tours in England and Wales*, LSE Reprint No. 14, (1932), 255.

5. For contemporary descriptions of these machines, see Hawkes Smith, W., *Birmingham and its Vicinity as a Manufacturing and Commercial District* (1836), Pt III, 11-16.

6. *Mattew Boulton Papers, Boulton & Fothergill Letter Book, 1771-3*, letter of 30 December 1770.

7. Hopkins, E., *Rise of the Manufacturing Town: Birmingham and the Industrial Revolution* (1998), 34-5.

8. Ibid.

9. Leland, J., *Intinerary*, 2nd edn, 1745, Vol. 4, 108.

10. Goodman, D., 'The Birmingham Gun Trade', in Timmins, S. (ed.), *Birmingham and the Midland Hardware District* (1866), 412, 413; Bailey, D.W. & Nie, D.E., *English Gunmakers; The Birmingham and Provincial Gun Trade in the 18th & 19th Centuries* (1982), 21.

11. Bailey, D.W. & Nie, D.E., op.cit., 20.

12. Dunham, K., *The Gun Trade of Birmingham* (1955), 16.

13. Dunham, K., op.cit., 15.

14. Bailey, D.W. & Nie, D.E., op.cit., 20; Goodman, D., op.cit., 392-3.

15. For a detailed account of the establishment and history of the Enfield works, see Pam, D., *The Royal Small Arms Factory, Enfield and Its Workers* (self publication, 1998).

16. Dent, R., *Old and New Birmingham* (1880), 112-13; and his *The Making of Birmingham* (1894), 257.

17. Turner, J.P. 'The Birmingham Button Trade', in Timmins, S. (ed.), op.cit., 435, 316.

18. Wright, J.S., 'The Jewellery Trade'; in Timmins, S. (ed.), op. cit., 435.

19. Census Returns, 1851.

20. Prosser, R.B., *Birmingham Inventors and Inventions* (1881), 77-8.

21. Aitkin, W.C., 'Brass and Brass Manufacture' in Timmins, S. (ed.), op.cit., 359.

22. Aitkin, W.C., op. cit., 229.

23. For the career of Edward Thomson, see Thomson, Sir E., *Memoirs during Half a Century Vol. I* (1845), and Gill, C., *History of Birmingham, Vol.I* (1952), 109-11.

24. *Children's Employment Commission, 1842*, Appendix to 2nd Report, Report by Grainger, R.D., 18.

25. Timmins, S., 'The Industrial History of Birmingham', in Timmins, S. (ed.), op.cit., 211.

26. *Children's Employment Commission, 1842*, Appendix to 2nd Report, Report by Richards, T., on Apprentices, 170, 171.

27. See the numerous references in Lane, J., *Apprenticeship in England 1600-1914*, (1996).

28. Index of Masters, Apprentices, and Trades, Birmingham Central Library.

29. Bailey, D.W. & Nie, D.E., op. cit., 20.

30. Richards' Report, 171.

31. Sidney and Beatrice Webb expressed the view in their *Industrial Democracy* (2nd edn, 1902), 476, that apprenticeship was in terminal decline at the end of the nineteenth century. This view is questioned in my 'Were the Webbs wrong about the decline of apprenticeship in the Black Country?' in *West Midland Studies*, Vol. 6, 1973. Also see More, C., *Skill and the English Working Classes* 1870-1914 (1980), 99-100, 103, for the argument that in 1906, 21% of all working males aged fifteen to nineteen were still apprenticed.

32. *Grainger's Report*, 18.

33. Ibid., 126, 129, 136.

34. Ibid., 146, 147.

35. Carus, C.G., *The King of Saxony's Journey through England and Scotland in the year 1844* (1846), 169, 170, 171, 174.

36. Faucher, L., *Etudes sur Angleterre, I* (1856), 502 et seq.

37. *The Leisure Hour,* 3 Feb., 1853, 88.

38. Timmins, S., 'The Industrial History of Birmingham', in Timmins, S., op.cit., 223.

39. Allen, G.C., *The Industrial Development of Birmingham and the Black Country* (1929), 114-15.

40. For further details, see Gill, C., op. cit., 283-290.

41. *Boulton Papers, Boulton & Fothergill Letter Book, 1757-65,* and M. Boulton *Letter Copy Book, 1766-8,* letter 10 July 1767.

42. Hutton, W., *History of Birmingham,* (2nd edn, 1783), 70.

43. Hopkins, E., 'The Birmingham Economy during the Revolutionary and Napoleonic Wars, 1793-1815', *Midland History* Vol. XXIII, 1998.

44. Duggan, E.P., 'The Impact of Industrialisation on an Urban Labour Market: Birmingham, England, 1770-1860', Wisconsin Ph.D. thesis, 1972, 226.

45. Mathias, P., op. cit., 224. See also Crouzet, F., *The Victorian Economy* (1982), 70.

46. *Report on the Sanitary Condition of the Labouring Population of Great Britain (1842),* 194.

47. Ibid., 211-12.

48. *Victoria County History, Warwickshire,* Vol. 7 (1964), 209.

49. Fletcher, L., 'Robert Owen's Equitable Labour Exchanges', Open University B.Litt. thesis, 1984, 89.

50. Hopkins, E., *Working Class Self-Help in Nineteenth Century England* (1995), 194, 196, 208, 209.

51. For a full account of the controversy, see Gill, C., op. cit., Chapter 11.

52. Briggs, A., *Victorian Cities* (1968), 115.

53. See in particular Briggs, A., *Victorian Cities,* (1968), Chapter 5; Briggs, A., *Collected Essays of Asa Briggs,* Vol. I (1985); and his article on Birmingham, *VCH Warks,* Vol. 7.

54. Behagg, C., 'Custom, Class and Change: the trade societies of Birmingham', *Social History* IV, no. 3 (1979), 459.

55. Hopkins, E., 'Birmingham during the Industrial Revolution: Class Conflict or Class Cooperation?', *Research in Social Movements, Conflict and Change,* (1993), Vol. 16, 123-4.

56. Ibid., 124.

57. Reid, D.A., 'Labour, Leisure and Politics in Birmingham ca. 1800-1875', Birmingham Ph.D. thesis, 1985, 250.

58. *Factory Inquiry Commission, 1833,* 1st Report, report on Birmingham by Mr Horner, 5; CEC, 1842, Appendix to 2nd Report by Grainger, R.D., 17, 19.

59. CEC, 1862, 3rd Report, xi, White's Report, 57.

60. Allen, G.C., op.cit., 166, 167.

61. See Samuel, R., 'The Workshop of the World. Steam Power and Hand Technology in Victorian Britain', *History Workshop,* (1977), 39, 60. See also Behagg, C., 'Radical Politics and Conflict at the Point of Production. A study of the relationship between classes', Birmingham Ph.D. (1982), especially 25, 59.

62. CEC,1843, Appendix to 2nd Report, report by Mr Grainger, 17, 18.

63. Ibid., 17, 18; 119, 126; 24.

64. *Report on the Sanitary Condition of the Labouring Population Of Great Britain, 1842; Report on Birmingham,* 216.

65. *Chadwick's Report, 1842,* 196, 193, 194, 195, 197.

66. Rawlinson, R., *Report to the General Board of Health... on the Borough of Birmingham* (1849), 23, 95.

67. *1844 Report,* 1-2, and Appendix, 2.

68. *Rawlinson's Report,* 51.

69. Ibid., 26.

70. Smith, D., *Conflict and Compromise: Class Formation in English Society 1830-1914. A Comparative Study of Birmingham and Sheffield* (1982), 276; Sanderson, M., *Education, Economic Change, and Society in England 1750-1880* (2nd edn, 1991),19; and see also *Grainger's Report, 1843,* passim.

71. Frost, M.B., 'The Development of Provided Schooling for Working-Class Children in Birmingham, 1781-1851', Birmingham M.Litt. thesis, 1978, 56.

72. Frost, M.B., op.cit., 32, 48; *Grainger's Report,* 190.

73. The extent of working-class education in 1850 will be returned to in Chapter Six.

74. Hopkins, E., *Rise of the Manufacturing Town...,* 162.

Economic Change

1. This was in 1741. Hutton declared, 'I was surprised at the place, but more so at the people. They possessed a vivacity I had never beheld. I had been among dreamers, but now I saw men awake. Their very step along the streets showed alacrity...': Jewitt, L., *The Life of William Hutton* (1872), 133.

2. But see Church, R.A., *The Great Victorian Boom 1850-1873* (1975) for a critical reappraisal of this concept.

3. Saul, S.B., *The Myth of the Great Depression 1873-1896* (2nd edn, 1985) provides a searching assessment of the extent of the Depression.

4. Allen, G.C., *The Industrial Development of Birmingham and the Black Country* (1929), 179, 197.

5. Ibid., 61.

6. Ibid., 179.

7. Faucher, L., *Etudes sur 1'Angleterre*, tome I (1856), 503.

8. Allen, G.C., op.cit., 188, 200.

9. Briggs, A., *History of Birmingham*, Vol.II (1952), 29.

10. *Victoria County History Warwickshire*, VII, (1964), 130, 131.

11. Ibid., 126-7.

12. The state of local trade during the Great Depression is commented on in the Chronicles of the Birmingham Chamber of Commerce. The worst years seem to have been 1874-1885, with some uneven improvement thereafter, and a final return to prosperity from 1895 onwards. See Wright, G.H., *Chronicles of the Birmingham Chamber of Commerce, 1783-1913* (1913).

13. Allen, G.C., 210.

14. Ibid., 215, 216.

15. Ibid., 216, 217.

16. Ibid., 218-19.

17. Ibid., 221, 222.

18. Ibid., 223, 225.

19. Wright, G.H., op.cit., 309, 310. The Council also advocated legislation on railway rates, and an international bimetallic currency.

20. Allen, G.C., 228, 250-2, 256, 259-60, 263.

21. Ibid., 265, 267.

22. Bailey, D.W. & Nie, D.E., *English gunmakers: The Birmingham and Provincial Gun Trade in the 18th and 19th Centuries* (1982), 25.

23. Ibid., 109.

24. Ibid., 26.

25. Allen, G.C., 296.

26. Allen, G.C., 298, 300. For the early history of the motor industry at Longbridge, see Church, R., *Herbert Austin: the British Motor Car Industry to 1941* (1979).

27. Allen, G.C., 304, 305, 306. The number of consumers grew during 1914-1919 from 8,746 to 11,000: *VCH, Warks*, VII (1964), 207.

28. Allen, G.C., 309. See also Cadbury Bros & Co Ltd, *The Factory in a Garden - Work and Play* (1926).

29. Allen, G.C., 192-3.

30. On these developments, see Allen, G.C., 315, 316, 322, and the *VCH, Warks*, VII (1964), 197-99.

31. *VCH, Warks*, 203.

32. Ibid., 141.

33. Ibid., 168.

34. Allen, G.C., 309.

35. Ibid.

36. Briggs, A., op cit., 45.

37. *VCH, Warks*, 147, 149, 145, 147, 145.

38. Ibid., 153.

39. Ibid., 147.

40. Allen, G.C., 327.

41. *VCH*, 141.

42. Briggs, A., op.cit., 48.

43. This is certainly true of the 1920s: oral information conveyed to the author by a retired employee, who added that Austin then reprimanded the foreman for the slack supervision of the apprentice.

44. Allen, G.C., 344-6.

45. Allen, G.C., 357.

46. VCH, 162.

47. Allen, G.C., 357-60. See also VCH, 157-162.

48. Briggs, A., op. cit., 65. The Alliance System is discussed again in the context of the development of the trade unions in Chapter 4.

49. Ibid., 135-6.

50. All the figures given for 1911 Occupations in this and subsequent paragraphs are taken from the Census for England and Wales, 1911, Vol X, Occupations and Industries, Pt II, 593-5. They exclude figures altered by the Birmingham (Extension) Order, 1911, which are set out, op.cit., 779-81.

51. Briggs, A., op.cit., 155. However, it must be reaffirmed that all the figures for Occupations discussed here do not include residents in the newly incorporated districts.

52. This was so even in the preceding century. See my article, 'The Trading and Service Sectors of the Birmingham Economy' in Davenport-Hines R.P.T. and Liebenau, J. (eds), *Business in the Age of Reason* (1987).

53. See Lodge, D., *Changing Places* (1975) for some ribald remarks when an attractive young female Birmingham University lecturer visits a Birmingham foundry floor.

54. Briggs, A., op. cit., 34.

55. Ensor, R.C.K., *England 1870-1914* (1936), 346.

56. Ibid., 38.

57. Taylor, A.J.P., *English History 1914-1945* (1965), 330.

THE CIVIC GOSPEL, AND AFTER

1. Ralph, J., *Harper's Monthly Magazine*, June, 1890.
2. There were five Improvements Acts passed between 1769 and 1828: Fraser, D., *Power and Authority in the Victorian City* (1979), 95. The first act in 1769 was known appropiately as the Lamp Act.
3. Quoted in Briggs, A., *Victorian Cities* (1968), 208. The members of the Council often met informally in the Old Woodman Tavern in Easy Row, so that for years the Council was known as the 'Old Woodman' Council (ibid.).
4. Briggs, A., op.cit., 211, 212.
5. Fraser, D., op.cit., 97.
6. Ibid., 99, 100.
7. Cherry, G.E., *Birmingham: A Study in Geography, History, and Planning* (1994), 75; Briggs, A., op.cit., 213, 214.
8. Quoted in Fraser, D., op.cit., 100.
9. Ibid.
10. Briggs, A., op.cit., 195-7.
11. Quoted in Wilson, W., *The Life of George Dawson* (1905), 151.
12. Hopkins, E., *The Rise of the Manufacturing Town...*, 139. Attendence figures are discussed more fully in Chapter Six.
13. Briggs, A., op.cit., 204.
14. Ibid., 202, 203.
15. Ibid., 204-5.
16. See Hennock, E.P., *Fit and Proper Persons: Idea and Reality in Nineteenth Century Urban Government* (1973).
17. Jones, L.A., 'Public Pursuit of Private Profit? Liberal Businessmen and Municipal Politics in Birmingham, 1865-1900', *Business History*, XXV, Nov. 1983. For a different approach and an attempt to interpret council policies in the light of modern theories of decision-making, see Jones, L.W., 'Aspects of Birmingham Community Power around 1900; A Study of Decision Making' (London M.Phil., 1992).
18. Leighton, D.P., 'Municipal Progress, Democracy and Radical Identity in Birmingham 1838-1886', *Midland History*, XXV, 2000.
19. See Fraser, D., op.cit., 101, for this argument.
20. The biographical details in this paragraph are taken from Marsh, P.T., Joseph *Chamberlain, Entrepreneur in Politics* (1994), principally at 10-11, 26, 38, 59-60, 75.
21. Chamberlain's reforms during his mayorality are described at some length in many works on Birmingham in the late nineteenth century. See in particular the works already quoted in this chapter by A. Briggs, D. Fraser, G.E. Cherry, E.P. Hennock, and also Bunce, J.T., *History of the Corporation of Birmingham, Vol. II* (1885).
22. Fraser, D., op.cit., 107.
23. Birmingham supplied most of the population of the area, but covered only a quarter of the total area of 34,343 acres. The total area of the works themselves rose to over 2,000 acres by 1900: Briggs, A., *History of Birmingham, Vol. II, Borough and City 1865-1938* (1952), 132, 134.
24. Briggs, A., op.cit. (1952), 77-81; and op.cit. (1968), 226-8.
25. Quoted in Fraser, D., op.cit., 108.
26. On the origins of the Caucus, see Briggs, A., (1968) 190; Fraser, D., op.cit., 104-5; Marsh, P.T., op.cit., 124. See also Tholfson, T.R., 'The Origins of the Birmingham Caucus', *Historical Journal*, II, 2 (1959).
27. Marsh, P.T., op.cit., 101-2. This author also points out that Chamberlain's supporters formed something of a clique in their own club, the Arts Club, which had seventy-five members, all Liberals, op.cit., 102.
28. For the subsequent history of municipal housing policy, see Chapter Five.
29. Marsh, P.T., op.cit., 95.
30. Briggs, A., op.cit., (1968), 232.
31. Briggs, A., op.cit., (1952), 119. This source also provides an extended examination of the Birmingham committee system.
32. Briggs, A., op.cit., (1952), 129.
33. Hennock, E.P., op.cit., offers a comparison between the numbers of large business men and small business men on the Council in the years 1896 and 1902. The former constituted 22.3% in 1896 and 16.7% in 1902; the latter 15.3% in 1896 and 16.7% in 1902, op.cit., 34, 56. There was therefore a minor but perhaps not especially significant decline in the numbers of large business men.
34. For a helpful account of the whole topic, see Briggs, A., op.cit., (1952), 89-91.
35. The creation of Greater Birmingham is described in detail in Briggs, A., (1952), 141-157.
36. The figure of 840,000 includes 314,000 in areas incorporated since 1851.
37. Cherry, G.E., op.cit., 83.
38. Briggs, A., op.cit., (1952), 112-115.

39. For the career of Sir Josiah Mason, see my account in the *New Dictionary of National Biography*, 1995.

40. A new history of the University of Birmingham is now available, Ives, E., Drummond, D. & Schwarz, L., *The First Civic University: Birmingham 1880-1980: An Introductory History* (2000).

41. Educational developments are dealt with separately and in more detail in Chapter Six.

42. Technical schools paid for by a halfpenny rate were authorised by the Technical Schools Act, 1889.

43. For further detailed discussion, see Chapter Six.

44. Briggs, A., op.cit. (1952) has a good account of the early history of Birmingham tramways, 92-97.

45. We return to the subject of town planning in Chapter Five. It has been observed that in spite of the Improvement Plan, in Birmingham the central office and shopping centre was smaller than in any other large English town: Muirhead, J.H. (ed), *Birmingham Institutions* (1911), 51.

46. Cherry, G.E., op.cit., 72-3.

47. See Burnett, J., *A Social History of Housing 1815-1970* (1978) generally on housing conditions before 1914.

48. Briggs, A., op.cit. (1952), 86-7, 26.

49. Fraser, D., *The Evolution of the British Welfare State* (2nd edn, 1984), 143.

50. Briggs, A., op.cit. (1968), 229.

51. Quoted in Cherry, G.E., op.cit., 86.

52. Briggs, A., op.cit., (1968), 194.

53. For a recent evaluation of his career, see Marsh, P.T., op.cit., 669-672.

54. Quoted in Marsh, P.T. op.cit., 672.

55. The phrase Civic Gospel is not always mentioned in modern accounts of the development of local government in England in the nineteenth century. For example, it does not appear in Waller, P.J., *Town, City and Nation; England 1850-1914* (1983), nor is there any reference to Unitarianism.

LIFE AT WORK

1. Bienefeld, M.A., *Working Hours in British Industry: An Economic History* (1972), 82.

2. Ibid.

3. Ibid., 116.

4. See Read, D., 'The Decline of St Monday, 1776-1876', *Past & Present*, 71, (1976).

5. It appears that John Frearson, a hook and eye manufacturer in Gas Street, was the first Birmingham employer to close his works at half-day on Saturdays in May 1851: Read, op.cit.

6. *Royal Commission on Labour, Fifth Report and Summary of Evidence*, 1894, Table VI, 104.

7. Corbett, J., *The Birmingham Trades Council 1866-1966* (1966), 54. The gas workers held a celebratory breakfast in the Town Hall. The Toast was – 'Here's to the Men who are willing to work, The employer who is willing to pay, And here's to the men who have striven to get, The gasmen their eight-hour day'.

8. *Victoria County History (Warwickshire)*, (1964), Vo1. 7, 183, 184.

9. Burnett, J., *Plenty and Want* (1966), 99, 101. For further detail of working-class food consumption at this time, see Hopkins, E., *Childhood Transformed: Working-Class Children in Nineteenth Century England* (1994), 279-283.

10. Benson, J., (1994) 12.

11. Allen, G.C., *The Industrial Development of Birmingham and the Black Country 1860-1927* (1929), 168.

12. For critical attitudes in the Black Country to working-class education, see Hopkins, E., 'Working-Class Attitudes to Education in the Black Country in the Mid-Nineteenth-Century', *History of Education Society Bulletin*,14, 1974.

13. The subject of education will be discussed further in greater detail in Chapter Six.

14. *Royal Commission on Labour, 1892, Fifth and Final Report, 1894, Pt 1, Summary Group C, Pt 1*, 247.

15. Ibid., 308.

16. For London, see Tawney, R.H., 'The Economics of Child Labour', *Economics Journa1*, 1909. For Birmingham, see Freeman, A., *Boy Life and Labour: the Manufacture of Inefficiency*, (1914).

17. Jackson, C., 'Report on Child Labour', in the *Report of the Royal Commission on the Poor Law* (1909), 22.

18. Sherard, R., *The Child Slaves of Britain* (1905), 333. This work is somewhat sensational in approach.

19. Hopkins, E., 'Working-Class Education in Birmingham during the First World War', in Lowe, R. (ed.), *Labour and Education: Some Early 20th Century Studies* (1981).

20. A joint report issued by the Government Low Pay Unit and Birmingham City Council, *The Hidden Army* (1991) claimed that of nearly 2,000 Birmingham children aged ten to sixteen, 43% had paid employment, three-quarters illegally.

21. Allen, G.C., op.cit., 342.

22. For the reduction in the size of the family, see Hopkins, E., *Childhood Transformed...*, 265-8.

23. At Cadbury's Bournville Works, George Cadbury insisted that no married woman should be employed. In his view, they could not be expected to combine satisfactorily the two tasks of housewife (and possibly mother) and factory worker: Stranz, W., *George Cadbury: An Illustrated Life of George Cadbury 1839-1922* (1973), 22.

24. See Webb, S. & Webb, B., *The History of Trade Unionism* (1894, new edn 1920).

25. Corbett, J., op cit., 25.

26. Ibid., 24-5.

27. Ibid., 75-6, 26.

28. Ibid., 32.

29. Ibid., 39, 40.

30. The Sheffield Outrages was a name given to violent measures taken in Sheffield by trade unionists against non-unionists and employers, extending even to murder. The *Hornby v. Close* Case threw doubt on the legal existence of trade unions. For a recent account of both subjects, and of the legislation which followed, see Hopkins, E., *Working-Class Self-Help...*, 127-134.

31. Ensor, R.K., *England 1870-1914* (1936), 133; Pelling, H., *History of British Trade Unionism* (1987), 61. The committee was set up in 1871, and not in Birmingham in 1869, as recorded in Corbett.

32. Corbett, J., op cit., Chapter Three.

33. For numbers in the new unions and the general significance of new unionism, see Hopkins, E., *Working-Class Self-Help...*, Chapter Seven, 'New Unionism and New Outlooks 1880-1900'.

34. Corbett, J., op.cit., 49.

35. Ibid., 57: Allen, G.C., op.cit., 365, 366; Briggs, A., *History of Birmingham, Vol. II* (1952), 64-5; Macrosty, H., *The Trust Movement in British Industry* (1922), 80.

36. Dalley, W.A., *The Life Story of W.J. Davis, JP* (1914), 211.

37. Corbett, J. op.cit., 67.

38. Hopkins, E., *Working-Class Self-Help ...*, 148.

39. Corbett, J., op.cit., 67. In 1890 a branch of the Fabian Society was established in Birmingham - the society's first provincial branch. By 1896 there were also two branches of the Independent Labour Party in the city: Barnsby, G.J., *Birmingham Working People: A History of the Labour Movement in Birmingham 1850-1914* (1989), 256, 263, 264. This author considers the ILP to have been the largest labour organisation in Birmingham before 1918; 264, 456. He also traces in detail the history of a number of other small socialist bodies in Birmingham such as the SDF, the Clarion Clubs, the Socialist Centre, the Labour Churches and so on.

40. Corbett, J., op. cit., 71; Briggs, A., op. cit., 194. It should be added that Stevens was president of the TUC in 1897, an indication of the high esteem in which he was held.

41. Corbett, J., op.cit., 72.

42. Ibid.

43. Briggs, A., op.cit., 63.

44. Ibid., 64-5.

45. Ibid.

46. Corbett, J., op.cit., 98, 101, 102.

47. Benefits could be substantial. For example, in 1908 the Tin Plate Workers Society, secretary J.V. Stevens, paid £1 per week strike pay, 12s per week unemployment pay, 8s per week sickness benefit, and £8 funeral benefit. Superannuation pay was 3s a week at the age of sixty, and 10s after twenty-five years membership. The great ASE, with more than 2,000 members in eight Birmingham branches, with a subscription of 1s 6d a week, paid 20s dispute pay, 10s sickness benefit, £12 funeral benefit, and pensions ranging from 7s to 10s a week: Barnsby, G.J., op.cit., 386.

48. *Rawlinson's Report to the General Board of Health*, 1849.

49. Hopkins, E., *Working-Class Self-Help...*, 56.

50. Corbett, J., op.cit., 80.

51. Hopkins, E., op.cit., 62-3.

52. Ibid., 39-40.

53. Ibid.

54. Ibid.

55. For helpful short accounts of the Liberal reforms, see Fraser, D., *The Evolution of the British Welfare State* (2nd edn, 1984); Thane, P., *The Foundations of the Welfare State* (1982); and Hopkins, E., *Industrialisation and Society, 1830-1951* (2000). For the standard account of the National Insurance Act, 1911, see Gilbert, B., *The Evolution of National Insurance in Great Britain* (1966).

56. Hopkins, E., *Working-Class Self-Help...*, 177.

57. Freeman, A., op. cit., 204-5 .

58. Tawney, R.H., op. cit.; Hopkins, E., *Childhood Transformed...*, 227, 229-30.

59. Clegg, H.A., Fox, A. & Thompson, A.F., *A History of British Trade Unions since 1889, Vol. I, 1889-1910* (1964), 141.

60. Kidd, A.T., *History of the Tin Plate Workers, and Sheet Metal Workers, and Braziers Societies* (1949), 85, 153.

61. More, C., *Skill and the English Working Class 1870-1914* (1960), 64, 99-100, 103. See also Hendrick, H., *Images of Youth: Age, Class, and the Male Youth Problem* (1990), 41-4, 65-72; and Knox, W., 'Apprenticeship and De-skilling in Britain, 1850-1914', *International Review of Social History*, XXXI, 1986.

62. Barnsby, G.J., op. cit., 395, 407-412.

63. Hopkins, E., *Working-Class Self-Help ...*, 169-171.

64. Ibid., 163.

65. Trade union officials were also members of the City Council by the beginning of the twentieth century - two of them by 1902, and five by 1912. In addition, there were two foremen and skilled members in 1902, and four in 1912: Hennock, E.P., *Fit and Proper Persons: Ideal and Reality in Nineteenth Century Urban Government* (1973), Table 8, 52.

66. Webb, S. & Webb, B., op,cit., 414, 419.

67. Dalley, W.A., op.cit., 189.

68. Hopkins, E., op. cit., 176.

69. Alan Fox has ascribed the slow development of trade unionism in the Birmingham area to social conservatism and the persistence of sub-contracting which acted as a brake on the growth of distinctly working-class organisations: Fox, A., 'Industrial Relations in Nineteenth Century Birmingham', *Oxford Economic Papers* (vii), 1955.

LIVING CONDITIONS

1. Cannadine, D., *Lords and Landlords: the Aristocracy and the Towns, 1774-1967* (1980), 111.

2. Ibid., 118, 121, 122, 100.

3. Thompson, F.M.L., *The Rise of Respectable Society: A Social History of Victorian Britain, 1830-1900* (1988), 181.

4. The full title of Chadwick's Report is the *Report on the Sanitary Conditions of the Labouring Population of Great Britain* (1842). For further details of housing conditions in the Reports of the 1840s, previously mentioned in Chapter One, see the author's *The Rise of the Manufacturing Town...*, Chapter Seven; and also my article 'Working-Class Housing in Birmingham during the Industrial Revolution', *International Review of Social History*, XXXI, 1986, Pt I.

5. See Rawlinson, R., *Report to the General Board of Health... on the Borough of Birmingham* (1849), and in particular, 23, 95, 29.

6. Vance, J.E. Jnr, 'Housing the Worker: Determinative and Contingent Ties in Nineteenth-Century Birmingham', *Economic Geography*, XLIII, 1967.

7. Hutton mentions their existence in his 1809 edition: see Hopkins, E., *Working-Class Self-Help...*, 21-22.

8. *The Morning Chronicle*, 10 March 1851.

9. 1844 Report, 1-2, and Appendix 2.

10. Children's Employment Commission, 1842, fo.s 175, 176.

11. *Chadwick's Report*, 1842, 211-13. For a general survey of rural diets at the time see Oddy, D.J., 'Food, Drink, and Nutrition' in Thompson, F.M.L. (ed.), *Cambridge Social History of Britain 1750-1950* (1990), Vol. 2, Chapter 5.

12. *The Morning Chronicle*, 7 October 1850, declared that 'In Birmingham a labourer must be skilled to have the slightest chance of obtaining a livelihood. Accordingly it is the mechanic, not the mere labouring man, who is in request'.

13. Dyos, H.J. & Wolff, M. (eds), *The Victorian City: Images and Realities* (1973), 367.

14. Rawlinson's Report, 48.

15. Hutton, W., *History of Birmingham* (4th edn, 1809), 71.

16. Ibid.

17. *Children's Employment Commission, 1842, Second Report, Mr Grainger's Report*, fo.s 20, 2.

18. Bunce, J.T., *History of the Corporation of Birmingham, Vol. II*, (1885), 457.

19. Ibid., 457-8.

20. Ibid., 462.

21. Ibid., 131.

22. See Bunce, J.T., 140-148 for a detailed description of the pan system, and of the disposal of the excrement collected which ended up in powder form ('poudrette') or dry manure.

23. Ibid., 147.

24. Vince, C.A., *History of the Corporation of Birmingham, Vol. III, 1885-1899* (1902), 117.

25. Ibid., 115.

26. Ibid., 128.

27. Booth, C., *Life and Labour of the People in London, Vol. II*, 1892, 20-1.

28. Vince, C.A., op.cit., 129.

29. *When We Build Again, A Study based on Research into conditions of Living and Working in Birmingham* (1941), Chapter Five, especially 45 and the map on Plate IV.

30. Ibid., 20-21, 44.

31. Chinn, C., *Homes for People: 100 Years of Council House Building in Birmingham* (1991), 19.

32. Ibid., 28.

33. Cherry, G.E., *Birmingham: A Study in Geography, History and Town Planning* (1994), 99.

34. Ibid., 99, 100.

35. Ibid., 99-105; Chinn, C., op. cit., 22, 26.

36. In 1908, 38% of the population of London occupied three rooms or less. Nearly a quarter of Newcastle's inhabitants had only only two rooms, and more than a quarter of Gateshead: Burnett, J., *A Social History of Housing, 1850-1970* (1978), 142-3, 152, 153.

37. Briggs, A., op.cit., 26.

38. Some of those aware of the housing problems of the time were inclined to ridicule the notion of Birmingham being the best-governed city in the world. Thus, according to the editor of the *Birmingham Gazette*, in 1901, 'Everyone who has lived in Birmingham a few years laughs at the idea that it is the best government city in the world'. (quoted in Walters, J.C., *Scenes in Slumland* (1901), 4).

THE SOCIAL SCENE

1. For a more extended discussion of these figures, see Hopkins, E., *The Rise of the Manufacturing Town...*, 136–140. See also Coleman, B.I., *The Church of England in the Mid-Nineteenth Century: A Social Geography* (1980), 41; and Mole, D.E., 'Challenge to the Church, Birmingham, 1815-1865', in Dyos, H.J. & Wolff, M. (eds), *The Victorian City: Images and Realities, Vol. II*, 1973.

2. Best, G., *Mid-Victorian Britain 1851-75* (1973), 196, 194.

3. Ibid., 217-18.

4. Cannadine, D., *Lords and Landlords: the Aristocracy and the Towns, 1774-1967* (1980); Briggs, A., *History of the Corporation of Birmingham, Vol. II, 1865-1938* (1952), 129.

5. All the figures in this and the suceeding two paragraphs are taken from Peacock, R., 'The 1892 Birmingham Religious Census' in Bryman, A. (ed.), *Religion in the Birmingham Area: Essays in the Sociology of Religion* (1975).

6. Hennock, E.P., *Fit and Proper Persons* (1973) has much useful discussion on the influence of Unitarianism in Birmingham during the nineteenth century. For the 1892 figures, see Peacock, R., op. cit.

7. Smith, D., *Conflict and Compromise: Class Formation in English Society: A Comparative Study of Birmingham and Sheffield* (1982), 114, 291.

8. Ibid., 109-111, 114.

9. Briggs, A., op. cit., 109.

10. Ibid.

11. Smith, D., op. cit., 179-180.

12. Skipp, V., *Victorian Birmingham* (1983), 122-3.

13. Bartley, P., 'Moral Regeneration: Women and the Civic Gospel in Birmingham, 1870-1914', *Midland History*, 2000, Vol. XXV.

14. Harris, J., *Private Lives, Public Spirit: Britain 1870-1914* (1994), 190, 191.

15. See Upton, C., *A History of Birmingham* (1993), 171-2; Briggs, A., op. cit., 313–14.

16. Miller, H., *First Impressions of England and its People* (1847), 231.

17. Kohl, J.G., *England, Wales and Scotland* (1844), 12.

18. Trainor, R.H., *Black Country Elites* (1993), passim.

19. Peacock, R., op. cit.

20. For the social composition of Unitarians, Quakers and Baptists, see Ram, R.W., 'Influences on the Pattern of Belief and Social Action among Birmingham Dissenters between 1750 and 1870', in Bryman, A., op. cit.; see also Hopkins, E., op. cit., 161-5.

21. Peacock, R., op. cit.

22. Skipp, V., op. cit.

23. Briggs, A., op. cit., 102.

24. Ibid., 104.

25. *The Schoolmaster*, 17 December 1872.

26. Chinn, C., 'Was Separate Schooling a means of Class Segregation in late Victorian and Edwardian England?', *Midland History*, 1988, XIII.

27. Skipp, V., op. cit., 177.

28. Vince, C.A., *History of the Corporation of Birmingham, Vol. IV, 1900-1915*, 288, 306.

29. Hopkins, E., 'Working-Class Education in Birmingham...' in *Labour and Education: Some Early Twentieth Century Studies* (1981).

30. Skipp, V., op. cit., 123, 124, 125-6.

31. Ibid., 131, 121.

32. Ibid., 134.

33. Ibid., 126. The full titles of the church societies were the National Society for Promoting the Education of the Poor in the Principles of the Established Church; and the British and Foreign Schools Society.

34. In 1876, the average consumption of beer per head of population was 34.4 gallons: Best, G., op. cit., 240. By 1871 there were within the borough of Birmingham 683 public houses and 1,193 beershops, that is, one establishment for every 174 inhabitants: Bramwell, W.M., *Pubs and Localised Comunties in Mid-Victorian Birmingham* (1984), Queen Mary College, Geography Department Occasional Paper, No. 22.

35. Reid, D.E., 'Interpreting the Festival Calendar: Wakes and Fairs as Carnivals', in Storch, R.D., (ed.), *Popular Custom in Nineteenth Century England* (1982).

36. For the Clarion Clubs in Birmingham, See Barnsby, G.J., op. cit.

37. Quoted in Springhall, J., *Coming of Age: Adolescence in Britain, 1860-1960* (1986).

38. Freeman, A., Boy Life and Labour (1914), 136.

39. Ibid., 141.

40. Birmingham was well served by local newspapers. In addition to the *Birmingham Gazette*, *Birmingham Mail* and *Birmingham Post*, there was a number of other local newspapers and magazines such as *The Dart*, *The Owl* and the *Town Crier*. The last-mentioned was a Labour Weekly which was published from 1919 to 1951.

THE GREAT WAR, 1914-1918

1. Brazier, R.H. & Sandford, E., *Birmingham and the Great War 1914-1919* (1921), vi, 5, 15, 27, 34. This work is a helpful source for Birmingham's military contribution, and in Chapters III and IV contains descriptions of actions in France, Italy and elsewhere in which Birmingham troops took part.

2. Allen, G.C., *The Industrial Development of Birmingham and the Black Country, 1860-1927* (1929), 374, 375, 377.

3. Briggs, A., *History of Birmingham, Vol. II, Borough and City 1865-1938* (1952) 214, 215, 217.

4. Briggs, A., op. cit. 217-218. See also Brazier R.H. & Sandford, E., op. cit. 124-127.

5. *Birmingham Post*, 5 July 1915, quoted in Briggs, A., op. cit. 225.

6. For much of what follows on the role of trade unions in Birmingham during the Great War, I am indebted to a Birmingham University BA (History) dissertation by Jenkins, N.R., 'The Trade Union Movement in Birmingham during the First World War' (1984).

7. Hopkins, E., *A Social History of the English Working Classes*, l815-1945 (1979), 213.

8. Jenkins, N.R., op. cit. Chapters I & II, and 24.

9. Ibid., Chapter I.

10. Hopkins, E., op. cit. 219.

11. See Jenkins, N.R., op. cit.Chapters II and III, especially 19, 20, 24, 34, 39, 41, 42.

12. Ibid., Chapter III, 'Conflict between the Skilled and General Unions'.

13. Hopkins, E., op. cit. 214.

14. Jenkins, N.R., op. cit. 50.

15. Ibid., 54-58.

16. Quoted from a Birmingham University BA (History) dissertation by Lacey, H., 'Women Workers in Birmingham, l911-1921' (1983), 24.

17. Ibid., 10. These figures are derived from Drake, B., *Women in Trade Unions* (1921).

18. Brazier, R.H. & Sandford, E., op. cit. l37.

19. Ibid., 138, 321.

20. Lacey, H., op. cit. 44.

21. Brazier, R.H. & Sandford, E., op. cit., 150, 151, 144.

22. Lacey, H., op. cit., 47.

23. Hopkins, E., op. cit., 217-18.

24. Ibid.

25. Lacey, H., op. cit., 47-48.

26. Enoch Powell retained a childhood memory of seeing battle casualties at New Street Station. It made a powerful impression on him. He also recalled seeing prisoners of war at work in the City: Heffer, S., *Like the Roman: the Life of Enoch Powell* (1998), 5.

27. Ives, E., Drummond, D. & Schwarz, L., *The First Civic University: Birmingham 1880-1980: An Introductory History* (2000), 166.

28. The University lost 178 students and staff in the First World War, and 120 in the Second World War: Ibid., 281.

29. Briggs, A., op .cit., 208-9.

30. Ibid., 205-6.

31. Ibid., 206, 207.

32. Hansard, 10 August 1917.

33. For further details of elementary education in Birmingham during the Great War, see Hopkins, E., 'Working Class Education in Birmingham...', and also an article by Hopkins, E. in Bourne, J., Liddle, P. & Whitehead, I. (eds), *The Great World War 1914-1945, Vol. II* (2001), on children in wartime.

34. Attendance, Finance, and General Purposes Committee Minutes, 26 January 1917.

35. Ibid., 28 November 1919.

36. Ibid., 29 October 1915, 26 November 1915.

37. *City of Birmingham LEA Scheme, 1920*, 1.

38. *Report of the Board of Education for 1916-17* (1918), 5: *Report of the Board of Education for 1917-18* (1919), 8.

39. Reports of the City of Birmingham Education Committee, 1914-1924, 62, 63.

40. Ibid., 72, 67.

41. Minutes of the Hygiene Committee, 26 October 1917; and Reports, 1914-24, 50.

42. *Reports of the Board of Education, 1915-16* (1917), 5, and for *1917-18* (1919), 8.

43. Minutes of the Attendance, General Purposes and Finance Committee, 23 May 1917; Minutes of the Education Committee, 28 September 1917.

44. Minutes of the Attendance, Finance, and General Purposes Committee, 21 December 1917, City of Birmingham Scheme (1920), and Minutes, Continuation Schools Sub-Committee, 30 May 1919.

45. City of Birmingham Scheme (1920), 57.

46. Briggs, A., op. cit., 223.

47. Brazier, R.H. & Sandford, E., op. cit., 323-4.

48. Ibid., 276.

49. Briggs, A., op. cit., 201.

50. Bourne, J., *Britain and the Great War 1914-1918* (1994), 1, 178.

51. Heffer, S., op. cit., 6.

52. Montague, C.E., *Disenchantment* (1922), 30.

BETWEEN THE WARS, 1918-1939

1. Priestley, J.B., *English Journey* (1934, Penguin edition, 1977), 321.

2. Briggs, A., *History of Birmingham, vol. II*, 'Borough and City 1865-1938' (1952), 271, 272.

3. Ibid., 300. Figure 12, on 297 provides a helpful map showing the location of industry.

4. *When We Build Again: A Study based on Research into Conditions of Living and Working in Birmingham* (Bournville Village Trust, 1941), 44 (hereafter WWBA).

5. See *WWBA*, Chapter V, 'The Population'. See also Walker, G., 'The Growth of Population in Birmingham and the Black Country between the Wars', *University of Birmingham Historical Journal*, I, 1947.

6. Briggs, A., op.cit., 282.

7. *Victoria County History, Warwickshire*, VII, (1964), 174 (hereafter VCH, Warks).

8. Hastings, R.P., 'The Labour Movement in Birmingham 1927-1945', Birmingham MA thesis 1959, 9.

9. *VCH, Warks*, VII, 141-3.

10. Briggs, A., op.cit., 282.

11. *VCH, Warks*, VII, 142. The figures quoted are Dr Smith's figures, which are at odds with her remarks quoted earlier.

12. Briggs, A., op.cit, 6.

13. *VCH, Warks*, VII, 142. The size of firms increased nationally in the 1930s, but even in 1936, there were only 519 factories employing over 1,000 workers, while 92% employed under a hundred, and 76.9% up to twenty-five: *Reports of the Chief Inspector of Factories and Workshops* (hereafter RCIFW), 1937, 22.

14. Briggs, A., op.cit., 285, 286.

15. *Birmingham Gazette*, 25 March 1933, 6 November 1933.

16. Clegg, H.A., *A History of British Trade Unionism since 1889* (1985), 534.

17. Littler, C.R., *The Development of the Labour Process in Capitalist Societies* (1982), 142-3.

18. Hastings, R.P., op.cit., 64-66.

19. *Labour Gazette*, (1919), 345-6. There was a striking overall national decrease in hours in 1919 of 40.4 million hours per week, hours being reduced for 6.3 million workers in all (*Labour Gazette* (1925), 116.

20. *RCIFW* (1935), 64.

21. The figures actually relate to the *Enquiry into Average Earnings and Hours of Labour*; October 1935, reported in the *Labour Gazette* (1937), 337.

22. *RCIFW* (1937), 73. See also *Labour Gazette* (1937), 337.

23. *RCIFW* (1920). Of course, not all industrial processes dangerous to health were noted by the inspectors. For example, in chrome plating the fumes produced rashs and eruptions around the nostrils and mouths of the women workers (oral testimony).

24. *RCIFW* (1927), 22-23.

25. Ibid., (1929), 18. The Inspectorate divided the city into East, South and West Districts.

26. Ibid., (1931), 21.

27. Accident figures taken from the *Factory Inspectors' Reports* of the period.

28. *RCIFW*, (1920), 86.

29. Ibid. (1938), 94.

30. Briggs, A., op.cit., 284.

31. *RCIFW*, (1920), 152.

32. *Labour Gazette* (1935), 330.

33. *RCIFW* (1934), 16. Oral evidence tends to confirm it was a temporary measure.

34. *RCIFW*, (1920), 155.

35. Aldcroft, D.H., *The Inter-War Economy: Britain 1919-1939* (1970), 366.

36. Figures taken from the *Labour Gazette* for the years indicated.

37. Hastings, R.P., op.cit., 6.

38. *Conurbation: A Planning Survey of Birmingham and the Black Country by the West Midlands Group* (1948), Table XXVII.

39. Hastings, R.P., op.cit., 7-9.

40. Conurbation, Table XXVII.

41. Williams, I.A., *The Firm of Cadbury 1831-1931* (1931), 114-116. For the work processes at Bournville in 1933, see Priestley, J.B., op.cit., 92-3. Priestley also mentions that membership of the various clubs and societies there was about 7,000.

42. Oral information from a former employee.

43. *Birmingham Choice*, 2 December 1988.

44. Briggs, A., op cit., 274.

45. Corbett, J., *The Birmingham Trades Council 1866-1966* (1966), 128-131.

46. Briggs, A., op.cit., 321.

47. Corbett, J., op.cit., 140.

48. *City of Birmingham Official Handbook*, 1938; *City of Birmingham Abstract of Statistics* (hereafter Statistics), No. 1 (1931-49).

49. *WWBA*, 50.

50. Ibid., 48-50.

51. See Hopkins, E., *Childhood Transformed...*, 101, and the authorities quoted there.

52. *City of Birmingham Official Handbook*, 1938, 167. The Central Wards comprised seven wards in the heart of the City. These were St Martin's and Deritend, Market Hall, Ladywood, St Paul's, St Mary's, Duddeston and Nechells, and St Bart's, all centred on St Martin's parish church in the Bull Ring. They were surrounded by the ten Middle Ring Wards which occupied approximately twice the area of the Central Wards. The Middle Ring Wards were in turn surrounded by the Outer Ring Wards, seventeen in number, which covered about three times the area of the Middle Ring Wards. As mentioned in Chapter Five, the Central Wards were twice as populated (62 persons per acre) as the Middle Ring (32 persons per acre), which in turn had a density twice that of the Outer Ring (15 persons per acre): see *WWBA*, Ch.8. See also Walker, G., op.cit.

53. *City of Birmingham Official Handbook*, 1938, 167. It should perhaps be noted that variations in mortality rates across the wards of cities were common enough at the time. For London, see Webster, C., 'Healthy or Hungry Thirties?', *History Workshop*, 13, (1982).

54. The national death rate for 1935-38 averaged 11.9. In Birmingham it averaged 11.6. The Birmingham death rates are set out in full in *Statistics*, 24.

55. *WWBA*, 16.

56. Jones, J.J., *History of the Corporation of Birmingham*, V, 323: *Statistics*, 67.

57. For further information regarding council house building, see Hopkins, E., 'Working-Class Life in Birmingham between the Wars, 1918-1939', *Midland History*, XV, 1990. Much of the material for this chapter has been drawn from this source. See also Cherry, G.E., *Birmingham: A Study in Geography, History and Town Planning* (1994), 112-124 on council housing.

58. *WWBA*, 31.

59. Jones, J.J., op.cit., 211.

60. Cherry, G.E., op.cit., 124. This work has an interesting discussion of the Council's change of view regarding the desireability of building flats, 122, 124.

61. *WWBA*, 53.

62. *WWBA*, (vii).

63. Soutar, M.S., Wilkins, E.H. & Sargant Florence, P., *Nutrition and the Size of the Family: Report on a New Housing Estate* (1942), 10-13.

64. *WWBA*, 68.

65. Ibid.

66. Ibid., Ch. X, 'Life on a New Housing Estate'; Black, H.J., *History of the Corporation of Birmingham* (1935-50), VI, Pt II, (1957), 387; Briggs, A., op.cit., 235, 236.

67. *WWBA*, 99. See also Burnett, J., *A Social History of*

Housing 1815-1970 (1978), 231-2, for the reaction of new tenants generally to their council homes.

68. Briggs, A., op.cit., 235; *The Home Market* (1936), 67; Hastings, R.P., op.cit., 133-7.

69. *WWBA*, 57-8.

70. Aldcroft, D.H., op.cit., 68.

71. *Annual Reports of the Birmingham Schools Medical Officer*, 1936, 10.

72. Ibid., 1938, 10.

73. Ibid., 1934, 8-10, and 1937, 8-9.

74. Soutar, M.S., Wilkins, E.H. and Sargant Florence, P., op.cit.

75. Ibid., l0-11, 13.

76. Ibid., 47, 15, 27, 48.

77. Briggs, A., op.cit., 234.

78. Clark, C., *National Income and Outlay*, 270, quoted in Mowat, op.cit., 492.

79. The 27.7% is calculated from the figures given in *WWBA*, 43.

80. Briggs, A., op.cit., 228.

81. Briggs, A., op.cit., 238-9; Black, H.J., *History of the Corporation of Birmingham VI (1936-50)*, (1957), Pt 1, 273.

82. Briggs, A., op.cit., 240.

83. Quoted in Hopkins, E., *Social History of the English Working Classes 1815-1945* (1979).

84. Briggs, A., op.cit., 241; Black, H.J., op.cit., 269, 283-9.

85. Black, H.J., op.cit., 284.

86. Briggs, A., op.cit., 240, 241.

87. Briggs, A., op.cit., 241.

88. See Hopkins, E., 'Elementary Education in Birmingham during the Second World War', *History of Education*, 1989, Vol 18, No.3.

89. Black, H.J., op.cit., 289.

90. Ibid., 242-3.

91. Sutcliffe, A. & Smith, R., *History of Birmingham 1939-1970* (1974), 333.

92. Briggs, A., op cit., 250.

93. Ibid., 256-7.

94. Ibid., 257-263.

95. Ibid., 264-9.

96. Birmingham Public Libraries more than doubled their issues from 1,960,999 in 1919-20 to 4,131,378 in 1939-40: *Statistics*, 103.

97. Soutar, M.S., Wilkins, E.H. & Sargant Florence, P., op.cit., 4.

98. Ibid., 41.

99. *Statistics*, 110.

100. Goodyear, D. & Matthews, T., *Aston Villa: A Complete Record 1874-1988* (1988), 262, 292; *Sunday Mercury*, 6 March 1988.

101. Birmingham and District Works Amateur Football Association, Golden Jubilee *Souvenir 1905-1955* (1955), 3.4.

102. *Sunday Mercury*, 5 June 1938.

103. Briggs, A., op.cit., 314.

104. Cyclist Touring Club, Birmingham and Midland District Association, *A Booklet to commemorate 50 Years of Progress 1899-1949* (1949), 16. I owe this reference and reference 101 to Cross, R., 'Working Class Leisure Activities in Birmingham between the Wars', Birmingham BA History Dissertation, 1989.

105. *Statistics*, l01.

106. See Crawford, A. & Thorne, R., *Birmingham Pubs 1890-1939* (1975).

107. See Briggs, A., op.cit., 307.

108. Quoted from the *Town Crier* in Richards, J., 'The Cinema and Cinema-Going in Birmingham in the 1930s' in Walton, J.K. & Walvin, J., *Leisure in Britain 1780-1939* (1983).

109. In 1939, Birmingham had seats for 115,000 – it is doubtful if any other town or city in provincial England had a larger number of cinemas in proportion to its population: Briggs, A., op.cit., 315.

110. *Statistics*, 89.

111. Priestley, J.B., op.cit., 78, 79, 80.

112. Ibid., 84.

113. Taylor, A.J.P., *English History, 1914-1945* (1965), 317.

114. *Daily Mirror*, 19 October 1939, quoted in Houghton, A.E., 'Birmingham's Evacuation in the Second World War', Birmingham BA History Dissertation, 1985.

Envoi

1. There is a detailed account of the events leading up to the passing of the 1911 Act in Briggs, A., op. cit., Chapter V, 'Greater Birmingham'.

2. For the 1911 Act and town planning in Birmingham, see Cherry, op. cit., 102-109.

3. In 1938 there were on the council, twenty manufacturers, seventeen company directors, sixteen solicitors and barristers, seven trade union and co-operative society officials, ten women, and thirteen members designated 'retired': Briggs, A., op. cit., 277.

4. A good deal of space in this book has been given to the subject of working conditions because of its importance to the average working man and woman. This has been well-put recently by a historian of early twentieth-century English history – 'The culture of the English working man was profoundly work-centred. For many, probably most, work was life': McKibbin, R., *Classes and Cultures: England 1918-1951* (1998), 162.

5. Soutar, M.S., Wilkins, E.H. and Sargant Florence, P., op. cit., 27.

6. For the activities of the smaller, left-wing political parties before 1914, see Barnsby, op. cit.

7. Simmons, J., *Soap Box Evangelist* (1972), 56, quoted in Rolf, D., 'Birmingham and Labour and the background to the 1945 General Election', in Wright, A. & Shackleton, R. (eds), *Worlds of Labour: Essays in Birmingham Labour History* (1983).

8. See the author's *Birmingham: The First Manufacturing Town in the World 1760-1840* (1989), afterwards reissued as *The Rise of the Manufacturing Town: Birmingham and the Industrial Revolution* (1998).

SELECT BIBLIOGRAPHY

This is not a complete list of all authorities consulted in the writing of this book. It is a select bibliography which is intended to guide readers to the principal Birmingham sources used for the text, together with a number of works supplying useful additional information. The place of publication is London unless otherwise stated.

OFFICIAL PUBLICATIONS AND OTHER PRIMARY SOURCES

Matthew Boulton Papers, Boulton & Fothergill Letter Books, 1757-65, 1766-68, 1771–73.

Census Returns, 1851–1931.

Chadwick's Report on the Sanitary Conditions of the Labouring Population of Great Britain, 1842.

City of Birmingham LEA Scheme, 1920.

City of Birmingham Abstract of Statistics, 1931–49.

City of Birmingham Official Handbook, 1938.

Harper's Monthly Magazine, June 1890.

Index of Masters, Apprentices, and Trades (Birmingham Central Reference Library).

Labour Gazette, 1919–39.

Minutes, City of Birmingham Attendance, Finance and G.P. Committee, 1914–18.

Minutes, City of Birmingham Continuation Schools Sub-Committee, 1919.

Minutes and Reports of City of Birmingham Hygiene Committee, 1914–24.

Rawlinson, R., *Report to the General Board of Health… on the Borough of Birmingham,* 1849.

Reports of the Board of Education, 1914–18.

Reports of City of Birmingham Education Committee, 1914–24.

Reports of the Chief Inspector of Factories and Workshops, 1918–39.

Royal Commission on Factories, 1833, Reports and Evidence.

Royal Commission on Children's Employment, 1840, Reports and Evidence.

Royal Commission on Children's Employment, 1862, Reports and Evidence.

Royal Commission on Labour, 1894, Reports and Evidence.

Royal Commission on the Poor Law, 1905–09, Reports.

Reports of the Birmingham Schools Medical Officer, 1918–39.

The Leisure Hour, 1853.

The Morning Chronicle, 1850, 1851.

The Schoolmaster, 1872.

BOOKS

Aldcroft, D.H., *The Inter-War Economy: Britain 1919-1939* (1970).

Allen, G.C., *The Industrial Development of Birmingham and the Black Country, 1860-1927* (1929).

Ashworth, W., *An Economic History of England 1870-1939* (1960).

Barnsby, G., *Birmingham Working People: A History of the Labour Movement in Birmingham 1850-1914* (Wolverhampton,1989).

Benson, J., *The Rise of Consumer Society in Britain, 1880-1980* (1994).

Best, G., *Mid-Victorian Britain, 1851-75* (1973).

Bienefeld, M.A., *Working Hours in British Industry: An Economic History* (1972).

Birmingham & District Works Amateur Football Association, *Golden Jubilee Souvenir 1905-1955* (Birmingham, 1955).

Black, H.J., *History of the Corporation of Birmingham VI, 1936–50* (Birmingham, 1957).

Booth, C., *Life and Labour of the People in London, Vol. II* (1892).

Bourne, J., *Britain and the Great War* (1994).

Briggs, A., *History of Birmingham, Vol.II, 'Borough and City', 1860-1939* (Oxford, 1952).
– *Collected Essays of Asa Briggs, Vol. I* (Oxford, 1965).
– *Victorian Cities* (Harmondsworth, 1968).

Bramwell, W.M., *Pubs and Localised Communities in Mid-Victorian Birmingham* (1984).

Brazier, R.H. & Sandford, E., *Birmingham and the Great War 1914-1919* (Birmingham, 1921).

Bunce, J.T., *History of the Corporation of Birmingham, Vol. II* (Birmingham, 1885).

Burnett, J., *Plenty and Want* (1966).
– *A Social History of Housing 1815-1970* (1978).

Bryman, A. (ed.), *Religion in the Birmingham Area: Essays in the Sociology of Religion* (Birmingham, 1975).

Cadbury Bros & Co. Ltd, *The Factory in A Garden – Work and Play* (Birmingham, 1926).

Cannadine, D., *Lords and Landlords: the Aristocracy and the Towns 1774-1967* (Leicester, 1980).

Carus, C.G., *The King of Saxony's Journey through England and Scotland in the year 1844* (1846).

Chambers, J.D., *The Workshop of the World* (Oxford, 1961).

Cherry, G.E., *Birmingham: A Study in Geography, History and Planning* (1994).

Chinn, C., *Homes for People: 100 Years of Council House Building in Birmingham* (Birmingham, 1991).

Church, R., *The Great Victorian Boom. 1850-1873* (1975).
– *Herbert Austin: The British Motor Car Industry to 1941* (1979).

Clark, C., *National Income and Outlay* (1937).

Clegg, H.A., Fox, A. & Thompson, A.F., *A History of British Trade Unionism since 1889, Vol. I, 1889-1910* (Oxford, 1984).

Clegg, H.A., *A History of British Trade Unionism since 1889, Vol. II, 1911-1933* (Oxford, 1985).

Coleman, B.I., *The Church of England in the Mid-Nineteenth Century: A Social Geography* (1980).

Conurbation: A Planning Survey of Birmingham and the Black Country by the West Midlands Group (1948).

Corbett, J., *The Birmingham Trades Council 1866-1966* (1966).

Crafts, N.R., *British Economic Growth during the Industrial Revolution* (Oxford, 1985).

Crawford, A. & Thorne, R., *Birmingham Pubs 1899-1939* (Birmingham, 1975).

Crouzet, F., *The Victorian Economy* (Cambridge, 1982).

CTC (Birmingham & Midland District Association), *A Booklet to Commemorate 50 Years of Progress 1899-1949* (Birmingham, 1949).

Dalley, W.A., *The Life Story of W.J. Davis, JP* (1914).

Davidoff, L. & Hall, C., *Family Fortunes: Men and Women of the English Middle Class 1780-1850* (1987).

Dent, R., *Old and New Birmingham* (Birmingham, 1880).
– *The Making of Birmingham* (Birmingham, 1894).

Bailey, D.W. & Nie, D.E., *English Gunmakers: The Birmingham and Provincial Gun Trade in the 18th and 19th Centuries* (1982).

Drake, B., *Women in Trade Unions* (1921).

Dunham, K., *The Gun Trade of Birmingham* (Birmingham, 1955).

Dyos, H.J. & Wolff, M. (eds), *The Victorian City: Images and Realities* (1973).

Edwards, E., *Personal Recollections of Birmingham and Birmingham Men* (Birmingham, 1877).

Ensor, R.C.K., *England 1870-1914* (Oxford, 1936).

Faucher, L., *Etudes sur Angleterre, I* (1856).

Fraser, D., *Power and Authority in the Victorian City* (1979).
– *The Evolution of the British Welfare State* (2nd edn, 1984).

Freeman, A., *Boy Life and Labour: The Manufacture of Inefficiency* (1914).

Gilbert, B., *The Evolution of National Insurance in Great Britain* (1966).

Gill, C., *History of Birmingham, Vol. I* (Oxford, 1952).

Goodyear, D. & Matthews, T., *Aston Villa: A Complete Record 1874-1988* (1988).

Government Low Pay Unit, *The Hidden Army* (1991).

Hardwick, H., *Images of Youth: Age, Class, and the Male Youth Problem* (1990).

Harris, J., *Private Lives, Public Spirit: Britain 1870-1914* (Harmondsworth, 1994).

Heffer, S., *Like the Roman: The Life of Enoch Powell* (1998).

Hennock, E.P., *Fit and Proper Persons: Idea and Reality in 19th Century Urban Government* (1973).

Holyoake, G.J., *Sixty Years of an Agitator's Life* (1892).

Hopkins, E., *A Social History of the English Working Classes 1815-1945* (1979).
– *Birmingham: The First Manufacturing Town in the*

World 1760-1840 (1989).

– *Rise of the Manufacturing Town: Birmingham and the Industrial Revolution* (1998) (re-issue of 1989 work).

– *Childhood Transformed: Working-Class Children in 19th Century England* (Manchester, 1994)

– *Working-Class Self-Help in Nineteenth Century England* (1995).

– *Industrialisation and Society: A Social History 1830-1951* (2000).

Hoppen, K.T., *The Mid-Victorian Generation 1846-1886* (Oxford, l998).

Hoppit, J. & Wrigley, E.A. (eds), *The Industrial Revolution in Britain, I* (Oxford, l994).

Ives, E., Drummond, D. & Schwarz, L., *The First Civic University: Birmingham 1880-1980: An Introductory History* (Birmingham, 2000).

Jewitt, L., *The Life of William Hutton* (1872).

Jones, J.J., *History of the Corporation of Birmingham*, Vol.V, 1915-35.

Kidd, A.T., *History of the Tin Plate Workers and Sheet Metal-Workers and Braziers Societies* (1949).

Kohl, J.H., *England, Wales, and Scotland* (1844).

Lander, E., *The Birmingham Gun Trade* (Birmingham, 1865).

Lane, J., *Apprenticeship in England 1600-1914* (1996).

Leyland, J., *Itinerary* (2nd edn, 1745).

Littler, C.R., *The Development of the Labour Process in Capitalist Societies* (1982).

Lodge, D., *Changing Places* (1975).

Macrosty, H., *The Trust Movement in British History* (1922).

Mann, H., *Religious Worship in England and Wales* (1854).

Marsh, P.T., *Joseph Chamberlain, Entrepreneur in Politics* (1994).

Marwick, A., *The Deluge: British Society and the First World War* (2nd edn, 1991).

Mathias, P., *The First Industrial Nation* (2nd edn, 1983).

McKendrick, N., Brewer, J. & Plumb, J.H., *The Birth of a Consumer Society* (1977).

McKibbin, R., *Classes and Cultures: England 1918–51* (Oxford, 1998).

McLeod, H., *Religion and Society in England 1850-1914* (1996).

Miller, H., *First Impressions of England and its People* (1847).

Mokyr, J. (ed.), *The British Industrial Revolution: An Economic Perspective* (1993).

Montague, C.E., *Disenchantment* (1922) .

More, C., *Skill and the English Working Classes 1870-1914* (1980).

Muirhead, J.H., *Birmingham Institutions* (Birmingham, 1911).

Pam, D., *The Royal Small Arms Factory: Enfield and its Workers* (1998).

Pelling, H., *History of British Trade Unionism* (1987).

Priestley, J.B., *English Journey* (1934).

Prosser, R.B., *Birmingham Inventors and Inventions* (Birmingham, 1881).

Rowntree, B.S., *Poverty: A Study of Town Life* (1901).

Sanderson, M., *Education, Economic Change and Society in England 1750-1884* (2nd edn, 1991).

Saul, S.B., *The Myth of the Great Depression 1873-1896* (2nd edn, 1985).

Sherard, R., *The Child Slaves of Britain* (1905).

Simmons, J., *Soap Box Evangelist* (Chichester, 1972).

Skipp, V., *Victorian Birmingham* (Birmingham, 1983).

Smith, D., *Conflict and Compromise: Class Formation in English Society 1830-1914: A Comparative Study of Birmingham and Sheffield* (1982).

Smith W.H., *Birmingham and its Vicinity as a Manufacturing and Commercial District* (1836).

Springhall, J., *Coming of Age: Adolescence in Britain, 1860-1960* (1986).

Souter, M.S., Wilkins, E.H. & Sargant, F.P., *Nutrition and the Size of the Family: Report on a New Housing Estate* (Birmingham, 1942).

Stevenson, J., *British Society 1914-1945* (Harmondsworth,1984).

Stranz, W., *George Cadbury: An Illustrated Life of George Cadbury 1839-1922* (1973).

Sutcliffe, A. & Smith, R., *History of Birmingham 1939-1970* (Oxford, 1974).

Taylor, A.J.P., *English History 1914-1945* (Oxford, 1965).

Thane, P., *The Foundations of the Welfare State* (1982).

Thomson, E., *Memoirs during Half a Century, Vol. I* (1845).

Thompson, F.M.L., *The Rise of Respectable Society: A Social History of Victorian Britain 1830-1900* (1988).

Timmins, S. (ed.), *Birmingham and the Midland Hardware District* (1866).

Trainor, R.H., *Black Country Elites* (Oxford, 1993).

Upton, C., *A History of Birmingham* (Chichester, 1993).

Victoria County History of England, Warwickshire, Vol. 7 (1964).

Vince, C.A., *History of the Corporation of Birmingham, Vol. III, 1885-1899* (1902).

Waller, P.J., *Town, City and Nation: England 1850-1914* (1983).

Walters, J.C., *Scenes in Slumland* (1901).

Walton, J.K. & Walvin, J., *Leisure in Britain 1780-1939* (1983).

Webb, S. & Webb, B., *The History of Trade Unionism* (1984, new edn, 1920).

– *Industrial Democracy* (2nd edn, 1902).

When We Build Again: A Study based on Research into Conditions of Living and Working in Birmingham (1941).

Williams, I.A., *The Firm of Cadbury 1831-1931* (1931).

Wright, A. & Shackleton, R., (eds) *Worlds of Labour: Essays in Birmingham Labour History* (Birmingham, 1983).

Wright, G.H., *Chronicles of the Birmingham Chamber of Commerce 1783-1913* (Birmingham, 1913).

Wright, W., *The Life of George Dawson* (1905).

Young, A., *Tours in England and Wales* (LSE Reprint, No.14, 1932).

ARTICLES

Aitkin, W.C., 'Brass and Brass Manufacture' in Timmins, S. (ed.).

Bartley, P., 'Moral Regeneration: Women and the Civic Gospel in Birmingham 1870-1914', *Midland History*, 2000, Vol. XXV.

Behagg, C., 'Custom, Class and Change: the trade societies of Birmingham', *Social History*, Vol. 3 (1979).

Chinn, C., 'Was Separate Schooling a means of Class Segregation in late Victorian and Edwardian England?', *Midland History*, 1988, XIII.

Crafts, N.F.R., 'British Economic Growth 1700-1831: A Review of the Evidence', *Economic History Review*, XXXVI, 2, May, 1993.

Fox, A., 'Industrial Relations in Nineteenth Century Birmingham', *Oxford Economic Papers*, (vii), 1955.

Goodman, D., 'The Birmingham Gun Trade', in Timmins, S. (ed.).

Hopkins, E., 'Were the Webbs Wrong about the Decline of Apprenticeship in the Black Country?', *West Midland Studies*, Vol. 6, 1973.

– 'Working-Class Attitudes to Education in the Black Country in the Mid-Nineteenth Century', *History of Education Society Bulletin*, 14, 1974.

– 'Working-Class Education in Birmingham during the First World War', in Lowe, R. (ed.), *Labour and Education: Some Early 20th Century Studies* (1981).

– 'Working-Class Housing in Birmingham during the Industrial Revolution', *International Review of Social History*, XXXI, 1986, Pt I.

– 'The Trading and Service Industries of the Birmingham Economy', in Davenport-Hines, R.P.T. & Liebenau, J. (eds), *Business in the Age of Reform* (1987).

– 'Elementary Education in Birmingham during the Second World War', 1918-1939', *History of Education*, 1989, 18, No.3.

– 'Working-Class Life in Birmingham between the Wars, 1918-1939', *Midland History*, XV, 1990.

– 'Birmingham during the Industrial Revolution: Class Conflict or Class Co-operation?' *Research in Social Movements, Conflict and Change* (Jai Press, London and Greenwich, Connecticut) (1993), Vol.16.

– 'The Birmingham Economy during the Revolutionary and Napoleonic Wars, 1793-1815', *Midland History*, XXIII, 1998.

– 'Josiah Mason', *New Dictionary of National Biography*, 1995.

– 'British Children in Wartime', in Bourne, J., Liddle, P. & Whitehead, P., *The Great World War, 1914-1945, Vol. II* (2001).

Jones, L., 'Public Pursuit of Private Profit? Liberal Businessmen and Municipal Politics in Birmingham, 1865-1900', *Business History*, XXV, Nov. 1983.

Knox, W., 'Apprenticeship and De-Skilling in Britain 1850-1914', *International Review of Social History*, XXXI, 1986.

Leighton, D.P., 'Municipal Progress, Democracy and Radical Identity in Birmingham, 1838-1886', *Midland History*, XXV, 2000.

Mole, D.E., 'Challenge to the Church: Birmingham,1815-1865', in Dyos, H.J. & Wolff, M. (eds), *The Victorian City: Images and Realities* (1973).

Oddy, D.J., 'Food, Drink and Nutrition' in Thompson, F.M.L. (ed.), *Cambridge Social History of Britain, 1750-1950* (1990), Vol. 2, Chapter 5.

Peacock, R., 'The 1892 Birmingham Religious Survey', in Bryman, A. (ed.), *Religion in the Birmingham Area: Essays in the Sociology of Religion* (1975).

Ram, A.W., 'Influences on the Pattern of Belief and Social Action among Birmingham Dissenters,1750-1870' in Bryman, A. (ed.), op.cit.

Read, D., 'The Decline of St Monday, 1776-1876', *Past & Present*, 71, (1976).

– 'Interpreting the Festival Callendar: Wakes and Fairs as Carnival', in Storch, R.D. (ed.), *Popular Custom in Nineteenth Century England* (1982).

Samuel, R., 'The Workshop of the World: Steam Power and Hand Technology in Victorian Britain', *History Workshop* (1977).

Tawney, R.H., 'The Economics of Child Labour', *Economic Journal*, 1909.

Tholfson, T.R., 'The Origins of the Birmingham Caucus', *University of Birmingham Historical Journal*, II, 2, (1959).

Timmins, S., 'The Industrial History of Birmingham', in Timmins, S. (ed.).

Turner, J., 'The Birmingham Button Trade', in Timmins, S. (ed.).

Vance, J.E. Jnr, 'Housing the Worker: Determinant and Contingent Ties in Nineteenth Century Birmingham', *Economic Geography*, XLIII, 1967.

Walker, G., 'The Growth of Population in Birmingham and the Black Country between the Wars', *University of Birmingham Historical Journal*, I, 1947.

Webster, C., 'Healthy or Hungry Thirties?' *History Workshop*, 13 (1982).

Wright, J.S., 'The Jewellery Trade' in Timmins, S. (ed.).

THESES AND DISSERTATIONS

Behagg, C., 'Radical Politics and Conflict at the point of production. A Study of the relationship between classes', Birmingham Ph.D. 1982.

Cross, R., 'Working-Class Leisure Activities in Birmingham between the Wars', Birmingham BA (History) dissertation, 1989.

Duggan, E.P., 'The Impact of Industrialisation on an Urban Labor Market: England, 1770-1860', Winsconsin Ph.D. thesis, 1972.

Fletcher, L., 'Robert Owen's Equitable Labour Exchanges', Open University B.Litt. thesis, 1984.

Frost, M.B., 'The Development of Provided Schooling for Working-Class Children in Birmingham, 1781-1951', Birmingham M.Litt. thesis, 1978.

Jenkins, N.R., 'The Trade Union Movement in Birmingham during the First World War', Birmingham BA (History) dissertation, 1984.

Jones, L.W., 'Aspects of Birmingham Community Power around 1900: A Study of Decision Making', London M.Phil., 1992.

Lacey, H., 'Women Workers in Birmingham, 1911-1921', Birmingham BA (History) dissertation, 1983.

Hastings, R.P., 'The Labour Movement in Birmingham, 1927-1945', Birmingham MA thesis, 1959.

Houghton, A.E, 'Birmingham's Evacuation in the Second World War', Birmingham BA dissertation, 1985.

Mole, D.E.H., 'The Church of England and Society in Birmingham c.1830-1866', Cambridge Ph.D. thesis, 1961.

Peacock, R., 'The Church of England and the Working Classes in Birmingham 1861-1905', Aston M.Phil. thesis, 1973.

Reid, D.A., 'Labour, Leisure and Politics in Birmingham, c.1800-1875', Birmingham Ph.D. thesis, 1985.

ILLUSTRATIONS

ACKNOWLEDGEMENTS

All the illustrations in this book have been supplied by the Local Studies and History Department of Birmingham Central Library, to whom I extend my grateful thanks, and especially to Mr Patrick Baird.

INDEX